HEART

OF A

STRANGER

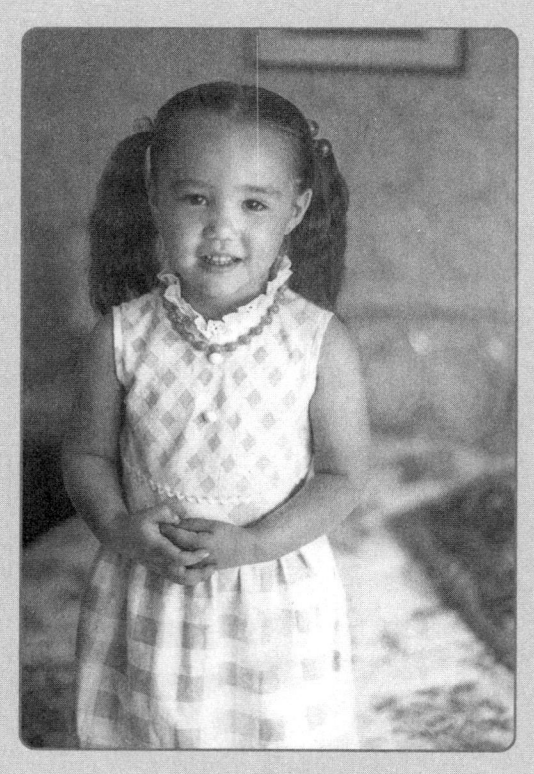

HEART

OF A

STRANGER

AN UNLIKELY RABBI'S STORY OF
FAITH, IDENTITY, AND BELONGING

ANGELA BUCHDAHL

PAMELA DORMAN BOOKS / VIKING

VIKING
An imprint of Penguin Random House LLC
1745 Broadway, New York, NY 10019
penguinrandomhouse.com

A Pamela Dorman Book/Viking

The PGD colophon is a registered trademark of Penguin Random House LLC.

VIKING is a registered trademark of Penguin Random House LLC.

Grateful acknowledgment is made for permission to reprint the following:
Translation of *Likutei Moharan* by Rabbi Nachman of
Breslov courtesy of Rabbi Jonathan Slater.

Song lyrics for "Pitchu b'hesed, pitchu b'ahava, pitchu b'tzedek"
courtesy of Rabbi Yoshi Zweiback.

Poem "One Tiny Seed" reprinted with permission of Rachel Goldberg-Polin.

Translation of "Kol Ha'olam Kulo" by Rabbi Nachman of
Breslov reprinted with permission of Aish.com.

Lyrics from "Sing Unto God" copyright © 1972 Farf, Inc. All rights reserved.
From the album *Sing Unto God*. Used with permission.

"Anthem" by Leonard Cohen © 1992 Sony Music Publishing (US) LLC. All rights administered by Sony Music Publishing (US) LLC,1005 17th Avenue South, Suite 800, Nashville, TN, 37212. All rights reserved. Used by permission. Territory: world.

Some sermons in this work were previously delivered by the author.

Set in Adobe Caslon Pro
Designed by Cassandra Mueller

LIBRARY OF CONGRESS CATALOGING-IN-PUBLICATION DATA
Names: Buchdahl, Angela, 1972- author
Title: Heart of a stranger : the story and spirit of an unlikely rabbi / Angela Buchdahl.
Description: New York, NY : Pamela Dorman Books/Viking, [2025] |
"A Pamela Dorman Book/Viking"—Colophon.
Identifiers: LCCN 2025006763 (print) | LCCN 2025006764 (ebook) |
ISBN 9780593490174 hardcover | ISBN 9780593490181 ebook
Subjects: LCSH: Buchdahl, Angela, 1972- | Rabbis—United States—Biography |
Women rabbis—United States—Biography | Asian American Jews—Biography |
LCGFT: Autobiographies
Classification: LCC BM755.B83 A3 2025 (print) |
LCC BM755.B83 (ebook) | DDC 296.092 [B]—dc23/eng/20250825
LC record available at https://lccn.loc.gov/2025006763
LC ebook record available at https://lccn.loc.gov/2025006764

Printed in the United States of America
3rd Printing

The authorized representative in the EU for product safety and compliance is
Penguin Random House Ireland, Morrison Chambers, 32 Nassau Street,
Dublin D02 YH68, Ireland, https://eu-contact.penguin.ie.

For my parents, Fred Warnick and Yi Sulja,
who traversed boundaries for love
and taught me to embrace the heart of a stranger.

Contents

AUTHOR'S NOTE

The Jewish tradition understands memory—and remembering—as sacred. We also understand that memory can be fluid, pliable, selective, and personal. In this memoir I have done my best to share the emotional truth of my memories as I experienced them, as accurately as possible. I recreated dialogue to the best of my ability. And I chose chapters and scenes from my life that I felt spoke to the particular theme of *Heart of a Stranger*. Every character in this memoir is real, but I have used pseudonyms in a few cases. Those pseudonyms appear as first names only.

Hebrew translations found in these pages are my own. Within those translations, any italics for emphasis are entirely mine.

HEART

OF A

STRANGER

INTRODUCTION

"*hat is a rabbi?*"

On December 29, 2021, reigning *Jeopardy!* champion Amy Schneider selected the $800 clue in the "I Am Woman" category. A picture of *me*, draped in a purple-striped prayer shawl, appeared in the box along with this clue: "Korean-born Angela Buchdahl is the first Asian American to be ordained a cantor as well as this leader of a Jewish congregation."

If you had told me as a little girl, newly immigrated with my Buddhist Korean mother and Jewish American father to a tiny Jewish community in Tacoma, Washington, that one day I would be featured as the *Jeopardy!* clue for "What is a rabbi?," I would have said, *That's impossible.*

This is the story of an unlikely rabbi. A story that could only happen in America. A journey that only became possible when I entered the world, in the seventies, thanks to its pioneers and revolutions. A story of loving parents who didn't let their wildly dissimilar families stand in the way of building their own, of mentors who told me to ignore the naysayers, of lucky breaks, stubborn determinism, and more than a touch of the Divine Hand.

Most people who go into the God business speak of a moment when they heard "the Call." You might imagine it to be a blinding flash of clarity, when God's voice is unmistakable, speaking directly, spelling out your future.

But it's rarely like that—even in the Bible, where God seems to call people all the time.

"Go forth from your land, from your birthplace, from your father's house, to the land I will show you . . . and you shall be a blessing" (Genesis 12:1).

Those words were God's call to Abraham five thousand years ago, when God instructed Abraham and his wife Sarah to leave everything behind—home, family, way of life—to follow God to an unknown place with a promise of blessing. The charge was clear; the purpose and path were not. Abraham and Sarah left all that was safe to pursue God's assurance of a lineage and legacy. Only when they crossed over the river Euphrates and became strangers in an unknown land could they give birth to a new people, *my people*, known as the Hebrews. Our name, *Ivrim* ("Hebrews"), translates literally as "those who cross over." The descendants of Abraham have been boundary crossers ever since.

My Jewish American father traveled far from home and met my Korean Buddhist mother in Seoul. Despite vast differences, they fell in love and married in 1968—one year after *Loving v. Virginia* made interracial marriage legal in every state. I was born in 1972, the same year that Sally Priesand, the first female rabbi in America, was ordained, following solely male leadership. That same year, Congress enacted Title IX, forcing schools across the country to increase equity for women. Yale, my alma mater, had only just achieved gender parity a few years before I arrived on campus. And I immigrated to America in the mid-1970s, just as the Reform Movement—a quintessentially American brand of liberal Judaism—changed its attitude and policies toward interfaith families like mine from outright rejection to outreach and inclusion. It's not an exaggeration to say that had I been born even a decade earlier, my very existence as a female Korean American Reform rabbi would not have been possible.

When I first felt pulled to become a rabbi, it didn't feel like a call.

More like a gasp: *What? Me? A rabbi?*

The first tug, at age ten, came through Jewish music: a vocalization of longing, release, pain, and praise that bypassed the intellect and channeled to every nerve ending in my body. When I sang Jewish music and prayer, I came alive and felt like God heard me. The sense of belonging was visceral, corporeal; through these melodies, I felt, and often witnessed, instantaneous community.

And then, at age sixteen, while on a summer program in Israel, I had a transformative reaction to the enduring exercise of Jewish study. When I was first guided through a piece of Talmud with its core text in the middle, surrounded in the margins by centuries of rabbinic commentary, so many thoughts started firing, my brain hurt. Ancient questions felt relevant, prescient. "How did they know?" I would ask of the sages who lived millennia before me. Once I realized that a rabbi's job was to immerse herself in this ongoing conversation, it became the only thing I wanted to do.

But the path to the rabbinate wasn't clear for a mixed-race Jewish girl from a town without many Jews. Despite feeling like the "Jewish representative" of Tacoma, the minute I ventured into the wider Jewish world, I learned that traditional Jewish law defined Jewish identity through matrilineal descent. Without a Jewish mother, the majority of Jews did not see me as "legally" Jewish. Even Reform Jews, who had recently adopted patrilineal descent as sufficient for Jewish status, took one look at my face and questioned how I could possibly be a *real* Jew. The deeper I got into Jewish leadership positions and into organized Jewish life, the more disorienting the thicket of legal strictures and Jewish signposts I didn't fully understand. That's where the angels came in: my hometown rabbi; a teacher here; a camp counselor there; friends who insisted I could do this, who said I could be one of Judaism's translators, despite there being no guide who resembled me. These champions waved off my rookie missteps and kept me focused on connecting more people to the same spiritual place that had become so essential for me.

I became a mother just months before I became a rabbi, and the responsibilities of caring for congregants and my own babies weighed on me with alternating gratification and guilt. With only male rabbinic supervisors in my career, this balancing act was also new territory. I saw the ways in which being a woman in this historically male profession challenged people's liberal and feminist assumptions, including my own.

And while I quickly learned that a rabbi's real routine was not going to match my romantic ideal of sitting all day long with ancient texts and talking about God and the meaning of life, I found the actual work even more compelling: drawing people's attention to the ways life is wondrous, pushing against complacency, opening avenues to a little more awe, and building and maintaining a real unwavering community. I am constantly moved in this job by the responsibility a rabbi is given to help a congregant see to the other side: whether navigating an ocean of grief, the shock of betrayal, the dread of a diagnosis, the transition to adulthood, or the earthquake of parenthood. Being a rabbi affords me a unique intimacy that comes with people's openness in life's key moments. Their vulnerability and trust is our covenant; I carry it carefully.

I became the first Asian American to be ordained a cantor in 1999 and the first to be ordained rabbi in 2001. Still, I did not set out to be a pioneer. The lure was the spell of ancient verses, the emotion of the music, the tug of a monumental story. I still pinch myself that today I am the senior rabbi of Central Synagogue in Manhattan, the first woman to lead this historic synagogue with the largest membership in the world and a livestream viewership that reaches more than one hundred countries. I am honored to serve one of the country's most engaged, vital, innovative, influential, and diverse Jewish communities. This position has given me the opportunity to offer Hanukkah Blessings at the White House for President Barack Obama in 2014 and President Joe Biden in 2023. I have been asked to serve as the Jewish voice in interfaith interviews on national television. But despite all this, there are still significant numbers of Jews who, if pressed, would say I'm not a Jew at all—at least not according to their legal definition. This belief has at times been said to my face, and it continues to show up in various media. The only response I've ever found is to continue to do what I do.

I never gave up because my ancestors' spiritual imperative and my parents' example taught me that the goal of life is not to be affirmed, settled, and comfortable. Rather, it's to find a purpose and pursue it. Almost always, this requires leaving what is most familiar and secure to wander into what is risky and uncertain. We hit barricades, get lost or diverted, but by persevering, we can become who we are called to be. Sometimes these journeys from the familiar are physical and geographic, but more often they are internal and emotional—a crossing of historic precedent, familial expectations, external barriers, or traditional gender roles. It would be easier to just stay put. No one likes to be a stranger; the desire to belong and stay safe is universal. But when we understand what it feels like to be an outsider, we cultivate a radical compassion for others who have been dismissed. We learn to press past the gatekeepers, turn exclusion into empathy, rejection into resilience. We stumble upon the blessings that come from inhabiting the heart of a stranger.

This book is part narrative memoir and part spiritual guidebook for boundary crossing. There is blessing on the other side of fear, and even as an outsider, we are never alone. I grew up feeling like an oddity—a freak on my worst days, and a pathfinder on my best. And yet when I studied the stories of my ancestors from a different era, from an extraordinarily divergent worldview, I'd feel the shock and comfort of seeing my own yearning in theirs. Of feeling connected to powerful threads and knowing that I have a tiny role to play in interweaving them.

My teacher Rabbi David Ellenson of blessed memory would often say, "All theology is autobiographical." I understood this to mean that the formative experiences of our lives—how we have loved, suffered, healed, forgiven—will necessarily color our core beliefs about whether God is loving and just, whether human beings are fundamentally good, whether or not we have agency to change our circumstances. So I share my story not as a blueprint but as a way of understanding how I have come to my convictions. Each chapter is followed by a *d'var Torah*—literally a "word of Torah"—with one Hebrew word anchoring a kernel of Jewish teaching. In these mini sermons, I've tried to convey some of Judaism's ancient wisdom, relevant today regardless of what faith, if any, you call your own.

My hope is that these texts resonate for you the way they've guided me. And that you will begin to see how *your* journeys are reflected in these stories.

When I immigrated to America just months before kindergarten, I remember classmates, noting my foreignness, asking me where I was from: "I'm Korean," I said proudly. Two years later when I returned to Korea for a summer visit, the children asked me the same question, to which I gave the same response. "No you're not," they retorted. I remember running to my mother, sobbing that I didn't have a home. She assured me: "Home is wherever your people are, Angela." This book is, fundamentally, about my zigzag quest to find belonging, and the realization that home is where you create it.

Abraham's expedition to "a land that I will show you," as God put it in the Bible, ended in Canaan, the Promised Land of Israel. There is this paradox: Abraham had to *leave* his birthplace to ultimately find his "homeland."

Sometimes we have to leave one home behind to build our truest one.

God—or some larger, unseen force in the world—has given every one of us the strength to make that pilgrimage, however daunting. When God promises Abraham, "You will be a blessing," the syntax matters: The guarantee is not that he will *receive* a blessing, but that he will become one.

Go forth. And you will be a blessing.

CHAPTER 1

The Mountain

I t's time to do the mountain," Mom announced to my father at the dinner table, where most of her pronouncements were made. My Korean mother, with her trim hair and trimmer frame, just under five feet tall, barely 110 pounds, clapped her hands and filled the kitchen with her infectious exuberance. My sister and I—ages seven and ten at the time—had no doubt which mountain she meant among the many Cascades encircling our city. Towering over fourteen thousand feet high, Mount Rainier dominated the Tacoma skyline, perched like a glittering crown atop the city below. Gina and I cheered; we were finally getting the keys to the palace in the clouds.

Mountains reminded my mother of her homeland; from everywhere you stand in Korea, you can see peaks. She also believed these masses of earth and rock carry a mystical, mythical power. According to ancient Korean shamanism, nature spirits reside in the hills, rivers, and trees. Starting in the fourth century, Koreans layered this shamanism with Buddhism, and we can see that amalgam in folktales. At bedtime, my mother filled my imagination with stories in which poor scholars were sages, the water held secrets, and tigers would spar with the Buddha. My mother's spirituality, like that of so many Koreans, was a mix of Confucianism, Buddhism, and animism—the belief that plants and other natural objects like rocks or rivers have souls. Where some might see contradictions among these philosophies, my mother just saw the connective tissue that bound all things, animate or not. Especially in nature, each atom could hold lessons for every other part of the ecosystem; wisdom, she insisted, was everywhere you looked.

Mount Rainier appeared to me like a massive climb, but my lanky father, with his gentle eyes and a game smile, insisted we could do it. "We won't start at the bottom," he assured us. "We'll start at Paradise."

"We're going to heaven?" I asked.

"Not quite. Paradise is the visitor center," my father clarified, adding that we could hike several different trails from the parking lot.

My deflation must have been obvious, because Dad reassured me that it *felt* a lot like Paradise up in the clouds. This mountain, his childhood set piece, had become a kind of personal metaphor: His family, part of a small Jewish community in Tacoma, had a tenacity and volatility that paralleled the geologic history of Mount Rainier in its eruptions and endurance.

For my Korean mother, our first mountain excursion was *an event*. She instructed my sister and me to help her prepare lunch. There would be no humdrum peanut butter sandwiches for our pilgrimage. We spent the morning wrapping rice and vegetables in kimbap hand rolls, packing up side dishes and kimchi, and marinating bulgogi—thin slices of beef for a barbecue.

"How do you plan to cook this when we get there?" I asked my mother.

"Charcoal and a little disposable grill," my mother said, as if that were obvious.

I could already feel the embarrassment of being the only family on the trail with a portable stove and dusty charcoal dangling from our packs. "Mom. I don't think Americans do that. We can just put the kimbap in baggies and be fine."

"Aiiii!" she exclaimed, throwing up her arms at the indignity of cold food on a trip of this importance. "And Americans also think baloney and a granola bar can be lunch! It's your first trip to the mountain! Dad will carry the charcoal." There would be no further discussion.

We woke early the next morning and loaded up our new maroon Buick with an Igloo of tea, food, and meat, the small gas grill rattling around in the trunk.

We passed the town's old paper and pulp mills, which infused the air with a sulfurous odor known as the "Tacoma aroma." Dad detoured to see "the Shop": Puget Sound Manufacturing, the family millwork business that my great-grandfather started in 1919 and that my uncles still ran sixty years later.

Trees had brought my Jewish ancestors—woodworkers by trade—to the state of Washington from Romania and Ukraine. My father never joined the family business but worked in proximity to lumber as the construction coordinator for the city's new pride, the Tacoma Dome, which in 1983 was the largest wooden-domed sports arena in the world.

I remember learning that its blue-and-white-diamond pattern was a modern homage to the city's iconic mountain. I inscribed my name on one of the rafters when Dad brought Gina and me to the site. The public was invited to scribble their signatures onto the last wooden beam that would be hoisted 150 feet to prop up the bubble. Taking special care with my cursive, I felt like I was sealing our family connection to history: *We are part of this.*

As we left Interstate 5 and turned onto Route 410, the city receded and the mountain grew strikingly lush and green. Forests of cedars, hemlocks, and Douglas firs were fixtures of our so-called Evergreen State. This was our first car with electric windows and Gina and I spent the greater part of the two-hour ride playing with the levers, racing each other to open and close our windows until Mom insisted we stop.

We parked the car and Mom loaded each of us with a knapsack weighted with bottles of water and containers of food from the Igloo. As we entered the trailhead and gazed up into the treetops, the mountain actually *did* look like a slice of heaven.

After an hour, it felt like we had been hiking for a day, but Mom never tolerated complaints, so Gina and I restrained ourselves to a few exaggerated sighs and foot-dragging. We had traveled far enough for the microclimate to change, from heavy foliage to snow and glaciers.

My mother instructed us to remove our backpacks and, before eating, sit and "appreciate the mountain."

"Feel the wind. Feel the rock under you. *You may think you are separate from this giant, but you are not. Be one with the mountain.*"

Gina and I looked at each other with raised eyebrows, suppressing our snickers. *Be one with the mountain?* That seemed silly. And impossible.

I looked at the tree in front of me, which was *a tree*, not a mountain. And yet, the tree and the mountain *were one.* Above me I saw snow, which I knew would melt away and be gone in a month. But for this moment, the snow and the mountain *were one.*

I closed my eyes and noticed the smooth stone holding me up. The way the wind stirred my hair and the branches at the same time. I felt the sheer thrill of actually sitting on this natural dinosaur, which I had seen from afar every day of my childhood. Then it hit me: For any other person looking at the mountain today, their view *would include me.* They might not know it, I thought, but *I am here,* indistinguishable from the mountain.

I thought of the Shema prayer we recite in synagogue, the one my rabbi called the "backbone of our faith." It ends with *Adonai Echad.* "God is One." In ancient times, pagans worshiped many gods. But Abraham founded a faith based on the surety that there is only one God.

As a child, I believed this to be a statement of superiority: Our God is *number one.* My misunderstanding was not entirely a result of immature, unschooled theology. Every Jewish service includes the *Mi Chamocha* prayer, which asks, "Who is like You, among the gods that are worshiped?" So I understood that there *were* other gods, but our God was best. *The One.*

But on that hike, my mother showed me that the verse we repeat— "God is One"—was never about preeminence or dominance, but rather wholeness.

"You might feel like a tiny speck on this mountain," she said, "but you are part of it. And when you breathe in the air, it becomes a part of you too."

Oneness is about unity, interconnectedness; if everything is one, then we all belong to this mountain, to the earth, and to each other. We are all gears in a fragile, interdependent system. This is not just the foundational principle of Judaism and my mother's Buddhism but a truth coursing through all religions.

My stomach grumbling, I opened my eyes to see a picnic blanket my mother had loaded with plates and Tupperware, the grill smoking.

"Use chopsticks to take the hot bulgogi off the grill," she instructed.

It sizzled in my mouth. The day's effort, which exhausted both my legs and head, only seemed to intensify the flavor.

"Chew, chew!" she slowed us. "I know you're hungry, but you must enjoy!"

My sister and I collapsed on the blanket after lunch, warmed by the fullness of our bellies, the blazing sun, and our mother's entreaty: *Be one with the mountain.*

She had no Buddhist community in Tacoma. But my mother made the mountain her temple and the grill her altar. She wanted us to taste her particular spirituality—forged in meditation, breath, presence, and a conviction that we are all One.

Echad
ONENESS

I walked into an apartment on the twentieth floor.

A hospital bed had been placed in the living room overlooking Central Park so that the dying man could look out the window onto the city that had been his home since birth.

His wife thanked me for coming. Children and grandchildren had gathered from all over the country.

I had been summoned to help usher this beloved patriarch into eternal life. I invited the extended family to gather around him. Relatives held his hand. He had been a real estate giant, but in the end it was not the skyscrapers he built, or the charity he gave, but this circle around him that would be his legacy.

And just as the biblical Jacob offered blessings on his deathbed, so did this man bless each person around him. Words of gratitude, praise, and comfort.

I delivered the viddui, a deathbed confessional that we also recite on Yom Kippur, our day of atonement. It's a simple prayer that encourages the dying to forgive the lingering harms of others, and in turn asks God to forgive our own shortcomings.

I invited the entire family to join me in saying the Shema, the last words a Jew is instructed to utter before leaving this earth.

Shema Yisrael. Hear, O Israel, Adonai is our God. God is One.

Why do we say this prayer before we die?

Perhaps because it encapsulates the monotheistic core of Judaism that undergirds all other beliefs.

A midrash—a rabbinic legend—tells of another reason that the Shema is said not just daily but specifically at our deathbed.

When the biblical patriarch Jacob—renamed "Israel" by God—was nearing death, his twelve sons all gathered around him. Jacob worried aloud that his children would not continue to tell his story or carry on his values.

But then something beautiful happened:

His sons drew close to him and loudly declared the first line of the prayer,

> *Shema Yisrael!* Listen, **Israel** (Jacob's other name).
> *Adonai Eloheinu.* Adonai is our God.
>
> *Adonai Echad.* God is One.

It's as if his children were saying, "Listen, Father. We will carry on your faith and story. None of us will leave your legacy behind."

Jacob uttered with his last breath, *"Baruch shem kavod,"* the second line of the Shema, which can loosely be summed up as "Thank God." He was reassured, finally ready to leave the world with the knowledge that Judaism in his family would not end with him. That is one explanation for why it is customary to say the first line of the Shema in a loud voice and the second line in a whisper, as Jacob did before he departed.

I remind all those gathered that dying is a return—to the Source from which all of us came. Whether you take a religious view that we originate from clay shaped by God's hand or a scientific view that we are made from the stardust of exploding supernovas, it all serves to remind us that we have the same beginning and end. Ashes to ashes. Dust to dust. I tell the family that when we say the Shema at the bedside of the dying, we remind them they are returning to Oneness.

We often think of ourselves as distinct from others. Individual, independent, self-sufficient. But in truth we are part of an undeniable whole, more entwined than we sometimes admit. We all begin and end the same way; that makes us one.

Rather than devastate us as we face an ending, this idea can be a source of comfort. If everything is one, then *you* are essential to—and inextricable from—that Oneness, intertwined with the stars you see and the earth you stand on. Shepherded by a force you may or may not believe in but whose power binds us together and promises unexpected strength to cross whatever boundary is before you.

CHAPTER 2

A War and an Education

Yi Sulja, my mother, was a boundary-crosser before I understood the notion, the first person to teach me about risk and resettlement.

Sulja was born in Japan in July of 1942, in the middle of World War II. While Japan was battling the world, Mom's home country of Korea was in a different struggle: a decades-long occupation by the Japanese Empire. Starting in the 1920s, Japanese colonizers forcibly brought Korean intellectuals, artists, and even female sex slaves back to Japan to serve their national interests. Since my great-grandfather was a Confucian scholar, he and his family, including the five-year-old Gae-ran, who would one day be my grandmother, were taken captive and brought to Japan. This is how my mother and many of her siblings would be born on foreign soil and obligated to take Japanese names.

Having spent most of her childhood and early adult life in Japan, forced to speak only Japanese in public, my grandmother started to feel Japan was her home. Nevertheless she was always viewed as a stranger—Korean, and lower class. With few professions available to her, Gae-ran ran a boardinghouse near Osaka and eked out a living.

One day, a handsome Korean resistance fighter showed up seeking lodging and food: It was the man who would become my grandfather, Yi Sam-dal, clandestinely running messages between the Korean independence movement and Korean nationals in Japan. Though not rich, he was a *yangban*, part of an elite, scholarly class versed in Korean history, Confucian classics, and literature. He carried himself like royalty, believing himself descended from Korean kings, though this status carried no weight in Japan. My grandmother, also the daughter of *yangban*, was a legendary cook, and apparently that sealed it for my grandfather. It was an unlikely match: She a pragmatic, astute businesswoman, and he an ideologue and dreamer. As my mother tells it, after marriage, her father continued his resistance work, and every time he returned to Japan from Korea, my grandmother would get pregnant and have another child. Gae-ran eventually gave birth to nine babies, seven of whom grew into adulthood.

When World War II ended, with Japan defeated and the occupation over, my grandfather was elated that finally their family could move back to Korea. My grandmother resisted; she felt comfortable in Japan despite her Korean lineage. Plus, she had a flourishing business, having added a bookshop to her small inn, while my grandfather was now out of a job. My grandfather proudly insisted they return to Korea. How could they not go back to their homeland?

When they arrived at my grandfather's small village, they found their neighbors did not fully accept this Korean woman who spoke with a Japanese accent. But my grandfather garnered a certain respect because he was one of the few in town who was literate. He became the town's storyteller, and neighbors would crowd into their hanok to hear his novelistic oratory, bringing a bottle of soju or a bag of rice as payment. He regaled them for hours.

Just as their rural town began to recover from both the occupation and the Second World War, the Korean War started. My mother's family was forced to flee once again, this time to a remote refugee camp outside Busan, Korea.

When I ask my mother about that time, she admits that it felt like an adventure. Later she realized how difficult this chapter must have been for her mother—pregnant, parenting five young children, able to pack only a few belongings, forced to live in leaky tents.

When Gae-ran delivered her sixth child, Pyongyung, in the wartime camp, the midwife screamed. Something was terribly wrong. Gae-ran believed that all the stress of war and dislocation during her pregnancy had caused what they called his "deformity"—a cleft palate. It was many years before they could afford to pay a surgeon to repair it.

My grandfather Yi Sam-dal died when my mom was just eleven, leaving Gae-ran to raise seven children alone. Older siblings watched over the younger ones and helped with cooking and cleaning while my grandmother opened a bookstore to support the family. From a young age, my mother was more interested in assisting at the bookstore than in the kitchen. She unpacked boxes, stocked shelves, and answered customers questions, reading as many books as time allowed, gaining a lens on the world beyond her small village.

Mom has always recalled a childhood that was happy despite its deprivations. On the banks of the Nakdong river, women washed clothes and children roamed freely. Mom was mischievous, often the ringleader of a band that would steal peanuts or a prize watermelon from a neighboring farm. Though she owned almost nothing, her days were buoyed by filched treats, retelling her father's tales, and reading volume after volume from her mother's bookshop.

My mother began to think about higher education—possible only if she passed a challenging national exam. Then and to this day, South Korea offers one definitive, centralized test, called *Suneung*, seen as the culmination of an entire academic career, which determines whether one may attend college. At twenty, Mom moved into a Buddhist temple for six months to prepare for the exam. Alone with the monks, she woke up each morning, meditated, completed chores, and then studied diligently. She scored the highest marks, receiving a full scholarship to Hyosung Women's College in neighboring Daegu. She went on to graduate studies at Ewha and Yonsei Universities in Seoul, two of the most prestigious schools in the country. Neither her parents nor a single one of her six siblings had ever attended college or even attempted to take the test.

Whenever she recounts this story to me, I can sense that she, too, had felt a calling of some kind. Once she glimpsed the world that education opened, she hungered for it.

Everything that came after stemmed from her original grit and rigor. My mother is diminutive in stature but inspires big awe; growing up, my sister and I both revered and feared her. Her parenting philosophy was summed up in her oft-said dictum: "Children are like bamboo; bend them while they're young."

My mother bent us plenty.

She was the strictest mom I knew among my friends, and the only one who used a switch from the yard on the back of our legs when she really disapproved of our behavior. The *sarangeh-mae*, "cane of love," was a classic Korean-mom punishment but totally foreign to my American friends, so I told no one about the three times she actually used it. But even as I found it embarrassing (and no longer recollect what I did to warrant the whacks), I do remember that my mother never resorted to the branch in fury. She would collect herself and dole out the discipline as a calm and careful form of loving correction, which is just how I experienced it.

Ironically, once I became a teenager, my mother went hands-off: She gave me no curfews, trusted me to spend weekends in middle school at a ski cabin with "the potheads," and never once punished me.

"I bend you while you're young, so now you're older, you grew straight! I don't worry about you."

I watch her these days, vigorously sweeping her floors at age eighty-two, firing the garden hose at her porch plants, expertly flipping a large watercress pancake and then cutting into it with kitchen shears, spooning out spicy gochujang sauce, insisting we sample the tea she brewed or the kimchi she fermented, and I see a hard-driving athlete who never tires, energized by her to-do list. I watch her direct my father—eighty-four as I write this—to haul large metal containers into their makeshift garden, where she's growing the herbs she cooks with every day. I watch how young Korean community leaders thank Mom for all the resources she created five decades ago at the Korean Women's Association for Korean immigrants who were overwhelmed by a new land and a difficult language. Tiny as Mom is physically, the first word that comes to mind when I think of her is "fighter."

Sometimes when I talk to a synagogue congregant facing something hard, I think about my mother's tenacity, the inner resources none of us know we have until we're forced to marshal them. Though she never warmed to traditional religious observance, Mom believed she could call upon some reservoir of strength that was beyond her. That might be the very definition of faith.

Gesher
BRIDGE

At Jewish summer camp, there was one song guaranteed to get everyone belting and bouncing on the chorus: *"Gesher Tzar Me'od"*—"The World Is a Narrow Bridge." An Orthodox American Rabbi, Baruch Chait, who moved to Israel and founded an Orthodox seminary, was the unlikely composer of this iconic and beloved song, ubiquitous in Israel and the wider Jewish world.

Chait composed *"Gesher Tzar Me'od"* for soldiers in 1973 during Israel's Yom Kippur War. Adapting the words of the eighteenth-century Rabbi Nachman of Breslov, founder of Hasidic Judaism, Chait sang:

"Kol ha'olam kulo, gesher tzar me'od." "The whole world is a very narrow bridge."

And crucially: *"Lo lefached klal."* "The main thing is to have no fear at all."

The words and the melody became an anthem of our people.

When I was young and felt invincible, it was easy to have no fear. I biked without a helmet. I danced in public. I skied mountain faces way beyond my skill. I overshared my innermost thoughts.

But as I got older, and experienced the fragility of my body, the betrayal of broken secrets, my first real heartbreak, the shame of failure, the finality of a loved one's death, I realized how narrow that bridge is, and how precarious. The charge to fear nothing began to seem willfully blind, naive, and maybe even dangerous.

Eventually I realized that the goal isn't to *never* feel fear but to not let fear win.

I recently learned that Rabbi Chait, when he set Nachman's words to music, had actually altered the words to say *lo lefached klal*, "have no fear." But Nachman originally used the verb "fear" in the Hebrew reflexive form: *lo yit'pached klal*, which offered a more profound truth: "The most important thing is not to bring fear *upon ourselves*."

We are in control of our fear. Fear is a choice.

There is a Talmudic teaching by the second-century BCE sage Ben Sira that cautions: "Do not suffer from tomorrow's trouble . . . as you do not know what a day will bring" (Yevamot 63b).

Ben Sira is not denying the pain and suffering from loss, betrayal, and illness that we might experience *today*, which is inevitable and real. But he suggests that our anxiety about the hypothetical future may be pointless. Ben Sira essentially states: Tomorrow, you may be dead, so why worry about something you may never have to face, about a world that may change before your fears come to pass? While his statement could seem a harsh response to our worries for tomorrow, he thrusts our mortality before us to shake us into the present moment instead.

My mother has always had this orientation. Maybe that's because so many of the things we fear *did* happen to her: She was a refugee. She lost her father while still young. She traveled to a new country in which she didn't always feel welcome. She has walked that narrow bridge and is still standing. She'd developed the muscle to focus on what was in front of her and not what might be.

Mom modeled the Buddhist maxim that we should not judge a moment as good or bad before understanding how it fits into the whole of our experience. My mother didn't tell us everything would be fine, but simply trusted that every one of life's events—joyful or calamitous—had something to teach. There is not only one positive outcome to any situation, she insisted, nor only one love in our lives. A painful hurdle, which we might at first wish never happened, might actually be the source of our greatest growth. Whenever I'm feeling anxious, this long view still helps. And when I'm overcome by fear, I push myself to keep moving forward.

Nachman describes the bridge as narrow on purpose: The narrowness leaves little room for error, which makes it seem more hazardous to cross. Life can feel unforgiving and shaky like that. But if you train your eyes on the rung just ahead of you and place one foot in front of the other, you do—eventually—get to solid ground.

CHAPTER 3

Love Wins

W hen he smiled, he had these terrible teeth."

My mother was describing the nice Korean doctor whom the local matchmaker had found for her, the one she refused to marry. "It was not only bad teeth," she tells me. "There was no way I could marry a typical Korean man. I was not going to cook his dinner and sit in the kitchen."

Korean marriages in the 1960s were arranged for economic stability, geographic desirability, and a good gene pool. But my mother had read too many Western novels—Austen, Hemingway, Fitzgerald—to settle for the smart doctor with a smile she couldn't imagine kissing.

When my father, Fred Warnick, a recent Stanford graduate in military uniform, arrived in Daegu through his ROTC placement, he was invited to give a talk at the Pine Tree Club on "college life in America." My mother and her fellow English literature graduate students frequented the Pine Tree Club's weekly meetings to practice their English and learn more about American life. The cliché of a dashing man in uniform held true; the friends were atwitter. Mom thought Dad was handsome, dignified. When one friend suggested Lieutenant Warnick meet them at the tea room for a weekly English conversational lesson, Dad remembers, "How could I turn that down?"

Her weekly class began with six of her girlfriends. One by one they dropped out until just Mom and Dad remained.

I have often wondered how they managed to fall in love when their worlds were nearly indecipherable to each other.

My father, Fred, the third of four children, was born in 1940 in Tacoma, Washington, a third-generation Jewish American. His Warnick ancestors, woodworkers all, built a prosperous millworking shop that made doors, fireplace mantels, and cabinets. The postwar era was good for their business. My grandfather Robert Warnick, a bit of a showman, enjoyed the prosperity of the postwar building boom. Often seen with a cigar in his hand and a sarcastic quip on his tongue, he bought one of the original Cadillacs with tailfins and wraparound chrome, owned the first color television on the block, and loved entertaining friends on Sunday evenings at their beach house on the Puget Sound.

Dad spent his childhood summers at that magical getaway, named "Aljafrel" for the four children in the family: Alan, Jack, Fred, and Elsa. The older children worked in the woodshop during the day and crossed the famed Narrows Bridge to Aljafrel every night. My father and his younger sister spent their days at the Sound with my grandmother, playing cards, lazing on the paddleboat, and swimming. When my father turned fourteen, he did what his two older brothers had done: went into the shop with their father for a forty-hour workweek, lunch pail in hand, learning the ropes, sorting lumber, running simple machines, and doing "gopher" work.

Grandma Phreda was the classic Jewish matriarch, playing mah-jongg, canasta, and bridge every week with the shul ladies, sprinkling Yiddish (her parents' mother tongue) into arguments to get her point across, making gefilte fish from scratch in a meat grinder. True to their generation, my grandparents socialized primarily with the few dozen other Jewish families in town.

My father has often said that his parents' Jewish identity was rooted mainly in being with other Jews. And while they weren't rigorously religious, his family never missed a major Jewish holiday, bar mitzvah, or yahrzeit—the anniversary of a loved one's death. Their Reform synagogue was central to their lives, a place where they didn't have to explain their difference or encounter coded antisemitism. Dad's brothers became the temple's secretary and president. Their Jewishness focused on family, history, serving others, and the hope of a Jewish state.

Eventually, my father chose not to follow his older brothers into the family millworking business; Al and Jack were running it well without him, and he'd long dreamed of studying architecture. An avid reader with a memory like an almanac, my father, Fred, was admitted to Stanford and traveled there for its distinguished architecture program.

All the while, back in Tacoma, the family millwork business was flagging. The industry was changing: Consumers no longer preferred just wood-paneled doors but metal and plastic, which the Warnicks didn't offer. Most wood manufacturers had moved to machine fabrication, but my grandfather refused to modernize, despite my uncles' entreaties. Eventually the business went bankrupt and my grandparents' marriage began to fray. My grandfather gave Grandma Phreda an ultimatum: *Side with me or your sons.* They divorced after forty years of marriage.

As the family business was on the brink of closing for good, the Tacoma Jewish community felt compelled to help: They believed in the company—Puget Sound Manufacturing—but no longer in its elder statesman. So a minyan of families from the synagogue each put up $10,000 of collateral for a $100,000 loan to revive the Warnick business under the next generation. They set only one condition: My grandfather could not step foot in the shop. Just as Phreda had, the Jewish community and the bank picked a side and went with the two young Warnicks in their thirties, whom they trusted to renew the business.

It is hard to imagine this degree of internal strain in such a close family. My uncle Jack remembers the times his father, no longer jovial or social, would show up despite being barred from the office. Jack or Al would duck out for a walk when they saw him coming to avoid having to confront him.

In the midst of this turmoil, my father—graduating college with debt, not knowing the full extent of how his family's finances were spiraling—enrolled in ROTC. The program stationed Dad in Korea, an ocean away from the struggles at home. He became enamored with the country and decided to stay after his service ended. Just as my father's relationship with my mother started to get serious, his family called him back home, sending a letter to the US Embassy in Tokyo, the only way to receive mail. Things were worsening in the business and his father, depressed and angry, began withdrawing from every family member and friend. My dad flew to Tacoma without saying goodbye to Sulja; he didn't know how to contact her in time and expected to be gone just a few months. He cried all the way home. His "brief return" turned into two years.

When Fred finally returned to Korea in 1967, Sulja was hurt by his long absence, even though he had begun sending letters a few months after he had disappeared without explanation. But she chose to focus on the fact that he had come back for her, even arranging a visit with her skeptical mother, Gae-ran. Fred used his broken Korean to convey his admiration for her culture and to make a promise to raise their children with a Korean heritage. Gae-ran was not convinced; she knew what it meant to start a new life in a new country and feared that prospect for her daughter. Fred assured her he would not take Sulja away from her—and he honored that vow until she died.

My parents united across a gaping divide in culture, nationality, class, and religion. It was almost as if they were raised in separate centuries. But whenever I've asked them how they possibly could have married, they answered simply: "We had similar values." Both respected tradition. Both revered their mothers and families. Both felt the transformative power of learning. Both were rooted in a bigger cultural story. When it came to the tentpoles of family life, my parents saw the world the same way.

But Korea was not so hospitable to couples of different backgrounds. At that time, a Korean woman's decision to marry an American man was viewed as disgraceful. Decades of American military presence since the Korean War had led to state-sanctioned prostitution. The government operated a program complete with medical screening and "escort" etiquette classes for poor, rural Korean women to serve as "personal ambassadors" for American GIs.

Over time, the children born of these unions became a source of national shame, and the government began sending many biracial children abroad to be adopted "for their own good." Since a Korean child's nationality came through the patrilineal line (unlike in Judaism), Korean norms held that the child of a Korean mother and an American father was essentially stateless.

In 1973, just after I was born, twenty-year-old Park Geun-sik, the child of an American soldier and Korean mother, born a "GI baby" in the Korean War, attempted suicide by leaping from a Seoul-bound train. His handwritten note made headlines; Park described his "cursed life" as a biracial child in the ethnically homogenous Korean society. He urged President Park Chung-hee to improve the plight of "undesirable" biracial children who were considered the lowest caste—bullied and sidelined and statistically far more likely to drop out of school, be unemployed, or take their own lives.

As a young child growing up in Korea before age five, I understood none of this prejudice; my world was confined to my extended family, which embraced us. Our home—a traditional *hanok* with sparsely furnished rooms set around a courtyard, a raised *ondol* floor that provided heat, and tiled roof—was the extended family's central gathering place because my *halmuni*, my grandmother, lived with us.

My earliest memories include frequent, noisy, joyful get-togethers with my mother's sisters, brothers, and so many cousins. I remember being squeezed by doting, clucking aunts forcing me to eat *just one more bite*. We would play *Yut Nori*, an ancient Korean game, tossing the four wooden batons that determine a player's movement around the stitched cloth board. We sat on the floor, heated from below through flues that extended from the kitchen cooking area to the chimney. The paper screen walls could not contain the smells of garlic and gochujang that filled every room when the women of the family gathered to cook. Without a television in the house, we entertained ourselves by taking turns performing Korean songs.

My father, the lone, tall American in a sea of Korean chatter, could have felt uneasy in this large family hubbub, but he loved being a fly on the wall, taking it all in. My aunties fussed over him, celebrating his every elementary Korean utterance as he gamely learned their native tongue. *Wan-suhbang, j'all hessum-needa!* "Warnick-husband is doing so well!" they would affirm. To this day, they describe my father as "the kindest man," and at our large family gatherings, when all the aunties and cousins bring over trays of galbi-gui, naengmyeon, and bulgogi, I watch my dad beaming, still delighted by his good fortune.

Though my mother swore she would never be a traditional Korean wife, when she married Dad in Korea in 1968, she and her sisters had no qualms about cooking, serving, and overpraising him. He, in turn, leaned into all things Korean. When Gina and I were toddlers, he loved teaching us about the kings of Korea, eating doenjang—the strangest, smelliest, spicy fish stew—and taking our extended Korean clan to picnic on the Seoraksan mountain, where I ran naked except for my diaper. For my father in the early 1970s, Korea became more than his wife's homeland or his daughters' birthplace; it was a mirror of his Jewish upbringing, with the same tumult of relatives and honoring of family, albeit in a different language. His adopted Korean *mishpachah* allowed him a whole new identity, where he could feel free of his Tacoma family's restraints or expectations.

But as I got closer to my first year in school, my mother, knowing the discrimination that biracial children in Korea faced from teachers and the inevitable bullying from students, would not wait to watch her children suffer the same harsh judgment. Though my father had assured Gae-ran that he would not take our family out of Korea, now she was gone—dead from a stroke—and no longer holding him there. My mother told my father that it would be best for their children to leave Korea, despite her heartbreak at abandoning family, her *hanok*, and every childhood friend. They arrived in Tacoma in 1977 when I was five and my sister three, shipping a boatload of Korean furnishings, including my mother's favorite silk screens, medicine chests, blankets and Korean pottery.

While Dad recounts a rosy reentry into Tacoma routine, Mom tells a starker story of dislocation and loneliness. She left everything familiar behind to come to a place she knew only from books. But America didn't resemble the stories she'd read at all. Everything felt foreign—from the giant supermarkets, which lacked all of the foods she missed, to our schools, where teachers looked down upon her because of her accent. Dad, who hadn't realized how much the business had strained the Warnick family, was busy trying to find work. Mom fell into a depression in those early years, feeling alien and anxious. Yet she put on a gutsy front for her two young daughters and carved out a sense of home, despite yearning for her original one.

My parent's unlikely courtship across cultures and their daunting relocation across the ocean tested their marriage. At times it shook their foundation, reverberating into fights that could reach high volumes and include thrown objects. But the truth is that love won when it came to Sulja and Fred: Not the kind with overt professions of adoration and flowers but the kind with ultimate trust and unconditional acceptance. Devotion emboldened my parents to ignore fences and naysayers, to keep insisting on finding common ground when they shared so little in common and to start a new family, no matter how unconventional, and a home where Gina and I felt we unquestionably belonged.

V'Ahavta
AND YOU SHALL LOVE

We all know the Golden Rule: "Do unto others as you would have them do unto you."

Sometimes it's phrased in the negative: "What is hateful to you, do not do to others."

My favorite formulation is found in Leviticus, in a section of verses known as the Holiness code:

V'ahavta l'reyacha kamocha: "You shall love your neighbor as yourself."

V'ahavta: "You shall love."

This command lies at the spiritual center of the Torah, and at the literal one as well: "Love your neighbor as yourself" is the middle verse found in the middle book of the Torah. It is literally the innermost core of our sacred text.

How can you command someone to *love*? The first thing to understand is that what is being commanded is not an emotion. We are not being commanded to *feel love* but to *do love*—a series of loving actions: Visit a loved one who is sick. Show interest in what matters to a friend. Remember a birthday or milestone. Honor someone's dignity when they are vulnerable.

Love, as it's commanded, means responsibility.

What would it take to love your neighbor as yourself? The neighbor who has a completely different story from yours, who might trust in a different God, or none at all, who talks and dresses and eats and votes in a way that is totally foreign to you.

My obligation to love stems from that Oneness of God asserted in the Shema prayer, and embodied by what my mother taught me on the mountain: If we all came from the same source, then we are bound to one another. Interconnected. So we must protect each other. Pitch in.

What would it look like to act on this sense of responsibility for your neighbor? The surrounding verses of this command guide us a bit: Don't cheat someone. Don't put a stumbling block before the blind. Don't judge another based on whether they are poor or rich. Don't profit off the blood of others. Don't make laborers wait for their wages.

We can reframe these in the positive: Call the person who has no companion. Bring food to the ill neighbor. Listen closely to a perspective you do not share. Give your time: tutor, feed, clothe, or counsel.

This is how we love: by performing loving actions, behaviors that recognize the value, dignity, and worth of every human being.

Many people think that loving our neighbor is the hardest part of this command. But focus on the last half of the verse: Love your neighbor as yourself.

As yourself.

It is a reminder that we can *only* love others as much as we love ourselves. If we have trouble valuing ourselves, we will be limited in how much we can value someone else. You can only love as much as you feel lovable. So bring compassion to your mistakes. Accept your shape, face, imperfections. Acknowledge that the to-do list is endless. Focus more on what you have than what you lack. Give yourself unproductive time. Rush less, control less, compare less, worry less. Be where you are. Get quiet enough to hear your heart. Remember you are worth hearing. You are worth loving.

Love your neighbor as yourself.

Love yourself as your neighbor.

CHAPTER 4

Tacoma

Our first home in America—a small unit in a nondescript two-story olive-green apartment complex—sat across the street from the synagogue where four generations of Warnicks had become bar mitzvah. It was the only synagogue for thirty miles.

Temple Beth El was designed to resemble a large tent, an echo of the makeshift shelters built by our ancestors as they wandered in the desert on the way to the Promised Land. The center pillar, a focal point of the sanctuary, soars to the ceiling with stained glass on all sides. There is a serene outdoor garden with benches and plant species from Israel and a large front lawn where children played Red Rover during summer day camp.

Upon arriving from Korea in 1977, we immediately joined Temple Beth El, and I began attending *Gan*, the nursery school. My parents chose Judaism for me and my sister, Gina, not as a renunciation of my mother's Buddhism but as an embrace of my father's extended Tacoma family. It was also, my mother believed, an easier way for us to become *American*. Temple Beth El had long been the Warnick sanctuary, and my parents agreed it was important for us to feel connected to a community beyond our family. I remember Dad telling me over and over that we *fully belonged*. "There is no such thing as half-Jewish," he'd repeat, as if to convince himself. "You are one hundred percent Jewish. You are also one hundred percent Korean. And one hundred percent American. You are all of it."

The rhythms of the temple became our own: weekly Sunday school, setting up tables and decorations for every holiday. We became fixtures at Shabbat services. I loved that the rabbi knew me and my place in so much Warnick history.

Whenever I walked in the door, I was greeted by surrogate Jewish aunts, uncles, and grandparents, in addition to my tribe of blood relatives, who pinched my cheeks, baked me mandelbrot, and cheered my milestones. I loved the wall of photographs that lined the corridors, one framed group tableau after the next, documenting every Confirmation class—the Reform ceremony when a tenth grader completes the "graduate" course after bar or bat mitzvah. Each of those snapshots was paired with a photo of the same students ten years earlier, at age five: their "Consecration" at Temple Beth El when they received miniature Torah scrolls.

I felt pride in how far back my Warnick family went on this wall, and that my kindergarten Consecration photo was already mounted alongside the dozen other Warnicks lining the hallowed hallways.

Temple Beth El showed me what a small, tight-knit Jewish community could be. Everyone knew one another, fed each other, danced the hora together, and showed up for every shiva. Every family contributed to a potluck bar mitzvah reception, volunteered to teach in the Sunday school, brought kugel to every bris, helped run the Purim carnival. There was a comforting, purposeful sense of teamwork, caretaking, and familiarity.

Mom made Temple Beth El her community, too. She took Hebrew classes, drove us to services, sang in the adult choir, and boiled wontons for the oneg. But Mom never converted. Judaism was introduced to her as a culture, even a race, which seemed impossible to merge with her immutable Korean core. A Korean immigrant could not, in Mom's mind, simply become an ethnic Jew; you were either born to it or not. I'm sure she also knew that her face, accent, and Korean cooking would always make her conspicuous, set her apart.

But I think the real reason my mother chose not to become a Jew is because, as friendly as everyone was to my mother in synagogue, they never quite treated her as *one of them*. Mom was a classic example of the *ger toshav*, what the Talmud calls "a resident alien," someone viewed as a permanent noncitizen who is welcome but never given a full-throated invitation to become a member herself.

I absorbed, even at a young age, the idea that while Jews might welcome the stranger, they keep them at arm's length. *We're so happy you're here, but you'll never be one of us.*

There is an old Jewish custom that instructs rabbis to turn away potential converts three times to test their resolve. And in most countries where Jews lived, our survival relied on the fact that we would not proselytize: We weren't considered a threatening club if we didn't try to solicit new members. But this insularity meant that Jewishness was transmitted primarily by birth and could be viewed as only biological, tribal. I didn't resent it so much as register it. There seemed a clear dividing line between who was family and who was a permanent guest.

I noticed that Mom was different from all the Jews. And that meant that I was different from all the Jews, too.

Maybe Mom's outsider status was the impetus that led her to welcome Korean strangers so doggedly. Over the course of eight years, Mom helped four of her siblings and their families immigrate to our town, assisting them with green cards, school enrollment, employment housing, and, importantly, where to buy Korean groceries—because food was our vocabulary and connection to the homeland.

Just as Mom made sure that no immigrant went hungry, she made sure no item of food went to waste. Long before "nose-to-tail eating" was trendy, before *Top Chef* made a sport of cooking from a jumble of ingredients, Koreans had a kind of cuisine that took the goal of discarding nothing to an art form. Unquestionably, Mom's frugality was shaped by living through the Korean War in base poverty. But it was also her reverence for food—and her mastery of what she could create out of smidgens—that made throwing anything out a crime. I would watch her open the fridge and take out leftover spinach salad, fried tofu, beef scraps—and of course handfuls of kimchi and more garlic—and magically transform it in broth to shirae-gi gook ("garbage soup") or with day-old rice into shirae-gi bap ("garbage fried rice").

My father had no such wartime excuse for his obsession with economizing. But his mother grew up a child of the Depression, so he also learned thrift as a virtue. He would repurpose all paper products, wrapping birthday gifts in old newspaper comics or reusing mail for letter-writing paper by flipping pages over to find clean space. He'd carefully slice the tops of envelopes, scratch out the address, and reclaim them. To this day, every correspondence I ever receive from my father—and there were countless camp letters and notes during college—are all on the backsides of paper with a slash through the original text, sent in a recycled envelope. At meals he would cut the flimsy paper napkins in half, challenging my sister and me to keep our fingers clean with the equivalent of a toilet paper square.

Despite my parents' frugality, when my aunt and her family of six arrived a few years after we'd settled, my mother treated them with typical Korean hospitality, meaning *like royalty*. Guests are not permitted to pay for anything, they're served the best of what you have, and their comfort trumps your own. In a move unthinkable by Western standards, my parents not only opened their small house but turned over their own bedroom to my aunt and uncle, the one closest to the only full bathroom we had. Mom and Dad moved upstairs to my father's study, where they slept on a Korean floor mattress and jammed their underwear and socks into desk drawers. Gina and I continued to share our bedroom in the former attic, while we reconfigured the basement so that my four cousins could sleep on Korean futons. The ten of us lived for six months in a 1,700-square-foot house with one shower.

Two years later, another set of cousins arrived: the three children of "Restaurant Emo," my aunt who owned a Korean barbecue. She wanted her children to get an American education but could not uproot her business and livelihood in Korea. So Restaurant Emo's kids lived with us for a year, and my mother became their legal guardian until the oldest, Hui Jung, turned eighteen.

Among the cousins who lived with us, my favorite was Joon Uk, whom we called Uki. He was the jester of the family, full of pranks and vitality, an electronics geek always up on the latest gadget. Uki and I were nearly the same age; when I left for college in New Haven, he graduated from high school with honors and enrolled at the University of Washington in Seattle to pursue a computer science degree. This was everything my aunt had hoped for when she sent him to America. While a student, Uki got a job at the local Best Buy, which not only helped pay for tuition but gave him a discount on all the gizmos he loved to explain to me in great detail.

At twenty-two, Uki was at the cash register when the store was robbed at gunpoint. He was shot in the head and died before the ambulance arrived. My mother had to drive up to Seattle to identify his body. His face was completely unrecognizable from the wound, but the watch he'd proudly bought himself for Christmas was unmistakable on his wrist.

I was living in Scarsdale after college when my mother called me with the news, one of the rare times I have heard her weep. Uki was her adopted son. She discouraged my coming home—I don't think she had room for my grief alongside her own. I curled up in bed alone and didn't move for days. Jacob, who was my boyfriend at the time, offered to stay at my side, but I didn't want his comfort. I was furious at the world.

Death was new for me. Grandma Phreda had left us a few months earlier, but she was eighty-four, and her passing was both calm and expected. Uki died in terror with a gun in his face, a senseless, violent end just as he was starting his life. Uki had been my childhood playmate. We binged together on the sugar cereal he snuck past my mom and danced in the basement to Duran Duran. How could he be gone? Such a spirit couldn't be snuffed out—so where was it? How could I keep him with me now that he'd disappeared?

I turned in a way I never had before to prayer, specifically the psalms, grateful that my Jewish tradition gave me the language and the permission to rage against God.

> From the deepest depths I cry out to you God.
>   (Psalm 130)
> I am weary from my groaning, every night my bed is
>   drenched with my tears. (Psalm 6)
> Don't hide Your face from me . . . Don't leave me.
>   (Psalm 27)

My mom had no such language to express her broken heart. Buddhist principles of equanimity and acceptance couldn't hold the weight of her suffering. She told me days later that her first impulse in the face of this unfathomable tragedy was to "cry out to Elohim"—a Hebrew name for God. In her grief, the language that bubbled up for my mother was Jewish. Her spirituality had always been quiet, private. But during her twenty years in the US, her religious *community* had been Jewish. When she felt unmoored, she reached for the ritual and reassurance of the tradition she'd come to share.

Mom later confided that Uki's killing was the only time—other than right before my bat mitzvah—that she seriously weighed conversion. Though she hadn't always felt part of Judaism in daily life, at this moment of grief, she needed it.

Ultimately, Mom abandoned that notion, unable to get past the sense that she would never feel part of a people she was not born into. But the experience stayed with me—the memory of her crying out for spiritual succor and finding it in Judaism. My great sadness is that she could never claim it for herself. But in a real sense, she embodied the Jewish ethos of crossing bravely to a foreign place. And it wasn't sufficient for her to make that trek alone; she gave others the courage.

Mom's "emigration operation" proved contagious. Within thirty years, the Korean population in the Seattle–Tacoma area would become the fourth largest in America.

The discipline and expertise of the immigrant's welcome became my mother's focus. She didn't stop after she brought much of her own family over. Mom co-founded the Korean Women's Association (KWA), a group she helped expand to thousands but that started with just a handful of women talking over tea in a living room. Together, the group shepherded waves of Korean immigrants into the US.

KWA became a crucial network for Korean newcomers looking to share meals and customs, to get help with paperwork, lodging, medical care, school enrollment, driving lessons, and the sad realities of domestic violence at the hands of some American husbands.

When my mother witnessed the indigent living conditions for Korean elders along South Tacoma Way—the city's most diverse, poor neighborhood—she submitted a proposal and won government funding for a low-income senior housing project in Tacoma. As KWA gained credibility with the state government and investors, Mom ultimately helped KWA launch and manage five building projects with more than 230 dwelling units for underserved seniors.

To this day, I am amazed at how an organization my mother co-founded during my childhood grew to become the second-largest social service organization in Washington state, with an $80 million budget and 1,500 employees in fourteen counties serving over fifteen thousand people a year—not just Koreans but new immigrants to Washington from multiple countries. Today, when I accompany Mom to the renovated KWA building in Tacoma, I'm bombarded by staff members eager to tell me that "Mrs. Warnick" is an inspirational "pioneer woman," a local icon. As a child I didn't appreciate her courage, creativity, or leadership, caught up in my annoyance at being dragged to the weekly dinner for elderly Koreans, where my sister and I were assigned rice duty—ladling out endless white balls to three hundred Korean seniors who came for company and a taste of home. We sat with our school books outside KWA meetings where traditional Yakwa honey cookies were laid out along with roasted barley tea. I watched Mom move around the room, asking the *ajumma* what they needed, hovering over someone trying to fill out a rental agreement or school application.

When Korean immigrants were too ashamed to discuss abuse at home by their husbands, Mom helped establish a domestic violence shelter. When there was no place to find Korean-language books, Mom created the first public Korean library in a KWA office space, a skill she learned from her days in Grandma's little bookstore.

Mom became certified to teach English as a Second Language and worked for thirty years in the Tacoma public schools, first instructing primarily Korean students and later immigrants from Vietnam, Cambodia, and Russia. In 1996, she established the first Korean language program in American public schools. Today there are hundreds. She taught Korean to local students and brought teens and school administrators on summer trips to see the country firsthand. She was South Korea's unofficial ambassador in Tacoma.

After retiring from teaching and several terms as KWA president, she and my father started a small business welcoming foreign exchange students to Tacoma. To this day, she matches dozens of young people with host families, placing them in schools and serving as their den mother as they acclimate to America for the first time.

Looking back, I see now that embracing the stranger was a form of spiritual practice for my mother. It went beyond a generous reflex; it fulfilled some deeper urge to shepherd, instruct, and protect.

Hachnasat Orchim
WELCOMING

Hachnasat orchim. The welcoming of guests is a core teaching of the Torah.

Judaism does not simply suggest we embrace outsiders It commands it.

Today, hospitality is something many of us prefer to do on our own terms—when it suits our convenience or requires little sacrifice. But that is not the standard set forth in our ancient texts.

When Abraham sent his servant Eliezer to find a wife for his son Isaac, Eliezar knew hospitality was *the* standard for Isaac's wife. So, he devised a test: As Eliezer traveled, he asked the maidens he encountered for water.

When Rebecca responded by offering a drink—not only for Eliezer but also his camels—she was considered worthy.

The ultimate example of open-handed hospitality comes when Abraham, newly circumcised at the ripe old age of ninety-nine, is not only healing from this delicate, painful procedure but is now permanently, physically marked as a stranger in a new land.

Rabbinic legend says that God intentionally made the desert oppressively hot to deter visitors from coming by and to discourage an elderly, recovering Abraham from looking for them. But Abraham nevertheless stands at the door of his tent, eagerly searching for anyone to welcome, despite the baking sun. Seeing how aggrieved Abraham is that no one is coming, God sends three angels in the form of men to pass by.

Abraham, in his compromised state, runs out to the strangers, bows before them, urges them inside. He slaughters a calf for them to add to Sarah's feast of curds and cake. He washes their feet with water, an ancient act of deep humility and welcome, and urges them *sa'adu libchem*—"to be refreshed"—which in Hebrew literally means to "nourish your hearts." The message is unmistakable: Welcoming the stranger means not just attending to their needs but honoring their dignity as well.

To me, Abraham and Sarah's hospitality seemed to strain plausibility, until I thought of it in the context of my mother's life. Abraham's welcome is not a paternalistic act of helping "those less fortunate." It nourishes his own heart.

This invitation and reception is itself a spiritual act of transformation—not for the angels *but for Abraham*. When Abraham welcomes these three wayfarers, he is no longer just the *stranger*; he becomes *the host*. The one who welcomes. When we open our doors—tents, houses, or communities—to welcome those who feel like outsiders, it changes the way *we feel*.

My mother was the stranger until she became the welcomer, acclimating her sisters who were more outsiders than she. Their newness made her realize she was no longer new. "I am the American now," she told me.

I have watched the same phenomenon unfold at my synagogue. Our volunteer greeters stand sentry at the doors to the sanctuary, welcoming the hundreds who arrive on a Friday night or Saturday morning, handing out programs for the service, saying, "Shabbat Shalom." It's a microcosm of Abraham and Sarah, but an important one: Our greeters, *shamashim* in Hebrew, tell me they feel changed by it. When you get to be the one who draws someone into a place, that place becomes yours.

I have also seen it happen with converts: One moment they feel insecure in their Judaism; the next they are dedicated learners, graduating to familiarity and eventually to expertise. For those who choose to start a family, their sense of belonging solidifies: They've become their children's teachers. The minute they start lighting Shabbat or Hanukkah candles—either with their kids or individually—they stop feeling like they're playacting a ritual that isn't their own. The convert now leads, models, anchors, and transmits.

I always return to a particular detail found in the rabbinic commentary about Abraham's welcome: He asks *God to wait for him* so he can go greet the three travelers. The Talmud says, "Hospitality toward guests is greater than receiving the Divine Presence" (Shabbat 127a).

It's no small thing that God stepped back for Abraham's hospitality. That was the greater good. When we put our fellow human beings first, we sanctify the encounter.

CHAPTER 5

Bedtime Prayers

I started leading nightly prayer services at eight years old, long before I would consider becoming a rabbi. Naturally, I included my little sister, Gina, because she was my best friend, first deputy, and co-conspirator in all things. And how could I *lead* worship if I didn't have at least one follower?

Gina and I shared an upstairs bedroom, a converted attic where the eaves on opposite sides of the room became the nooks for our twin beds. We decorated the angled ceiling by Scotch-taping the Scholastic Book Club animal posters that were included with the purchase of three books—something we begged our father to allow every month and he obliged. Dad put up curtain rods and we bought translucent white curtains with flowers on them, tied on each side. When we wanted privacy, we would close the curtains, creating a cozy puppy-and-kitty-filled cubby under our slanted canopy.

We each had our own desk and closet on our side of our room, and I had to walk through Gina's half of the room to get to mine. I believed fervently that there was no reason she had to walk into my territory, and I reminded her of that on many occasions. Yet, much to my chagrin, she continued to encroach. Finally I unspooled a masking tape line down the center of the room and insisted "No Trespassing." She complained that I had to go through her side just to come in and out the door, so my rule was unfair. We negotiated an accommodation: I was permitted one daily pass through her section and would allow her one in return. If either of us exceeded that amount, we owed the other five cents. The sibling desire to annoy and intrude now came at a cost, but we were both willing to pay it, as the little bowl of nickels on the bureau between us attested.

But when it got dark, and Gina and I settled into our beds, reviewing our day, giggling over something funny that Mom said, the walls came down.

I talked to God pretty regularly on my own: walking home from school, playing on the shores of the Puget Sound, making up songs for God while swinging on our backyard play set. But this ritual of bedtime prayers felt more official because I recited the same words every night, and some of them were *ancient*.

I understand in retrospect how unusual it was for me to start praying at such a young age. But as a child, whenever I learned of signposts or *tasks* of a Jewish life, I would inevitably take them on, urging my family to adopt a stricter routine.

My teacher Ms. Tovah at Temple Beth El said that I would get a star on the sticker chart at Sunday school for every blessing our family did on Shabbat: lighting candles, blessing challah, or making kiddush over wine or grape juice. So the candlesticks started coming out every Friday evening instead of our typical haphazard practice of "whenever we remembered." In my new policing of family Sabbath, I forgave the fact that we rarely had challah bread, unavailable in any Tacoma supermarket, but instead blessed the rice Mom made as part of her "traditional" Shabbat dinner.

Of course I wanted the Sunday school gold star. But it wasn't just the prize that motivated me. I felt excited to make my Jewish experience more committed, more true—to feel like I was "doing Jewish" the way Jewish should be done.

I also gleaned Jewish lessons through children's books, devouring classics like *Ella of All-of-a-Kind Family*, *It Could Always Be Worse*, and *The Carp in the Bathtub*, which romanticized New York Jewish life and its close-knit, early-immigrant striving. Our public library stocked very few Jewish-themed stories, but our synagogue had a "bookmobile" cart that moved between classrooms on Sunday, filled with volumes we could borrow. One was about Rachel, a serious Jewish girl who did lots of mitzvot (commandments); each night she'd recite the Shema before bed.

"Gina," I whispered to my sister as we settled under our covers that night. "Did you know that Jewish children are supposed to say the Shema before sleep?" She shook her head. "We should do that," I announced. "Let's start now."

Gina was always game. Night after night in our pajamas, I led us in unison as we covered our eyes with our small hands: *Shema Yisrael, Adonai Eloheinu, Adonai Echad.* Hear, O Israel, Adonai, our God, is One.

Later, in third grade, as I was flipping through the back of the Temple Beth El telephone directory, I came upon a "Bedtime Prayer for Children" and brought it up to our room like a purloined treasure.

"We should add this," I said earnestly. Gina, ever the sport, nodded intently.

> *Before I sleep I close my eyes to Thee, O God*
> *I thank Thee for Thy blessings all, which come to us*
> *   Thy children small*

O keep me safe throughout the night, that I may see
the morning light . . .

I still can recite it verbatim. It may have been a Protestant-inspired "Jewish" prayer, but I liked what it said. The words made me feel held, heard, watched over.

Yet something was still missing from our cobbled-together worship. I decided we needed to include unscripted, personal prayers so we could pray for the people we loved by name. I wanted to ask for God's protection, especially over Gina, whom my mother always insisted was my personal responsibility. She ranked first in my litany of requests.

When Gina was five, Mom gave her a short pageboy haircut. Naturally athletic and strong, it fit her scrappy inclinations, which included playing dodgeball and soccer with the boys at recess rather than hopscotch and swings with the girls. But it meant that people confused her for a boy, which she didn't like. Gina had a different mixture of my parents' features, a more narrow face, fuller mouth, stronger nose. Her ethnicity was hard to identify; she was frequently asked if she was Native American or Hispanic and rarely assumed to be Asian. People often stared, trying to figure her out. Around middle school, she grew out her lustrous hair, discovered lip gloss, and grew into an arresting beauty. And people kept staring.

Gina also had a particularly sweet and trusting heart. I remember her at six, running to me in tears, having spotted a dead bird in our alley. She insisted that our father give it a proper burial in our backyard while I recited the Kaddish. Sometimes even a dead bug or popped balloon spotted on our walk home made Gina stop short and demand we take a moment to grieve. She felt connected to the souls of all things, which is why she became a vegetarian at an early age; she couldn't bear eating animals. I never envied Gina her striking looks; there was never a question that she was the more beautiful sister, and her loveliness felt like one of God's unique gifts to her. What I did envy sometimes—and still do—is her tenderness. Despite the fact that the rabbinic roles of consoler and pastor feel natural to me, I have observed that Gina is more instinctively kind than I am, more emotional, gentler. Certainly, her penchant to experience things more deeply has made her such an extraordinary musician, friend, and sister.

So my extemporaneous prayers always began by asking God to watch over Gina, Mommy and Daddy, my grandma Phreda, and my friends Hilary, Marlette, and Phuong. I then asked God for world peace, more patience to practice piano, help on the next day's math test. I didn't actually expect that God would magically provide these things, but somehow I felt certain that articulating my wishes—to a greater force—was a critical step in realizing them.

Thus began our bedtime liturgy. I led my sister in the same recitations every night:

- The Shema
- The synagogue telephone directory's Bedtime Prayer for Children
- Personal prayers

We would conclude by singing an elaborate "amen" in the harmony we heard and copied from our temple choir.

Our little bedtime service lasted for years. Even when I entered high school and Gina and I finally got our own rooms, we did not stop.

"Gina! You ready for the Shema?" I would yell across the hall with our doors open.

To this day, when we reunite from opposite coasts (Gina directs a music department in LA), my sister and I say our nightly prayers together before we go to bed. Neither of us has forgotten a word. It is still our special language, a cable of connection, for two little girls trying to find their way to speak to God.

I believe that all children are born with faith. Some combination of society, parenting, and peer pressure often knocks it out of us. But those who discover belief always had it; in a sense, we just had to relearn what we already knew.

How many young children start off talking to inanimate objects—stuffed animals, imaginary friends? How often do adults look into an infant's eyes and have the sense they understand something we don't? A child's inclination to believe—in the tooth fairy, Moses parting the Red Sea, Santa Claus, or God—is not necessarily about deity as a being but about the world having some enchantment, some hidden power.

Lailah—"night"—is the only female angel in our tradition. She is described in the Talmud as the Angel of Conception: She selects an appropriate soul to be matched with every infant that is born. While the baby is forming, the angel allows it to view its own lifetime, from one end to the other, and to understand the entirety of our sacred text at a glance.

But this knowledge is overwhelming to the new soul. The baby does not want to leave the womb.

Shhhhhh, Lailah reassures.

At the moment of birth, Lailah puts her finger on the upper lip of the newborn and causes the infant to forget everything. That is why we are said to have a little indentation above our mouth: the philtrum, the mark of Lailah. She extinguishes the candle and coaxes the child into the world.

The mark of Lailah is a reminder that the depth of our entire life experience and the world's secrets are already inside us, waiting to be restored. Which means we spend our entire lifetime relearning a wisdom we always had.

I have conversations all the time with congregants who feel a visceral sense of faith or connectedness to something larger. But I also talk to many who don't, who feel neither God's presence nor the lack of it. Many more are searching for something ineffable, transcendent.

As far-fetched as Lailah's parable might be, for me it captures something true: Finding meaning doesn't have to feel like a foreign expedition. It can feel like a return to the most familiar place on earth.

When my husband, Jacob, and I had our first child, Gabriel, we tucked him in every night by reciting the Shema. On Fridays we would bless our three kids with the traditional prayer for children while holding our hands over their heads. Even now, after my children have left home for college, I have sometimes held my hands up to the phone to bless them from a distance.

It is difficult to explain the instinct that led me to pray as a child. When I talk about prayer with congregants, I encourage them to think less, to tune in to the cadence of the ancient Hebrew language, to speak aloud— and without inhibition—to an unseen power. It is more about conversation than petition; I urge them to put aside their usual measures of logic and rationality, to speak as if someone or something is listening. Lailah brought us into the world, gave us our story, and then made it disappear. We each find our way back to what we have known inside all along.

Emunah
TRUST

The Hebrew word most often translated as "faith," *emunah*, is more accurately translated as "trust."

Faith and trust might seem interchangeable, but the key difference between them is revealed in the Torah when *emunah* first appears.

When God calls Abraham to leave his birthplace, God makes a covenantal promise to him that the land he enters will be given to him and his many descendants.

Abraham and Sarah follow God's call, years pass, and Abraham and Sarah—still without any heirs—begin to lose hope that this promise will ever be fulfilled.

Abraham questions God: "My Lord God, what can You give me, since I remain childless?" (Genesis 15:2).

God responds, "Look up to the heavens and count the stars, if you are even able to count them . . . so shall be your offspring" (Genesis 15:5).

God doesn't ask him to *believe* something but to *do something*—to step outside himself, look up, count.

I imagine that, as Abraham looks up to the heavens and begins numbering the vast expanse of stars, this action inspires awe, gives him confidence in the Creator, and renews his resolve to keep trusting in God, to keep moving in the direction God pointed.

His upward gaze and counting become a kind of prayer.

The text continues: *Vehe'emin*, and "Abraham *trusted* in the Lord" (Genesis 15:6). In a moment when Abraham is clearly feeling doubt, he nevertheless puts his trust in God.

Therein lies the difference: Faith is a noun, something you can have or possess, as in "I have faith in God." Or conversely, "I *don't* have faith."

Trust, on the other hand, is a verb. It is something you *do* or *act upon*. It is a choice and a deliberate response, as in "I trusted, so I followed."

Many Jews, when asked if they believe in God, have trouble answering. The better question is: Do you trust that there is a force for good in the world? Will you act upon that trust?

It is often said that Judaism is a religion that cares more about *deed* than *creed*, meaning that the Torah is less concerned with telling us *what* to believe than *how* to behave. Faith happens after—or as a result of—the action commanded by God. *We believe after we do.*

The Torah's description of Mount Sinai—that powerful moment when the Israelites receive God's law—drives this home. Moses's followers say, *"Na'aseh v'nishma."* We will do and then we will understand. The doing comes first. The understanding will come later. Or maybe it won't. But nevertheless, we will have done the right action anyway.

When people tell me they don't believe in God, or aren't sure if they do, I understand their hesitation. There is often resistance to the idea of the divine. I say that the belief itself is not essential to living a life of faith. I am more interested in asking: What kind of spiritual aliveness might you feel if you did certain acts that felt godly—kind, selfless, reparative—even if you reject the idea of being commanded by God? How would you behave in the world if you trusted that there was a God who was watching? A God who cared?

I've maintained my nightly prayer ritual for almost fifty years even though I don't actually believe that God will answer my prayers like a genie granting a wish.

But I trust that articulating my deepest wishes and hopes orients my heart and energy in the right direction and strengthens my aspiration to make them real.

Does it matter whether or not Abraham believed in God? You might say that it does. But more important is that Abraham *trusts* in God and behaves as if there is one.

He trusts God when he is called to leave his home.

He trusts God when he counts the vast stars of the night sky.

He trusts God when called to bring his son Isaac to the mountain.

He walks through the world with *emunah*.

What would it mean to walk through the world with trust in a greater force that was good?

CHAPTER 6

Ruthie

The new music instructor poked her head into our Hebrew school classroom. With brown curly hair and a guitar slung across her back, it seemed she had traveled in on some different breeze like Mary Poppins. We didn't get a lot of new faces in our Tacoma congregation, let alone teachers in their twenties.

"I'm Ruthie," she introduced herself, "and I won't have a job if I don't get you all to sing!" Ruthie urged every student to join her children's choir, meeting in the library after Sunday school.

I was both intrigued and suspicious. Communal singing, in my past experience, was uninspiring. Our small temple couldn't afford a cantor, so the wonderful (but tone-deaf) rabbi and a non-Jewish professional trio sang transliterated Hebrew out of old hymnals. Their operatic, high-pitched choral arrangements seemed designed to *discourage* participation and alienate modern ears.

But something about the elfish glint in Ruthie's eyes, the way she was clearly an adult but not too much of one, made me want to try her choir.

When Gina greeted me after Sunday school, breathless—"Did you meet Ruthie? I'm joining!"—well, that sealed it. If Gina wanted to stay after religious school, I would too.

The following week, a dozen kids waited expectantly in the library. Ruthie began by teaching us a song that, from its first bars, grabbed me in a way no other ritual or hymn ever had. A young composer named Debbie Friedman from Utica, New York, had set the English words of Psalm 96 to music. "Sing Unto God" was the title track on her first album, developed while working at Jewish summer camps and released in 1972, the year I was born. Unbeknownst to me, it had upended ritual music with its propulsive beat, funky groove, and unapologetic elation. Though the album rocked the Jewish landscape, the revolution took a few years to reach the Jewish hinterlands of Tacoma.

The music Ruthie taught us borrowed from the folk genre and sounded like Joan Baez, Neil Young, and Simon and Garfunkel—music I actually chose to listen to on the radio. Debbie's song especially made my body move despite itself.

> *Rejoice in the Lord all ye righteous*
> *And cry out to the Lord with joy*
> *Sing out from your hearts, O sing praises to God!*

It had a driving energy and vocal leaps that required us to sing *big*. This new anthem made me feel exhilarated.

It wasn't just the song but *how* Ruthie led it—teaching us to make it our own, one phrase at a time. "Where is the joy?" she'd implore while vigorously strumming her guitar. "Sing with your shoulders!"

I'll never forget our astonishment at the sound we made when we mastered our two-part harmony. Ruthie beamed. She pulled me aside for special attention, and I felt noticed when she said I had a "distinctive strength' in my voice.

My sister and I went on to obsessively rehearse every song Ruthie taught us. I would imitate Ruthie, directing Gina—"You take the melody; I'll handle the harmony!" We practiced in our bedroom, at the kitchen table, while walking to the bus stop.

Ruthie arranged for our nascent choir to record an actual eight-track cassette tape, which was offered for sale to members of our congregation. Wearing headphones in a real studio, singing into a professional microphone, I felt like a rock star. My family listened to the finished tape over and over in the car. Because Ruthie took my voice seriously, I started to see myself differently. Maybe I could do something that mattered.

And then Ruthie was gone without explanation—just as suddenly as she'd appeared. After three years of her contagious energy, our little congregation began to wilt back into its old sound. I was bereft but decided to take up the guitar to follow her example and keep her music with me.

For years after Ruthie's departure, I begged my temple educator, Joan Garden, for another Ruthie. Joan explained that Ruthies "didn't grow on trees" in Tacoma, Washington; Jewish music education was not exactly a flourishing field. After several years of my laments, Joan hit on a solution: "*You* lead us!" The temple offered to get me some song-leading experience, covering my flight to Camp Swig, a Reform Jewish camp in California. I would join a brand-new "working camper" program called Avodah, which allowed me to stay for the full summer at little cost.

Fourteen years old, I flew by myself with a duffel and barely used guitar, not knowing what I was getting into. During the day, I was part of the morning chore rotations—washing dishes, babysitting staff children, gardening and pruning, or the dreaded bathroom scrubbing. Between work shifts, afternoon learning, and daily song sessions, I would steal time in my bunk or the outdoor wooden benches and work my way through the catalog of Jewish and Israeli songs in our orange Camp Swig songbook. Fortunately, most could be played with just six "campfire" chords. I took adolescent pride in the fact that I was not a paying camper who returned home after two or three weeks. We in the Avodah corps were quasi staff, riding around on golf carts with the maintenance team and rubbing shoulders with the idolized song leaders and cool, older counselors on the worn sofas in the staff lounge.

Among the towering redwoods and the fragrance of wild fields, I looked forward to our daily morning prayers. I saw how communal Shabbat song sessions could animate kids to pound the sticky tables in a crowded dining hall or dance outside on the grass. This musical language—unselfconscious, unfettered—became its own kind of emotional bond. We were in an uplifting bubble, just us, praying in a sanctuary that was all ours. I felt my voice grow stronger, and I tried mightily to help the campers find their own. The experience made me realize that the fleeting thrill of singing with Ruthie in services could be the way that Judaism felt *all the time*.

I was invited back to Camp Swig over the course of three summers as a song leader: strumming for hours each day, from morning prayers to an afternoon song session to gentle lullabies at bunk bedtime. When the mess hall walls shook, it was the song leaders who conducted the swaying and the harmonies. When Shabbat descended at camp, we song leaders would stand onstage before the great lawn filled with hundreds of campers dressed in white to welcome in the Sabbath bride—the metaphor for the divine presence. These were perfect days. Song leaders were revered at camp, and we felt sure there was no better place on earth.

When I returned to Temple Beth El, Jewish songbook and guitar pick in hand, I rotated through Sunday school classrooms, trying to recapture some of that camp magic with the younger students, willing my newly calloused fingers to keep up. When I led our temple summer campfire I reveled in my newfound ability to get a bunch of American kids excited about Israeli folk songs. I was a poor Ruthie replacement, but in Tacoma, I was all we had, and for the time being, that seemed to be enough.

Savlanut
PATIENCE

When it came to the mundane patience required for lines at the grocery store, driving in traffic, or being placed on hold by his insurance company, my usually gentle, easygoing dad could easily become agitated, even rude. Only slow, audible breaths—in and out of his nose—seemed to bring him back to himself.

But when it came to the repetitive discipline of rehearsing music, he was endlessly patient. My father loved playing piano since childhood, but a teenage football accident left his pinkie finger permanently fixed at a right angle. He nevertheless was determined to conquer the Chopin Nocturne, Op. 9, No. 2, with its trills and waltzing bass lines, and would sit at the piano for many hours to coax his large hands to play delicately.

I watched him intently as a child, and by age five asked him to find me a piano teacher. He was thrilled to sign me up. Every single day without exception, as I plunked away on our Yamaha upright, he sat beside me. It didn't even feel like practicing; he made it a game, asking me to check the time signature, find the notes, calculate the rhythms, put it all together. "Try it again. And again. Once more." If I did well, he would neatly inscribe a five-pointed star on the music sheet. If I mastered it, he would reward me with the greater prize: a six-pointed star.

"A Jewish star for that performance!" he would cheer.

Looking back, I can't fathom how many hours he listened as I laboriously worked my way through the *A Dozen a Day* technique series, attempting to perfect "Three Blind Mice" and "Twinkle, Twinkle." By the third grade, only because of his help, I mastered the iconic "Für Elise" by Beethoven.

Gina started lessons at age five, and Dad once again sat sentinel with her. Countless more hours were spent on that hardwood piano bench, bolstering his two earnest amateurs on the keys. As the second child, Gina had to use my piano books, already marked up. When she earned her stars, Dad would carefully inscribe a "G" inside them, distinguishing her achievements from mine.

The biblical word for "patience," often used to describe God, is *erech apayim*, which literally means "long in the nose." This seemed nonsensical at first, until I imagined God, like my father, needing to take deep breaths whenever the Israelites made God angry. But the modern Hebrew word for patience is *savlanut*, which comes from the root "to suffer" or "to bear a burden." Patience means carrying a load with equanimity, or perhaps helping another person bear theirs.

Dad cultivated both kinds of patience—the nasal breathing and the weight-bearing. I don't tell people enough how he caught me when I buckled, helped me carry the load of rejection, whether from a mean girl in school or a teenage boy who clearly preferred a different face: "Well, I think you're beautiful, and some guy will be very lucky," Dad would insist. When Jewish youth-groupers told me I wasn't actually Jewish, he would assuredly affirm: "You're as Jewish as they come!"

Of course I dismissed his pep talks as a father's obligation and lack of objectivity. But when I became a parent myself, I heard myself boosting my kids the way Dad had me. I started to appreciate what it took to read a child's favorite book six times in a row, or play Go Fish one more time, or just sit, watching my son's piano lessons or my daughter's floor hockey games. I finally appreciated the unconditional love of my father's patience.

Dad finally moved off the piano bench to a nearby chair once I was in high school. Closing his eyes, he would simply take it in, no longer instructing. Now there was just music.

I think about what it means to have true patience. It's not just about slowing our anger or being able to sit still. It's noticing who might be carrying a burden and taking on some of the weight. When we are patient, imagine that we lift just a bit of someone else's load.

We remind them that they are not sitting alone on the bench.

CHAPTER 7

Minister Emo

My mom fell smack in the middle of seven children. While she adored her three brothers, her life centered around her three sisters—all "Emo" to me, which means "aunt" in Korean.

To distinguish between them, as literally as can be, Minister Emo was a minister, Restaurant Emo ran a restaurant, and the oldest, Hawaii Emo, formerly lived in Hawaii.

Minister Emo was originally the most devout Buddhist in the family. But when Mom helped her emigrate to Tacoma from South Korea, she joined a Korean Christian church, mostly to socialize with other Korean Americans. Emo's Buddhism stayed strong for several years, until one winter she got seriously ill and several Korean church families nursed her back to health, cooking and praying for her. Emo believed fervently she'd been saved by Jesus. So she formally converted to Christianity. Her growing zeal ultimately led her to become a minister, and she ran a small Korean-speaking church in Tacoma's Korean neighborhood.

For years as a young girl, I went to her house every day after school, where I gobbled up Emo's spicy tteokbokki, played with her four children, and worried that I might burn in Hell for eternity.

I could not escape feeling like a heathen at Emo's house. On every wall hung pictures of Jesus, always with blond hair and blue eyes, looking nothing like anyone in our family. There were etchings of a bloody, crucified martyr with nails in his hands and feet and a crown of thorns cutting into his head. I would stare at these pictures in awe and horror while Emo let me know that Jesus endured all this torture for my sins. Minister Emo was committed to saving my soul.

"Your father is a nice man, and it's not his fault he was born Jewish," Minister Emo would say. "Angela, you can be Jewish in this life, but I want to save you from the fires of Hell in the afterlife, which is for eternity."

I was petrified. Hell sounded like, well, *hell*.

"When the moment of judgment comes, you need to say you take Jesus into your heart. Say that you believe, and you can be saved." I didn't fully buy my aunt's ominous prophecies. It just didn't make sense that people like my father—the kindest, most ethical, honest man—would be consigned to Hell because of the accident of his Jewish birth. There had to be millions of other good people who had never been exposed to Christianity, and I could not imagine they all would be consigned to the inferno. When I asked my aunt about that, she said, "This is why missionaries go around the world: to save people." But I could not believe in a God who damned innocent children in Africa or Asia to Hell simply for not knowing Jesus.

My aunt was an indefatigable proselytizer, converting Mom's two older sisters, who became devout Christians. My cousins also absorbed and reinforced the gospel. Even as my immediate family stayed unshakably Jewish, I did have a nagging worry: What if Minister Emo knew something we didn't? The stakes for being wrong felt so high. Were we actually doomed?

My father's faith was not fervent like my aunt's. It was less about belief—I'm not sure I ever heard my father talk about God—and more about a sense of obligation to his inheritance. Dad never a missed Friday-night Shabbat service or Sunday-morning Torah study. He was the last to leave the hall after the oneg reception, packing it in only after greeting every last congregant. Dad reminded me of a variation of that old joke: "Mr. Goldberg went to synagogue to talk to God. Dad went to synagogue to talk to Mr. Goldberg." Dad's weekly synagogue attendance was more about the people than the prayers.

My father's Judaism wasn't about a deity or dogma. It was a series of actions played out every day. There was a devoutness in his charitable giving, as he sat before a mountain of solicitation envelopes each month, sorting through petitions from worthy causes like the March of Dimes, the Multiple Sclerosis Foundation, the Tacoma Youth Symphony, and the Soviet Jewry movement. Money was tight, and his checks were usually for $5 to $10. But he wrote dozens of them. He felt strongly that it was his obligation—not charity but tzedakah: a commandment to create justice through giving. My father would hand us coins to drop into our blue Jewish National Fund box so that we could accumulate the requisite $5 to plant a sapling in Israel by the time *Tu B'Shvat* arrived—the new year for the trees. He also purchased a sapling in the Holy Land whenever a baby was born in our family or congregation. While he had not yet been to Israel himself, he reminded us that had this ancient home of the Jewish people existed as a refuge before World War II, we would not have lost six million in the Holocaust, over a third of the world's Jewish population. Somewhere in Israel, there is a JNF forest my father helped seed, to mark new life in defiance of Hitler and to nurture a fledgling Jewish nation.

I didn't tell my parents about Minister Emo's evangelizing until much later. I knew Emo simply wanted to "save" me, and I didn't want to get her in trouble. Besides, Daddy would have said that Emo's faith, while important to her, had nothing to do with ours. We were not going to Hell; that was one thing my father took on faith. I don't think he ever worried about his soul.

My mother also seemed unconcerned about damnation. She holds the Confucian belief that one must avoid extremes and always choose the middle path. While she saw the value that religion brought her sisters, she rejected their absolutism regarding who would be "saved" or not. Drawing on her Buddhism, my mother is certain that we each have a unique, inborn wisdom, one that can only be tapped through withstanding life's tests and being awake to the world around us, not through any bible or preacher. She said it was our task to find our inner voice. It is easily missed. The clearest goals or beliefs can be obscured by the white noise of a comparing mind and a judging eye or by fear and insecurity. Meditation helps quiet that static. It's how my mother maintains her equilibrium and her dignity, despite all the external critics telling her she wasn't American enough, educated enough, sociable enough. She reminded me that Judaism believes every person is made in the image of God, and when we tap into that divine spark, we can access a wisdom that is uniquely ours. I suppose that I am sort of a spiritual mutt. God speaks in many languages—that's no platitude but a truism in my DNA—lessons gleaned from my Buddhist mother, Jewish father, and born-again aunt. No one owns Divine Truth, and I am always suspicious of any religion that claims it does.

What all faiths share is *seeking*—trying to understand the *how* of the world: How are we to live? How are we to contribute? How do we protect the most vulnerable? How should we go about revealing each person's individual light? How can we hear that personal sacred voice?

M'chayei Metim
RESURRECTION

Religious traditions often borrow divine concepts from each other. Resurrection is an ancient doctrine of Jewish belief, but as it became central to Christian theology, rabbinic Judaism distanced itself from the idea, and many Jews today are not aware that it's a core belief of Judaism.

M'chayei metim, or "resurrection of the dead," is first mentioned in the Hebrew Bible in the prophetic books of Isaiah and Daniel. Maimonides, the medieval philosopher, ranks belief in resurrection as one of the thirteen core principles of Jewish faith. And it's been incorporated into a prayer called the *Gevurot*, "God's Strength," which Jews recite daily.

Later rabbinic sources assert that when the Messiah comes, a time that's envisioned as the halcyon era of the future, all the dead will be resurrected, beginning on the Mount of Olives, right outside where the ancient Temple stood. At that time, all the dead bodies that are not already in Israel will miraculously roll through underground tunnels to the Holy Land. This process is said to be spiritually painful (even if you're dead), and avoiding the rolling is one of the reasons that Jews from around the world choose to be buried in Jerusalem. Another reason, of course, is to be among the first brought back to life.

The concept of resurrection was met with great discomfort by rational, post-Enlightenment Reform Jews. They rejected resurrection, along with the revivalist, supernatural body-rolling, in the 1885 Pittsburgh Platform, the first declaration of Reform Jewish principles.

But the controversy over resurrection was much older than this. Professor Neil Gillman of the Jewish Theological Seminary suggests that as early as the first century BCE, there was so much conflict around the idea of revival from the dead that the rabbis inserted the *Gevurot* prayer into the daily liturgy to force Jews to articulate this concept repeatedly.

Many hundreds of years later, those early Reformers who spurned resurrection did not remove the *Gevurot* prayer altogether but rather changed the words to make it palatable so that *m'chayei metim* ("you give life to the dead") became *m'chayei hakol* ("you give life to all").

For most of my life, I recited this line, "You give life to all," without giving it much thought. It's a positive statement and entirely unobjectionable.

But a few years ago, I had an experience that left me unsatisfied with those familiar words. On a family trip to the

Arenal, Costa Rica's youngest and most active volcano, I learned that all the ash from the volcanic activity caused severe destruction in the immediate aftermath. But there were actually benefits to the environment in the long term. These volcanoes contribute to an exceptionally rich and fertile soil that creates lush forests, productive farmland, and yes, even *resurrection of the dead.*

I noticed that the farmland was encircled by perfect rows of the strangest-looking trees: The trunks were thin, identical in height, each topped with a tuft of branches sprouting in every direction like a bad haircut.

Rather than growing from seeds, these trees had started as fence posts, built to contain livestock, to mark property borders. But in the fertile soil of the Arenal, this dead wood—with a kiss of the miraculous—took root, sprouted, and literally came back to life.

Suddenly the Gevurot prayer felt concrete: God *can* bring live trees out of inanimate fence posts; the dead are revived. I saw it with my own eyes. And of course "resurrection" can happen in all manner of ways—a parched field, dry and cracked, greening again after a rainy season; hearts that stop and are resuscitated. *M'chayei metim,* "you give life to the dead," is actually the traditional blessing you say upon seeing a friend you have not seen for more than a year. Even dormant friendships can be revived.

Our ancestors knew how to interpret resurrection metaphorically: Prayer breathes life into what we think is beyond saving. I've seen countless times that even the impossible is

79

possible. After that trip to Costa Rica, I invited congregants to consider returning to the traditional language of the *Gevurot* prayer: "You bring the dead to life." Because our prayers *should* be audacious enough to contain our hope. What we think we've lost can be reborn.

CHAPTER 8

Inheritance

Yes, I was that dorky outlier who really, really liked Hebrew school. Since Temple Beth El was the only synagogue within a thirty-mile radius, I looked forward to seeing my Jewish classmates, some who came from as far as Olympia or even Aberdeen, over an hour's drive away. I loved the Hebrew prayer cards we could each master at our own (competitive) pace. I worshiped the teenagers I knew from the temple summer camp, who became our instructors once they completed Confirmation in tenth grade. Walking into synagogue always felt like coming back to my own clubhouse. I was embraced there, understood, captivated by speaking in a language of ritual, music, and prayer.

Our rabbi, Richard Rosenthal, born in Germany in 1929, was just nine years old when he witnessed Kristallnacht. During the sickening violence of that terrible night, his father was beaten so badly that his own son could not recognize him. Young Richard fled with his parents to America and, as he grew up, chose rabbinic ordination because his family survived. He felt obligated because he was spared.

During his forty-one years in the Tacoma pulpit, the gift of his intelligence, integrity, humor, and longevity conferred stability in our small community. He made the world seem reliable and safe. I still miss talking to him.

But for all Rabbi Rosenthal's many attributes, the man could not carry a tune. And the synagogue had no budget for a cantor. So, like many students of my generation, I learned my bat mitzvah portion from a nasally recording on a cassette tape. Every week I would go to Rabbi Rosenthal's office and chant the new verse I had practiced. If I hadn't fully mastered the section, I would more or less make it up. But no matter how I mangled the cantillation, Rabbi Rosenthal told me my chanting was marvelous.

And then one day, out of nowhere, he added, "Angela, you should think about becoming a rabbi."

Excuse me? I looked across his big desk. Rabbi Rosenthal was the only Jewish authority I'd ever known, and he embodied solemnity. With a bushy, graying goatee, hair sprouting out of his ears, thick glasses, a tweed blazer, and a deep voice, he was right out of central casting. I, on the other hand, was a freckled biracial teenager experimenting with feathered hair. From my vantage point, the life of a rabbi consisted of ponderous sermons, dusty books, and talking to grown-ups over herring at the kiddush.

I just couldn't see it.

But when the day of my bat mitzvah arrived, something shifted. I had invited fifty classmates to attend, most of whom had never been to a synagogue, let alone a bat mitzvah, and suddenly I was thrust into the role of host and tour guide. I was proud of my Jewish home, excited to show them around, walking my guests to the wall of Consecration class pictures and inviting them to pick me out at age five when I began my Hebrew studies. There was a picture of my grandfather from the 1920s in a Jewish youth movement basketball uniform, proof of my deep roots.

I explained that the lobby's towering central column—carved with Hebrew letters and framed by panels of stained glass—included the liturgy of martyrs, in homage to the six million Jews murdered in the Holocaust. I told them how my rabbi barely escaped Nazi Germany as a young boy. This temple and its people were part of an important story, and I wanted to make sure it was understood.

Entering the sanctuary to begin the service, I gasped at the sight of it, filled to overflowing. Extra folding chairs were being set up. Yes, I had sent invitations to people from outside the synagogue, but as was the custom, I didn't send personalized invites to the Beth El community. *B'nei* mitzvah kids were simply announced in the bulletin, and congregants were welcome and expected to show up. And they did. Not only was my entire Hebrew school class there but scores of my father's and grandmother's generations as well. Being a Warnick in Tacoma meant I had *yicrus*—good lineage—and I felt newly proud to be the fourth generation to come of age in this community.

The peak moment of a bat mitzvah service is when a child is called up for an aliyah, the call-and-response blessing before and after reading the Torah. Aliyah literally means "ascent" and is considered a spiritual elevation, the highest honor one can receive in the Jewish community. In any Shabbat service, several people will be asked to have an aliyah, but the privilege is only granted after the age of thirteen. So a bat mitzvah service is the symbolic demonstration of Jewish adulthood, the chance to make a public commitment and uphold Jewish tradition and identity.

I asked my cousin Greg if he would honor me with the first aliyah at my service. Greg was my cool, older cousin who paved the way for me in all things—taking me to my first *Rocky Horror Picture Show* and explaining the Warnick family dramas when I needed translation. Like everything else in our relationship, Greg had gone ahead of me on the bar mitzvah track. His father, Alan, had stood next to him on the bimah that day but died soon after from leukemia, making Greg's entry into adulthood more literal and palpable than any of us would have wanted. Uncle Alan's absence was its own presence at my bat mitzvah, but seeing Greg ascend to the Torah, standing on his own before a congregation who remembered Alan, filled me with gratitude.

Though I had watched others recite this familiar blessing countless times, when it was my turn to have the final aliyah, I suddenly grasped what it means to rise to one's birthright, to be called up to perpetuate a people, to join a history. I felt like the community was lifting me onto their shoulders, just as they'd carried my father's family for four generations. The Torah seemed to be drawing me closer as its parchment was unfurled. This moment came with responsibility: to make ancient words matter for my friends. Mine was the only bat mitzvah most of them would ever attend, and I fervently wanted them to "get" what was magical about this religion and rite of passage. As I chanted Torah, the job of a rabbi was suddenly revealed and shining—meaningful, enduring, even noble.

The lunch reception in the social hall felt fancy because my parents splurged on a swan ice sculpture. The buffet was a fitting potluck: wontons made by my Korean aunties, mini cheesecakes, rugelach, and fudge squares by my adopted synagogue *bubbes*.

There was no DJ, no hora, no photo booth or sweatshirt party favors like some of today's more elaborate parties. But when I sat in the back seat of our maroon Buick driving home, clutching the kiddush cup from the synagogue and the Tower Records gift cards from classmates, I knew that on this particular morning, I had taken my place in an epic story.

My arrival in America as a five-year-old seeded a persistent desire for connection—to the people we came from and the people we joined. I've always liked the feeling of rootedness, but it sometimes was hard to feel anchored when my family path included so much immigration and wandering. But on my bat mitzvah day, I was firmly tethered to something no one could take away: inheritance. It was mine everywhere and anytime. I would now have to protect it and pass it on.

If my father and mother had not decided to raise us as Jews, the Jewish thread of my family would have snapped: four thousand years stretching back to Sinai and ending with me. I don't think I understood the enormity of this when I was thirteen. But I began to feel it more with each passing year, and I carry that sense of imperative to this day.

As a member of the clergy for the last twenty-five years, whenever I prepare a bar or bat mitzvah student as they stand on the *bimah*, flanked by parents and grandparents, about to physically receive the Torah by holding it in their arms, I talk about legacy and decision-making. I remind them, "Judaism is not just something you're given; it's something you choose. When the ceremony is over and the party guests have gone home, you will be left with a Jewish identity that is largely up to you. How will you decide what it means?"

Simcha
JOY

First-timers at my synagogue at a Friday-night service frequently remark with a little too much shock: "I didn't know Judaism could be so . . . *joyful*!"

I find the comment surprising and more than a little dispiriting. Because there is no religious feeling without joy, and their question reveals how infrequently they've felt it.

The Talmud goes so far as to say that "a person *should not stand to pray* in a state of sadness or laziness, nor from laughter, conversation, or frivolity . . . but only in a state of joy found in mitzvah" (Berakhot 31).

As a rabbi who sees struggle, illness, depression, and loss on a daily basis and who has faced pain in my own life, it's too simplistic to say this rabbinic teaching is about urging someone to buck up. That is not what Judaism expects, nor what any rabbi should suggest. But I invite you to consider how to place joy at the *very center* of your spiritual quest.

Joy is so central to Jewish ritual that *many* of the core life cycle events—from baby namings to bar mitzvahs to weddings— are simply called a simcha, "a joy."

I'm not talking about the fleeting boost that can come from a friend's compliment or a great cup of coffee. I'm talking about a soulful uplift that comes from genuine connection.

Rabbi Lord Jonathan Sacks pointed out that the word "simcha" in the Torah is never applied to individuals. Rather, simcha happens *in relationship*—brought about by human interactions, communal gatherings, festive meals, or holiday rituals.

Coming together in an authentic, loving way with other people, nature, or God generates simcha.

The Chassidic tradition teaches that the cultivation of simcha should be the primary aim of a religious Jew. The ancient psalmist instructs: *"Ivdu et HaShem b'simcha,"* "serve God with joy." Being joyful is not just an optional bonus in Judaism; it is the very foundation of a spiritual life.

Deuteronomy lays out a list of horrific punishments, curses, and natural disasters that will plague the Israelites if they do not serve God "with joy and good heart" (Deuteronomy 28:47).

Imagine those curses being the motivation for joy!

We know joy is not always easy to access, and we shouldn't minimize the effort required. Kierkegaard wrote, "It takes moral courage to grieve; it takes religious courage to be joyful." The sharp awareness of the hardships of the world, and our vulnerability in it, makes seeking joy an act of courage and faith.

The eighteenth-century Hasidic Rabbi Nachman of Breslov showed us what that courage might look like. A charismatic leader with thousands of devoted students, he also endured bouts of debilitating depression. Knowing firsthand how difficult it was to seek joy when in despair, Nachman advised, "If you don't feel happy, pretend to be. Even if you are depressed, put on a smile. Act happy. Genuine joy will follow."

Dr. Alan Schlechter, an NYU professor of the Science of Happiness, told me that Rabbi Nachman's suggestion is now called "behavioral activation" and is one of the top treatments for depression today. "The method insists we start doing the things that can bring us joy, even if they are not making us feel the way they used to," Schlechter told me. "In the doing, the feelings will change."

Simcha comes from the word *sameach*, which also means "joy" or "happiness." You can break down that word into two other Hebrew words: *sham*, "there," and *moach*, "your brain"—"where your brain is at." This teaches that simcha can be a state of mind, not simply the result of planned events or circumstances outside our control.

Rabbi Nachman, despite his depression, understood simcha as the ultimate religious obligation. He knew that joyfulness was a daily choice, a decision to actively rejoice in the face of suffering, believing that real joy is possible.

CHAPTER 9

Jerusalem Summer

When I was a junior in high school, my aunt Lily clipped an ad from *Hadassah Magazine* and placed it in front of me on our kitchen table.

"You should apply," she pronounced. "At the very least, it's a free trip to Israel next summer."

I had no other plans, so I picked up the listing. It described the Bronfman Youth Fellowship, a selective program in Israel founded by the business giant and philanthropist Edgar Bronfman Jr., meant to offer a deep dive into Jewish learning and Israeli history. Twenty-five "promising" high school juniors were chosen each year from across North America. I was intrigued and thought I might be atypical enough to stand a chance; how many other Korean Jews would apply? I did have some semblance of a Jewish résumé already: president of my Tacoma B'nai B'rith Youth Organization chapter, Jewish summer camp counselor, Sunday school music teacher. I had also become the self-appointed "Jewish representative" at my high school (as one of only two Jews in the student body, I answered any questions about "what Jews do"). And at the winter concert for parents, after we played "Sleigh Ride" and "Here

Comes Santa Claus," my band conductor would pause, turn to me, and announce—with something like surprised glee—"Angela, our flutist, also happens to be Jewish!" That was my cue to walk over to the stage pedestal to light the menorah I'd carried from home in my backpack. I took my time igniting the shamash candle and using it to light the others; I admired the flickering flame, the lone Jewish beacon in a sea of wreaths and jingle bells. Instead of bemoaning the short shrift given to Hanukkah, I took pride in being different.

I flew down to California for the Bronfman finalist interview and met Rabbi Michael Paley, the founding director of the fellowship, known for his charismatic teaching and jovial warmth. He was the first Orthodox rabbi I had ever met, and he gently asked if I realized that traditional Jewish law traces identity through matrilineage. This was genuinely news to me. Rabbi Rosenthal had never once suggested that my Jewish identity was in question nor that anyone else might question it. I found it hard to respond.

Paley looked almost apologetic. He assured me that the Reform movement has accepted Jewish status through *either* the mother or father. "But you should know," he added, "there may be Jews on this trip who do not consider you a Jew." I wasn't sure where he, as an Orthodox rabbi, stood on my Jewish status, but I didn't have the courage to ask.

His sentence reverberates to this day and prompted a question in my mind that replays: Who is this jury that determines whether I am in or out?

I was accepted into the program. But I had been warned.

When I arrived in Jerusalem, it didn't take long for me to see that most of the other Bronfman fellows were another breed. Many were fluent in

Hebrew, easily deciphered a page of Talmud, and seemed to know every other Jew on the planet.

There were students like my roommate Debbie, an Orthodox Jewish girl from Brookline, Massachusetts, where everyone in her neighborhood was equally—and visibly—observant. I hadn't known that an insular religious world like hers existed in America with all-Jewish classmates, all-kosher grocery stores, a real suburban shtetl.

As we unpacked our spare shared room in the Youth Village, the hostel where we were all bunking, Debbie asked how many Jews were in my Tacoma high school.

"Only my friend Hilary and me," I answered. "But my sister will be a freshman next year, so that will increase our population by fifty percent." As soon as I said it (three Jews in a school of 1,300!), I realized I was describing a foreign world to Debbie, the reality of being a minority on one's home turf. I could not have been prouder that Gina and I were among the few but committed, though I could tell that Debbie was digesting how un-Jewish my surroundings were.

"You mean there is not even one Jewish boy to date in your whole school?" she asked.

I decided this was not the moment to mention Sam, my Protestant boyfriend in Tacoma. Instead, I proudly described my high school building, a former nineteenth-century French Renaissance–style hotel we called the "Brown Castle." (It really was both a castle and brown.) In the gully below the school building was a large stadium bowl from which it took the name Stadium High School. Since my father, grandfather, and a dozen other Warnicks had all attended, our home was filled with Stadium pennants, yearbooks, letter jackets, and other prized memorabilia. The bowl was inaugurated by President Theodore Roosevelt, and as a civic showpiece it was once a required stop for dignitaries coming through Washington state. In recent decades, it was more often home to Friday-night games for a notoriously unsuccessful Tigers football team. But after my colorful monologue, there was only one detail that stood out to Debbie.

"You mean you go to football games on Friday nights . . . on Shabbat?" she asked.

"I have to play in the marching band," I responded defensively.

The truth is that before she asked, I hadn't seriously considered going to synagogue on Friday nights rather than the football game.

I realized we were mutually baffled by each other's childhoods. Thinking it might help explain the experience of a rare Jew in Tacoma, I told Debbie that the previous autumn, student body elections had been calendared for Yom Kippur, and I'd successfully appealed to the principal to move the vote to accommodate what Jews considered the holiest day of the year.

Debbie seemed impressed: "That's *chutzpadik*."

"When you're in a small Jewish community, you feel as if all Judaism rests on your shoulders. Like if I wasn't going to be Jewish, no one was. And by the way, the principal did reschedule the elections." I gilded the lily by adding that I ended up winning the class presidency.

Looking at Debbie's face, I could tell that she admired my political moxie more than my religious fervor. All she gleaned was that my life was filled with secular pursuits: non-Jewish friends, foods, and football games. For Debbie, nothing in her life happened outside of Judaism: She lived according to a Jewish calendar, had only Jewish friends, listened to Hebrew rock music (never on Shabbat), and even crocheted kippot in her free time. The schism became even clearer when it came to religious observance in our own dorm. I listened to my Walkman on

Saturdays; Debbie observed a prohibition on electronic devices during the Sabbath.

Debbie said we weren't operating in the same Jewish system. I understood that she was just laying out the rules she'd been taught, not making a personal indictment. But it still felt like one. And when she got to the point of analyzing my lineage, she declared exactly what Paley predicted someone would: "Jewish law determines Jewish status through one's mother. And your mom is not a Jew."

There it was. No longer just theoretical. She was letting me know that according to her boundaries of halacha (Jewish law), I was on the outside. My friend, my peer, could look me in the eye and tell me that I wasn't the real thing. It was disorienting to hear her speak it out loud.

This opinion wasn't just Debbie's, or solely that of Orthodox Judaism. Outside of my liberal Reform bubble, the majority of the Jewish community did not count me as a Jew. And this gutted me.

I later reflected on this painful realization with another person in the program, a former camp friend who had grown up in a more liberal Orthodox community. "Don't worry," she assured me. "You can always convert."

The idea of going through a conversion to become what I already was and *had been all my life* was more than an insult. It felt like a repudiation. If I wasn't a Jew already, what had I been all along? My whole being rejected the notion that I would have to convert. While I wasn't expert in Jewish law, I knew enough Torah to remember that in biblical times, when Hebrew patriarchs had multiple wives and maidservants, Jewish lineage was traced through the father, not the mother. Matrilineal descent was a later standard, codified in Jewish law only by the first century. Biblical precedent strengthened my conviction that having a Jewish father, and living a Jewish life, was enough to make me a Jew.

The intense weeks of the Bronfman program included speakers who have stayed with me—poet Yehuda Amichai, writer A. B. Yehoshua, feminist icon Alice Shalvi, politician Naomi Chazan—luminaries who shaped the intellectual and cultural ethos of modern Israel.

When we student fellows would sit together after these lectures, often on the grass outside the Goldstein Youth Village in Jerusalem, the conversations were heated and emotional. The program had tossed us together at the height of our adolescent questioning. We were encouraged to manage and accept the differences between us, and yet we were challenged by mentors whose main message was "Interrogate everything." Whether intended or not, the trip put us in a state of existential angst for five weeks.

What strengthened my Jewish resolve was immersing myself in Jewish text itself. It was a part of my inheritance I had never fully mined: the granular dissection of verses, the rigorous ethical demands, ancient disputations that felt utterly relevant. Rabbinic sages spoke from the page, responding to the big questions of life I wanted to explore. My head throbbing from turning the words over and over, I was never so excited by text study. If this is what Jewish learning was all about, I wanted more of it.

Somehow the discipline and exhilaration of study felt like God's way of telling me not to doubt my Jewish core. Even when others kept forcing me to doubt an identity I'd never questioned before, I managed to hold fast to some kind of Jewish anchor. Throughout that Israel summer, moving through the country's *shuks* and shuls, vineyards and beaches, hills and ruins, I felt my connection to Judaism deepen. Israel's myriad versions of Jews—from Iraq, Morocco, and Ethiopia; taxi drivers, street artists, and soldiers—reassured me that I might find myself among that riot of Jewish diversity. The beauty and palpable Jewishness of the place affirmed what I'd been taught about the "ingathering of exiles," the intrepid power of a tiny, mighty people, the possibility of belonging. It felt like a home that had been waiting for my return.

Three months later, my cohort gathered again in New York City. During a break from intense Torah study, I took a walk with Rabbi Michael Paley, who had inspired me as a teacher and mentor while I was in Israel. Meandering through the busy midtown streets, just blocks from Central Synagogue, where I would work two decades later, I could feel the Jewish cultural influence in the city—from the corner-side knish seller to the Broadway theaters. "I would love to become a rabbi someday," I blurted out to Paley. It was the very first time I'd uttered those words aloud.

I paused, anxious to hear his reaction.

"That seems to fit the plan," he said somewhat cryptically. It was neither encouragement nor dissuasion. Rather, his reply seemed to be an acknowledgment that there was some higher order at work, a path that I was already on. I don't know what I expected when I chose to suddenly confide in Rabbi Paley on that sidewalk, but in hindsight, his spare answer was a gift. I heard his response as an invitation to press forward.

My mother was less encouraging. "You have three strikes against you: You're a woman. You are Korean. You have a non-Jewish mother. Why choose this fight?" While she voiced anxieties around my ability to ever get hired as a rabbi, I suspected that she also worried that becoming a rabbi would mean my full immersion into a world she could not enter.

Gina confronted exactly what my mother feared when she was selected for the same Bronfman fellowship three years later. While my challenges made me want to become a rabbi, hers had the opposite effect: It made her question her relationship to the Jewish community entirely.

On her program's final Saturday evening, several classmates asked Gina—known for her strong singing voice and guitar skills—to lead them in their last Havdalah, the service that would conclude not only the Sabbath but their entire summer journey together. Some of her more traditionally observant peers were troubled: Gina was female and not Jewish, according to their legal definition. That meant her leadership of these blessings would not be legitimate in their eyes and would not fulfill their religious obligation to recite these prayers.

Rather than having the courage to explain this to Gina directly, they instead gave her a role in her own deception. One pulled her aside and asked that when reciting the blessings, she replace *Adonai Eloheinu*—God's name, which is only to be used during prayer—with the substitution *HaShem Elokeinu*, which is an alternative reference for God that doesn't meet the requirements of Jewish law. That switch, he knew, would render the prayers invalid according to tradition. Gina, deferring to his greater ritual knowledge, agreed without understanding the implications.

As the sun went down, the group gathered on the lawn, singing in a circle, with only the braided Havdalah candle illuminating their faces as darkness fell. Gina, now quite comfortable within the group, led them with her deft strumming and clear voice, respectfully replacing the words of blessing as she had been asked, while an observant male classmate quietly uttered the "true" blessings with God's proper name under his breath. In the dim light, she was oblivious to the looks of confusion on many of her friends' faces, as she unwittingly played into his charade.

Her friend Aaron grabbed her hastily after the service and asked if she realized what she'd done. When he explained it, Gina was mortified, having suddenly been cast as the unschooled Jew, her public embarrassment the necessary price of upholding the law.

The modern-day prophet Rabbi Abraham Joshua Heschel taught that there are those who are "willing to break a din (Jewish law) to save a Yid (a Jewish person)." And there are those who are "willing to break a Yid to save a din."

Those students broke a Jew that night.

Even now, when I think about that group of students who were willing to sacrifice my sister's dignity in order to uphold their sense of legal strictures, I burn up inside.

Most Orthodox Jews believe that Jewish law must be adhered to in its entirety and that we are not to question God's will even when we cannot fully grasp it. Yet even the most traditional Jews appreciate that Jewish law has evolved and they are not following the literal word of Torah. There is not one Bible-believing person today who stones fellow citizens because they don't keep the Sabbath, for instance, or who continues to sacrifice goats in a fiery pyre. The Torah remains sacred, but revelation— God revealing the laws and teachings to humanity—is an ongoing story.

I personally understand biblical text and subsequent commentaries as divinely inspired writings, written down by men over the ages. In order for it to be the living word of God, it has to live in every generation. Each interpreter and believer discerns Torah's meaning using their own moral compass, the guidance of Jewish precedent, and teachers they trust. If our reading of Jewish law requires us to destroy the honor of another human being, we must be misunderstanding God's will. The starting place for all creation derives from the assertion that every person is made in the image of God; that principle is fundamental and explicit, the foundation for all that comes after.

My sister does not live as a practicing Jew anymore. If pressed, she would unequivocally say, "I am Jewish," but she has never joined a synagogue as an adult. Events in our lives led us in different directions. And I would point to our Bronfman summers as the fork in the road that showed just how fragile identity can be.

Mashber
CRISIS

Maybe you've heard the Jewish proverb, "Never let a good crisis go to waste."

Winston Churchill is often credited with that saying, but the Jewish tradition anticipated this sentiment by more than three thousand years.

If there is one thing to learn from Jewish history, it's that Jews were built for crisis: The texts and liturgy, most of which were written during a famine, exile, crusade, or pogrom, remind us—in a moment of crisis—that it isn't unprecedented.

We've been here before.

My teacher Melila Hellner-Eshed from the Shalom Hartman Institute helped me unpack the Hebrew word for crisis: *mashber*, which appears three different ways in the Bible. Taken together, they offer a road map from crisis to rebirth.

The first appears in the Book of Exodus.

Moses has been atop Mount Sinai for forty days while God inscribes the law on two stone tablets. The Israelites, who are waiting impatiently at the foot of the mountain, start to doubt Moses's assurances of God's protection. They build a golden calf to worship, just in case Moses doesn't come back. When Moses does rejoin the group, carrying the Ten Commandments, he sees the faithlessness of his people and smashes the tablets in anger. The Hebrew verb used here is *vayishaber*—"to break."

Only after seeing Moses's destruction do the Israelites reject their idol worship. Only after seeing God's inscribed commandments in rubble do they commit to following them.

Out of breakage comes belief. The Israelites get a second chance.

Mashber appears a second time, in the Book of Jonah the prophet.

Here God instructs Jonah to go tell a citizenry of sinners in Nineveh that they must repent. Jonah doesn't want the assignment because he is not invested enough in these foreigners to help them, so he tries to evade God and the task by jumping on a boat. God sends a violent storm, and when Jonah tells his fellow passengers that he's the cause, they throw him overboard. Jonah should certainly have drowned, but God delivers a great fish to swallow him, and Jonah finds oxygen inside the fish's belly. He finally gets a moment to breathe.

Jonah prays to God from the belly of the whale, saying, *Y'soveveini kol mishbarecha*: "Your breakers swept over me."

Mishbarecha—from *mashber*. Here the root Hebrew word for "breakers" is akin to "waves": a giant, pounding, merciless ocean, which can overwhelm and engulf us.

Jonah takes respite from the storm there for three days. In the quiet, dark belly of the whale, he prays, reflects, and is transformed. Newly willing to follow God's command, he goes to Nineveh to give its sinning people a chance to save themselves.

When we are in crisis and it feels like the giant breakers of life are coming down on us, we're frightened by our inability to come up for air. When we are underwater, what we need more than anything is a kind of sanctuary to gain some perspective. And to take a breath.

The last appearance of *mashber* appears in the book of the prophet Isaiah, where it is translated as a primitive delivery chair. Isaiah claims this is a day of distress: *Ki va-u vanim ad mashber*, "the babes have come to the birthing stool," but there isn't the strength to deliver.

How brilliant of our ancestors to understand crisis as the *seat of new birth*. But Isaiah writes that at this most regenerative, hopeful, high-stakes moment, on the verge of birthing life, sometimes we feel we don't have the strength to push past the agony.

Anyone who has actually been in labor knows that there is a moment when you don't feel like you're birthing; you feel like you're dying. That line between life and death is not imaginary. There is real peril and indescribable pain in every miraculous birth. At some point, despite the fatigue and the fog, like our mothers before us, we know we need to summon the strength to push forth new life.

So when we are in crisis—*mashber*—here are three steps for renewal:

Break. Breathe. Push.

Every birth begins with a breaking.

CHAPTER 10

Which Box Do I Check?

When I filled out my college applications, I was only allowed to check one box for racial identity. There was no option to mark "Jewish" or "mixed race" (or "unicorn," for that matter), so I chose "Asian American." It certainly didn't sum up my identity, which I was still trying to sort out, but I came to realize that one box almost never does.

Both of my parents emphasized the importance of education, and I thought they'd be over the moon when I was admitted to Yale. But Mom cried, "If you go east for college, you will never come back!" Dad, a Stanford alumnus, piled on: "What's wrong with my alma mater?"

Despite their protestations, after my Bronfman summer, I was magnetically drawn to Jewish life closer to the epicenter of New York City. I assured them, naively, that once I had completed four years on the "other" coast, I would certainly be returning to our Pacific Northwest.

On my enrollment forms, I requested "interesting" roommates. I got five of them. When we first met, I, too, put each of them in an oversimplified box.

1. Liz: Urban Pittsburgh.
2. Ana: Recent Romanian immigrant.
3. Jianling: Mainland China.
4. Elizabeth: Yale legacy from DC.
5. Esther: Korean American from Cleveland.

Esther and I were the most similar, and not just because we had Korean mothers. We both played flute and swam for our high school teams. We both came to campus with permed hair, an unfortunate fashion holdover from the eighties. We didn't look all that much alike, but people confused us all the time.

Like me, Esther was deeply connected to her religious community. But like the vast majority of Korean Americans, she was Christian. Unlike Minister Emo, who was always proselytizing her born-again gospel, Esther kept her faith to herself. But I noticed how she'd bow her head and make a quiet grace before every meal or when she slipped the rubber bracelet embossed with *WWJD* on her wrist in the morning.

Esther got involved right away in Korean American Students at Yale (KASY) and invited me to join her for a meeting. I hesitated. I'd been back to visit Korea three times since emigrating but hadn't kept up the language and knew that being mixed race still carried a stigma with Koreans.

Finally one night, Esther convinced me to accompany her to a KASY event. As reassuring as it was to see a roomful of people who looked like me, I instantly became the outsider. "We are all gathering at the Korean church this Sunday and having bibimbap lunch afterward," they announced at the end. The Korean community had room for one religion at the time, and it wasn't mine.

That box didn't exactly fit. Even though it was the one I'd checked.

My roommate Elizabeth encouraged me to lean into what it means to be a strong woman on campus. She'd grown up in the suburbs of Washington, DC, attending Sidwell Friends, a Quaker private school whose ranks later included Chelsea Clinton and Sasha and Malia Obama. Elizabeth grew up in a family of four daughters and immediately found a home in the Women's Center at Yale.

The center was right off Old Campus, where most freshmen lived, and one could drop by for gummy bears, tampons, pregnancy tests, and a little radicalization. Elizabeth was helping organize a Take Back the Night march, an annual event protesting sexual violence on campus. I marched with Elizabeth and several hundred women, shouting, "Enough is enough!" and "The way I dress is not a yes!"

Though the reality of violence against women seemed entirely clear-cut and inexcusable, the other issues activating the Women's Center didn't galvanize me. I'd been raised to believe I could match a boy in any pursuit—music, leadership, or academics—as long as I gave it my all. Naively believing that the work of the feminist movement was essentially done, I was blind to the inequalities even on Yale's campus: Only a handful of the female faculty were tenured in contrast to their male counterparts, and spending on women's athletics was a fraction of men's. Yale admitted women for the first time in 1969, announcing their commitment to admit "future leaders," which for Yale meant one woman for every seven male students. It was only in 1972, the year I was born, that President Nixon signed Title IX into law, the landmark civil rights legislation that prohibited sex-based discrimination. The federal government gave Yale seven years to come to parity. It's hard to conceive that when I arrived on Yale's illustrious campus in 1990, only ten years had elapsed since the university's first balanced class.

So I did check the female box, but that didn't mean I focused on the barriers still facing women; they hadn't hit me personally. Yet.

Of all the self-declaring categories, the Jewish box felt most like me. I'd come to Yale intent on investigating and deepening my Jewish identity. In the early 1990s, Yale's student body had a sizable Jewish population, a vibrant Jewish studies program, and a Hillel that was buzzing and popular despite its remote off-campus location in a windowless basement. I eagerly attended a Shabbat dinner with Karen, a Bronfman alum one class ahead of me. Heading to the Kosher Kitchen, I was told to expect oversalted chicken soup, head-spinning intellectual debates, and a lot of raucous singing after dessert. But one ritual had not been explained in advance.

When we finished the familiar Shabbat blessings over the candles and wine, people were invited for a ritual handwashing. This was not my custom, so while others walked to nearby sinks, I stayed at the table, chatting with those who remained. People went strangely silent around me and looked away. Karen shot me a glance with a quick shake of her head, signaling, *Stop talking, Angela*. I cut myself off midsentence.

Someone started a wordless melody and others joined in. I was confused. Didn't I just learn that we're supposed to be silent?

Only after we made the blessing over the challah did Karen lean over and whisper, "You're not supposed to talk between the handwashing and the *motzi* blessing. But singing without words is acceptable."

I thanked her for explaining the nuances of traditional Shabbat practice so that I would not embarrass myself again. But it was a moment that stayed with me; even when you're in, you can still feel left out.

Over time, through song leading and music, I found a role in Jewish campus life. I led the Reform Shabbat minyan: a liberal, egalitarian prayer group. I served as the cantor for the Reform High Holiday services in an overflowing Dwight Hall chapel. I was frequently called upon to lead songs for special rituals, from Holocaust remembrance to the opening of the new Slifka Center for Jewish Life on campus.

But I never felt at home at Hillel. Everyone there seemed to belong to another club. They had this distinctive way of talking—a confidence in conversation, sparring easily and cutting each other off with humor and without offense. When they played Jewish geography, it never took more than one degree to find someone in common, unless you were trying to connect to Jewish Tacoma. Even when student leaders asked me to conduct worship, I worried that I would be exposed as a fraud because of my halting Hebrew or by missing some cultural reference familiar to everyone else. My lack of traditional religious literacy or full Jewish pedigree pegged me in my mind as a counterfeit Jew.

In the Book of Judges, the Gileadites vanquish their rivals, the Ephraimites, and set up a blockade on the banks of the Jordan River to catch any enemies who might try to flee. The border guards demand that each person who wants to cross say the word "shibboleth"—an ancient password. The meaning was not the point but rather the pronunciation. The conquered Ephraimites, who had no *sh* sound in their language, pronounced the word as "sibboleth" and were thereby unmasked as the enemy and promptly slaughtered (Judges 12:1–15).

The shibboleth was a necessary password to cross the border. Tribes used secret signals back then, and we still do: The right clothing, cultural references, or accent helps each tribe easily identify their own. Who is let in or let through. Who is not.

Though I had been raised as a Jew my whole life, the reality of my Buddhist mother, Reform Jewish father, and my small-town synagogue upbringing all made me an outlier from the typical immigrant Jewish story. I couldn't pronounce "shibboleth." Jewish to my core, I still wouldn't get past the guards.

So here I was: too many identities without feeling comfortable in a single one. I wasn't awakened enough to see myself as a feminist. I didn't have the Korean American religious connection to feel part of that community. I wasn't fully feminist, fully Korean, or fully Jewish.

After leading High Holiday services during my junior year at Yale, a good friend came up to me afterward and said, "You know, Angela, you just look Jewish to me now."

I know she intended it as a compliment. And in some ways, these were words I'd longed to hear for years. But I also knew that for her, it meant that she no longer saw me as Korean.

When you carry multiple identities—in your face, your name, your DNA—it confuses people. They want to know which box is yours. But as the poet Adrienne Rich wrote, "Responsibility to yourself means refusing to let others do your thinking, talking, and naming for you."

Zehut
IDENTITY

What does it mean to become a "Jewish adult"?

When I sit with a child on the cusp of becoming bar or bat mitzvah, I often ask, "What makes you *you*?"

At only twelve, they usually respond with a blank stare. When pressed, they offer their after-school classes, sports, or hobbies. It's a good starting point, and no doubt these activities say a lot about who they are as seventh graders.

But I invite them to go deeper. Not just to name the things they do, but to tell me the stories of who they are—the hurdles, happy places, quirks, and superpowers that have shaped them. And this always elicits very different answers.

"I'm a good listener."

"I know how to make people laugh."

"I am a connector of friends."

I tell the students, "Knowing what makes you *you* is at the heart of what it means to become a Jewish adult. While a bar or bat mitzvah means coming to the age of responsibility for the commandments, these are not simply about fasting on Yom Kippur or lighting candles on the Sabbath. The overarching demand of Judaism is that you partner with God in making this world a little bit better. And the true obligation of becoming a Jewish adult means figuring out the particular job that you're on this earth to do."

I remind each young person in front of me, "There has never been another person exactly like you, and there never will be again." If they can absorb that *no one else* has their distinct talents and hurdles, maybe they can see why they're so needed in the world.

This tale of a Hasidic rabbi named Zusya captures the challenge of this mandate.

Rabbi Zusya, a gentle, open-hearted man, lived a humble existence. But Zusya died having felt constantly deficient and inferior. When he came before the heavenly tribunal, Zusya cried, "I am unworthy, for I was not like Moses, the prophet. Nor Jeremiah, the writer. Nor Akiva, the scholar." And the heavenly voice replied, "That is not the concern. Zusya, *why were you not more Zusya?*"

In other words, don't measure your worth by anyone else's; the yardstick is only you. Not your profession, your income, what you look like. The Hebrew word for "identity" is *zehut*. It comes from the simple *zeh*, meaning "this."

Your identity is *this*.

Your zehut is your distinctiveness, grounded in celebrating your "this"—meaning what exists, who you are—not "that," meaning that other person over there.

So much in our society and media is constantly urging us to compare ourselves to everyone else, to obsess over our deficiencies—all the things we don't possess, cannot do, or are not good at. Self-esteem gets suffocated by self-criticism. But our eccentricities, and, yes, the things we're convinced we lack, are the very qualities that forge character and make us singular. They enable us to do what only each of us can do. When we stand before the heavenly tribunal, it might be easy to feel as inadequate as Zusya if we look at those we admire and expect ourselves to be like them. But we won't be asked why we weren't that. We will be asked why we weren't this.

Zehut. Your "identity" in Hebrew is *thisness*.

You are the only version of *this*. Embrace it.

CHAPTER 11

Hitting the Wall

When I was eleven, my mother put kimchi on our ritual Passover plate. She thought it was a reasonable substitution for the horseradish "bitter herbs," since both elicit a similar sting in the mouth, the same clearing of the nostrils. "Kimchi—just like maror, only better," she pronounced. She also liked to spoon kimchi on gefilte fish and matzah.

They say "you are what you eat," and Mom's kimchi substitution only proved how mixed up I was. A reminder that we were never going to be a "normal" Jewish family.

Before my last year in college, I went back to Israel precisely because the religious questions that saturated the air there helped me sort through my Jewish identity more than in any other place. As a religious studies major, I received a Dorot Fellowship to do research in Jerusalem for my senior thesis on women in the cantorate. I wanted to explore how the fairly recent introduction of female cantors and songwriters had changed Jewish life—worship, views of God, synagogue leadership. But my research got off to a rough start. Several people had suggested I interview an influential Orthodox Israeli songwriter, so I tracked her down. When I called her on the phone, she had questions for me before I could ask any myself—namely, where I was born, where my parents were from. Before I knew it, she'd ended the conversation: "My whole life is Torah, and I can only teach Torah to Jews. So I'm sorry, I can't do an interview with you." The irony was that she herself was a convert to Judaism and had once not been a Jew herself. But I will never forget her words, the sound of unapologetic certitude, the smack of exclusion.

I took comfort in being surrounded that summer by my longtime friends who shared a Jerusalem apartment with me. I had known Batya since my Bronfman summer in 1989, when we were sixteen. But she had changed. Batya arrived a semester ahead of me to study in a traditional women's yeshiva and was experimenting with becoming a *ba'alat teshuva*—a newly religiously observant Jew.

By the time I joined her in our small apartment one block from the town center, she was strictly kosher and Sabbath-observant, which meant no turning on lights or music from sundown Friday to sundown Saturday. She followed even the most exacting prescriptions, like avoiding tea bags because the water "cooks" the tea, thus breaking the rule against cooking, and pre-ripping toilet paper since cutting is not allowed on Shabbat. She had the zeal of the newly converted.

"Here is the cabinet for 'meat' dishes," she instructed me. "Here is the cabinet for 'milk' dishes. Chicken is meat. Eggs are 'parve,' which means 'neutral'; you can eat them with either meat or milk. Fish is parve, too, but we usually eat that with a dairy meal. And we only have one sink, so when you wash the meat dishes, please put this sink liner in."

"Sink liner?"

She showed me a plastic basin. I had been keeping kosher for the last three years, but this level of regulation was daunting.

I'd grown up with a mother who did not know how to cook without putting treyf (nonkosher food) into just about everything. My Korean grandmother taught all her daughters to cook well, and my mom's sister, Restaurant Emo, had opened a pork barbecue restaurant in Daegu. That gives you a sense of their diet. Just about every Korean soup has shellfish thrown into the stock. Even kimchi, the fermented pickled cabbage dish that epitomizes Korean cuisine, is usually made with shrimp paste. I certainly did not keep kosher as a child.

But when I went to college, having declared that I wanted to be a rabbi, I decided that I wanted to embrace the laws of kashrut, albeit in my own modified way that gave room for me to eat off the dining hall plates. I welcomed the mindfulness required at each meal to stay within the parameters, the resourcefulness it often required when kosher options were not readily available. I loved paying attention to what I was eating, embracing difference, ingesting a little holiness into this everyday act. And of course, there was an unmistakable pull to identify outwardly as a Jew, even though most of my Jewish friends in college didn't keep kosher themselves.

I remember coming home after my first semester at Yale and announcing to my mother that I was now keeping kosher. She didn't take the news well. Food was a gesture of love, and my new commitment felt like a rejection—not just of the Korean culture we share but of something precious she had relied on to nourish and raise me.

"But what are you going to eat?!" she lamented.

"Mom, it's pretty simple, just no pork or shellfish. You don't have to worry so much about the milk and meat thing since you never cook with dairy anyway."

"You mean you are giving up King Crab?"

This had become my mother's absolute favorite indulgence since moving to the Pacific Northwest.

"Yeah, sorry, no crab. No oysters. No scallops."

She shook her head, grieving my lost delicacies.

Mom made an effort, at first, to avoid cooking my forbidden foods, creating kosher-style dishes. She made her kimchi with anchovies instead of shrimp. She left the clams out of the doenjang stock. But she never quite understood why I was denying myself the joys of favorite foods, and she wearied of the absolutism.

"Mom, this salad. It has shrimp on it. I can't eat this."

"*Wah*. It's just a little bit of shrimp!"

"Yeah, that's not how this works, Mom. A little bit of shrimp is still shrimp."

I grew accustomed to just picking out any obvious treyf from my mother's cooking, not being too demanding about interrogating every ingredient. I decided that keeping peace in the house, and being able to continue to eat my mother's cooking and my Korean aunties' family meals, was its own sacred act. I would work this respect for my mother into my more flexible kosher practice.

But that summer in Jerusalem, Batya made it crystal clear that my level of kashrut wasn't kosher.

"You can't just pick out the shellfish! The whole meal becomes contaminated. Even the plates, the cutlery, the sponges can all become tainted. This is why we have separate dishes, utensils, pots, and pans."

I would enter the kitchen hesitatingly, hyper-focused on reaching for the right plates, washing things separately. But one evening when I was making dinner, I accidentally used the wrong mixing spoon in a meat pot.

"You're using a parve spoon in a meat pot!" Batya exclaimed.

"I'm so sorry. But I haven't even put the meat in the pot yet," I explained.

"It doesn't matter; the pot is a meat pot."

"But you said that this is a parve spoon. It's neutral. It's not like a milk spoon in the meat pot, right?"

"*No*. You've ruined the spoon from being parve. It can't just be washed off," she cried.

"I'll buy you a new spoon," I offered.

"I'm going to call the rabbi's wife to ask her what I'm supposed to do with this now!"

My face got hot. I felt mortified. Ashamed.

Here I had been keeping kosher since freshman year, teaching my mother the rules, but now realized I'd never actually studied what it means to *really* keep kosher. Even the rabbi's wife would discover I was an imposter.

And yet. There was also part of me that understood I never wanted to keep that level of strict observance. Not if it meant that the impure status of a mixing spoon would matter more than the feelings of another person. Not if it meant I could never eat in my mother's kitchen.

Our third roommate, Judith, was another friend from college. She came from a vibrant Jewish home. Her parents were leaders in the 1960s national *havurah* movement, in which young baby boomers created small alternative, do-it-yourself Jewish communities as their countercultural rebellion against institutional Judaism. As these *havurah* participants matured, many of them ultimately ended up leading Jewish institutions. Judith's mother, Dr. Paula Hyman, was a prominent Jewish feminist scholar and my thesis adviser at Yale. Judith was fluent in Hebrew and grew up visiting Israel every summer with her mother, surrounded by a circle of elite intellectuals and thought leaders.

Among them was Rabbi Jacqueline Koch Ellenson, a wonderful mentor of women rabbis, and her husband Rabbi David Ellenson, of blessed memory, who would go on to become a beloved president of Hebrew Union College. "Jackie," as Judith called her, came over to our apartment early one morning and invited us all to accompany her to pray with Women of the Wall. This was a pioneering group of Jewish feminists who wanted to pray with ritual garments and read Torah at the Western Wall in Jerusalem, which was reserved for men in its central space. These iconic stones are part of the retaining wall of the Second Temple, one of the holiest sites for our faith, where Jews have pilgrimaged for millennia.

It seemed obvious to me that women should have an equal right to pray as they desired at this holy site, but the traditional rabbis controlling the Wall forbade it. The prayer space is divided unevenly, with a much larger men's section and a *mechitza*, a partition, between the genders. Men wrapped in prayer shawls hold services with Torah scrolls and pray with *tefillin*, leather prayer straps; women are barred from doing the same.

But in 1988, a group of brave women donned prayer shawls, entered the women's section, and began to pray. No one paid them much attention at first, but month after month they returned, and as they grew in number, so did the outrage and abuse. Men from the other side of the barrier would scream, curse, and threaten the women for the simple act of singing out loud, wearing a tallit, or holding a Torah scroll—considered subversive acts, violating tradition. Women were heckled, shoved, spat upon, called prostitutes, and even arrested for "disturbing the peace."

Decades later, the group is still fighting for their basic right to pray at the Wall. But they became one of the most widely covered media stories in Israel. Former Chief Rabbi Ovadia Yosef decried, "There are stupid women who come to the Western Wall . . . These are deviants who serve equality, not Heaven. They must be condemned and warned of."

A *rabbi* said that. About women who simply want to pray. It always shocks me when clergy act as watchguards, defending their territory, rather than as guides, accompanying seekers into the tradition.

By 2017, the Supreme Court of Israel ruled that if the government could not find "good cause" to prohibit women's reading Torah at the Wall, then women would be able to do so. That year, after Prime Minister Benjamin Netanyahu promised to establish an egalitarian prayer section where men and women could daven together, he did an abrupt about-face, bowing to ultra-Orthodox pressure and reneging on the agreement.

Very few Americans knew about the movement back in 1993, but Jackie did. She invited Judith and me to participate in this burgeoning struggle. Judith wrapped tefillin on her arm and head, another subversive act for a woman. Men hissed at Judith from the other side of the *mechitza* and even women on our side glared with disgust.

I grabbed a prayer book and joined the circle as the service began. But the women were speeding through the words so quickly, much of it under their breath. I kept looking over at Judith's siddur to see what page we were on. I tried mumbling along, but so many prayers were unfamiliar and my Hebrew was not strong enough to keep up. I was an outsider among the outsiders: a less literate Jew among expert pioneers. The women of the group glanced over at me with little interest. I was certain they were judging me as a visitor out of her depth.

When they got to the familiar Shema prayer, which they sang a bit slower, I joined in a little too loudly, trying to assert my place in the group. Then it was back to the quick murmur of traditional prayer.

After the service, the group ascended into the Old City to find a more private place to read Torah. In these years, the women did not dare risk opening the scroll at the Wall itself, fearing a violent reaction from the ultra-Orthodox. We walked into the ancient remains of the Hurva Synagogue, its name meaning "ruin," built in the sixteenth century and rebuilt in the nineteenth, which had a reading table. The site was a symbol of resilience, having survived multiple destructions by our enemies and 116 years of inactivity.

The leaders of Women of the Wall knew Jackie and gave her the honor of an aliyah. Then the group turned to Judith and invited her to have an aliyah as well. They turned to a woman who clearly seemed like a matriarch in the group and offered her the third.

"Would anyone else like an aliyah?" the leader inquired. She looked around the small group but did not meet my eyes.

This was it—my chance to show these women that I was not just a visitor, a stranger to Judaism, but one of them.

I raised my hand. "I would love to have an aliyah."

The leader motioned me to come stand next to her, beside the open parchment scroll. I felt my heart beating loudly in my chest. Though I had recited these words so many times and heard them chanted just minutes before, I was nervous.

I started out with the opening line, which is an invitation: *"Bar'chu et A-do-nai ha-m'vo-rach"* (Bless the Lord who is blessed). The group of women responded in unison: *"Ba-ruch A-do-nai ha-m'vo-rach l'o-lahm va-ed"* (Blessed be the Lord who is blessed for all eternity).

Then I continued the prayer that I knew by heart: *"Asher natan lanu . . ."*

Except those were the wrong words.

"*Bachar banu!*" came the chorus of women, correcting what had clearly been my mistake.

My face flushed as I absorbed their collective edit and quickly hurried through the rest of the prayer. I had set this up as a test and totally flubbed it, certain I'd proven all their assumptions. *May a hole in the ground open up and swallow me.*

"Don't give it another thought," Judith said as we walked away.

But she could not possibly understand how I felt. She had always been an insider.

I came home and called my mother, using up five expensive long-distance minutes in unintelligible heaves of crying while telling her of all the little daggers from the summer: The rejection from the Orthodox songwriter, the scrutiny I felt from my longtime friend and roommate who seemed to judge everything I did as insufficiently Jewish, my botched blessing at the Hurva Synagogue, which had "ruined" me.

"I don't know why I keep fighting for this," I sobbed. "Everywhere I turn in the Jewish community I feel judged or told I'm not the real thing. I want to be a rabbi, but I'm not sure I want to be a Jew anymore. I don't have a Jewish name; I don't have a Jewish face. No one would even notice or care; I could just stop being Jewish right now."

My mother paused, absorbing my pain, and responded simply, "Is that really possible, Angela?"

Her question took me aback. I always thought I could just stop being Jewish at any time, like a borrowed coat that I could simply take off and give back. No one thought I was Jewish, anyway, despite the fact that I asserted it in every conceivable way.

It wasn't until my mother posed that naked question—can you actually stop being a Jew?—that I realized my Jewishness was not superficial, but bone deep. Judaism penetrated the way I thought, and shaped the way I moved through the world. I couldn't stop being Jewish any more than I could stop being Korean or stop being a woman. It is wholly who I am.

"It's actually not possible," I said to my mother, wiping my tears and catching my breath. I had never felt so relieved to have no choice in the matter.

Shikhecha
FORGOTTEN

Jews are often described as a people of memory—not only because we tell and retell our history in rituals, holidays, and literature, but because we are frequently commanded, *Zachor!* "Remember!" *Remember* the Sabbath. *Remember* how we left Egypt. *Remember* our covenant with God. "Remember" appears more than 150 times in the Torah. This insistence underscores the very human tendency *to forget*.

Most of us bemoan forgetting as a failure of our memory system—a source of frustration and even shame. But forgetting is an important feature of our brains, not a malfunction. With hundreds of thousands of daily inputs, we could not filter the information we actually need if we remembered every color, word, sensation, or experience of our lives. Something has to rise to a level of significance for our minds to actually decide to store it as a memory.

If, as we all learned in science, the human traits that endure are those that are integral to survival, then what essential purpose does memory serve? From an evolutionary perspective, it did not exist merely for the sake of nostalgia. It was essential to recalling what sounds our predators made, where food could be found, how to build, teach, mate, protect, and live another day.

Recent brain science has shown that forgetting also turns out to be crucial for our survival. A set of neurons are dedicated to active forgetting, deciding which things must be dropped to make room for what our memory needs to prioritize for our health and endurance. Post-traumatic stress disorder is seen as an injury to the forgetting function. When we cannot forget—and in fact, continuously replay an intense grief, injury, or betrayal—we can become frozen in place, unable to go forward.

Though the Torah does not explicitly instruct us "to forget," we are told not to bear a grudge and not to take revenge, which implies more forgiving than forgetting. But there is also a prominent commandment in the Torah that refers to *shikhecha*, or "forgotten crops." These sheaves intentionally left behind in the field by farmers were required by agricultural law to provide a safety net for the most needy. This law reminded the Israelites that the harvest didn't wholly belong to them.

"When you reap the harvest of your field and forget a sheaf," says Deuteronomy, "do not return to retrieve it. That bundle of wheat must be left for the stranger, the orphan, and the widow in your midst."

The *shikhecha* isn't caused by absentmindedness; the forgotten crop has a purpose. The command shows there can be a higher benefit to forgetting: for example, "forgetting" a criminal record after someone has served their punishment so that they might proceed with their lives. Or "forgetting" a grudge in order to repair an estranged relationship. Or "forgetting" some of the land you are purchasing in order to donate it to a land trust.

We can gain from what we leave behind. Sometimes we need to discard the sheaf on the field. Forget on purpose.

CHAPTER 12

Don't Call It Conversion

The amazing thing about realizing your worst fears is that hitting "rock bottom" is a form of *landing*. After plenty of tears in Israel and a true sense of futility and loneliness, I had my mother's voice in my head, telling me to dust myself off. I realized, after all that, *I was still Jewish*. And little by little, something solid began taking hold underneath me. I recalled the words of the Psalmist: "I cried out to you from a narrow place, and you answered me from a wide open space" (Psalms 118:5). I left Jerusalem that summer feeling like I was ready to ask different questions, no longer "Am I enough?" but "How do I move forward?"

A form of an answer came via two messengers, as if sent from the universe to clarify the next chapter of my Jewish life.

I met these two angels in San Antonio, Texas, just months after my intense summer in Israel, when I flew to Trinity University for a gathering of Jewish educators. College students like me had been recruited to attend so that we could be exposed to some of the best in the country: rabbis and teachers whom we'd read, watched, and admired.

A highlight of the conference, convened by the Coalition for the Advancement of Jewish Education, was a session called "Choir," led by none other than the legendary Debbie Friedman, who wrote the soundtrack of my Jewish childhood. It was a perfect fusion of star-power and pastoral care. I would be singing alongside the troubadour of Reform Judaism, whom I'd never before seen or met in person.

During our first session in a nondescript classroom, fifty chairs encircled one single seat, where Debbie was perched with her guitar. "We are all broken," she said, strumming softly. "Once we acknowledge that, we can start the healing." For most of my life, I would have instinctively dismissed her words: *I'm not broken.* I was happy enough. Unrebellious. Studious. Upbeat. But after this senior summer in Israel, my cracks were showing.

Once Debbie began singing, tears flowed without warning. She had composed a melody to accompany words from our morning liturgy, *Refaeinu Adonai N'nerafe*, "Heal us God and we will be healed," and the song penetrated. Self-conscious at first, I then noticed that many others were crying too.

Debbie seemed completely unsurprised by this emotional response. She just encouraged us to keep singing those words, over and over. With every refrain, I felt another fault line open inside me. I came back each day of the conference, looking forward to the catharsis, finally able to acknowledge pain I had never confronted, vulnerability I'd tried to conceal. Having been doubted and questioned for so long seemed to me like a small hardship in the scheme of things, one that did not entitle me to claim suffering. But I hadn't realized how destabilizing and soul-crushing it was to be told repeatedly that you are not who you truly believe yourself to be My Korean and Buddhist DNA would always somehow put me outside the Jewish tent, and make me a stranger even to myself.

At the same instant it struck me: *Feeling like the stranger might be the most Jewish thing about me.*

The second angel at that conference was Rabbi Elliot Dorff, a Conservative rabbi and scholar, who taught a session on ethics. I was taken by his mastery of Jewish texts, the humanity and compassion he embodied, so I asked if he would be willing to talk to me about conversion. I suspect he understood this was not just a theoretical conversation for me, but he never pressed me about my own background or Jewish status.

In 1983, when I was eleven years old, the Reform Movement's leadership made the historic decision to accept patrilineal descent for Jewish identity. Practically, this meant that if your mother or father was Jewish, and you were raised in the Jewish tradition, you were considered legally Jewish, no conversion required. I asked Rabbi Dorff what he thought of the ruling. He said he appreciated the Reform Movement's desire to accept all children of intermarriage, but objected to framing conversion as something remedial. Instead, he preferred that conversion be viewed as a positive act of commitment, or *recommitment*, something to seek.

I countered that it didn't *feel* positive to suggest or require conversion of someone with a Jewish father, who had been raised as a Jew all her life. It seemed like a negation of the Jewish life they had already been living.

He responded that my lens on conversion reflected the Christian understanding, which stems from the Latin *conversio*, meaning "a turning around" or "complete change." It is true that the Western view of conversion is seen as a total transformation, or repudiation of what has come before. But Rabbi Dorff said that Judaism sees *giyur* differently: not as a total transformation but as an acknowledgment and embrace of the Jewish soul that has always been in you.

This perspective was not only a clarification but a gift. I could now understand *giyur* not as turning into something new but as a reaffirmation of the Jew I always was.

My challenging summer in Israel had brought me as close as I ever came to turning away from Judaism. But desperation brought home how much being a Jew meant to me—how inescapable that identity was. I decided to finally consider *giyur*, even though I didn't feel pressured by anyone to do so, even though I believed I was already fully a Jew. Even though I would always resent being repeatedly asked, "So, you converted, right?"

Ultimately my mother's incisive question, Debbie's music, and Rabbi Dorff's reassurance made *giyur* feel like the right path, even inevitable.

I was now secure enough in my Judaism to acknowledge that my mother and half my family were not Jewish, that Mom's Buddhist Korean philosophy influenced the Jew I had become. Instead of trying to assert that I was the same as any Jew with two Jewish parents, I could celebrate the many threads that make up my Judaism.

I called my hometown Tacoma rabbi, Richard Rosenthal, and told him that I had decided to have a *giyur*, which I viewed as a "reaffirmation ceremony." His first reaction was to declare that I had always been Jewish in his eyes. But he would of course help me put together a *beit din*, the traditional "rabbinic court" of three rabbis who judge one's sincerity and readiness. That December, during senior year winter break, my family and I drove to a Seattle synagogue because it had a ritual bath, the mikvah, while Tacoma had none. In the low-slung redbrick Sephardic Bikur Holim congregation with a candelabra on the roof, I would immerse myself in the "living waters" as part of my traditional *giyur* ceremony.

Rabbi Rosenthal brought along Rabbis James Mirel and David Fine to fill out the *beit din*. They were all Reform rabbis who accepted me—before any conversion—as a Jew of patrilineal descent. I realized of course that this Reform *beit din* would still not make me a Jew in the eyes of most Orthodox Jews. I knew that if I wanted a *giyur* that would be accepted by even the most traditional denominations (Israel is another matter because conversion there is regulated by the Chief Rabbinate), I would have to go before an Orthodox *beit din*, and commit to Orthodox practices, which was not my Jewish observance. But I did not undertake this ceremony to gain external approval; it was a way of ritualizing the internal journey I'd been on.

I sat nervously in the small, dimly lit waiting room outside the mikvah, in a simple dress with no makeup, no nail polish, no deodorant or perfume, wearing glasses rather than contact lenses, since the mikvah requires us to strip down to our most natural state. The three rabbis of the *beit din* sat with my family on leather couches as Rabbi Rosenthal invited me to explain why I was taking this step. I said I was ready to acknowledge and no longer apologize for the fact that my Jewish soul had been shaped by both my parents. I thanked my father for the gift of a Jewish inheritance he was so eager for me to love just as he did. I thanked my Buddhist mother for the gift of a spiritual vocabulary that had infused my own. I affirmed that in America today, we are all, in a sense, "Jews by choice," that we can opt into this rich legacy or discard it at any moment. I was not a "new Jew," but I felt newly secure in my Jewish belonging; this ancient ritual became the exclamation point.

While the *beit din* listened, as is customary, from the adjoining room, I stepped into the deep mikvah, naked, the warm water rising up to my neck. Every mikvah contains a flow of "living water" drawn from the rain or natural sources, recalling the powerful ancient waters of the primordial deep, the flood, the Red Sea—with all its potential for renewal and redemption. In order to immerse my entire body as the ritual requires—from the soles of my feet to every hair on my head—I had to lift my toes off the pool floor and curl in a fetal position.

Baruch Atah Adonai . . . al ha-Tevilah. "Blessed are you . . . who has commanded us concerning immersion."

I uttered the blessing and then dipped again.

I wanted to linger in the mikvah a little longer, feeling the womb of living water carrying me over the threshold from my childhood Jewish identity into this more grounded one. I stepped out of the pool, toweled off, dressed, and rejoined the rabbis with my family to sing the sheheheyanu—our blessing of gratitude and praise.

Sheheheyanu, v'kiyamanu, v'higianu lazman hazeh. "Thank you for giving us life, for sustaining us and enabling us to reach this moment."

It was a moment of reaffirmation, yes, but also rebirth.

No one dictated this path. I had chosen it.

Shevarim
BROKENNESS

In the project of Creation, as told in Genesis, God constructed an ideal world of celestial lights, oceans, and plants (declaring them "good") as well as human beings ("very good"). But Adam and Eve quickly fell from grace in the Garden of Eden, and we humans have been struggling ever since.

Of course, if we have to measure ourselves against an original state of perfection, we will never escape our own inadequacy. We will live lives of apology for all that we are not.

But Kabbalah, the Jewish mystical tradition, offers a different creation narrative, one that acknowledges the very impossibility of perfection.

In the beginning, God's presence filled the universe.

Because God was everywhere, there was no room for anything else.

So God had to contract, like a sharp inhale, in order to make space in which to create the world.

The mystics called this divine contraction tsimtsum.

In that newfound space, God created darkness.

God then poured a stream of Divine Light into ten vessels.

But these vessels could not withstand such awesome, primordial energy.

They shattered, showering holy sparks everywhere.

Human beings were created to find these splinters of divine light, to make a repair—by helping God gather the shards together, to restore and recreate the world.

What a strange, chaotic, and beautiful creation narrative, one that asserts that brokenness, not perfection, is our true inheritance.

Our task is not to search in vain for some lost paradise but to look for tiny sparks of light in the divine debris that is all around us. To find holiness in the broken fragments.

Many of the greatest artists, athletes, musicians, and thinkers have had physical challenges. Beethoven wrote his finest symphonies while going deaf. Virginia Woolf expanded our concept of literature and Vincent van Gogh our way of seeing color while they both struggled with mental illness. The physicist Stephen Hawking used a wheelchair and computer-assisted speech to help the rest of us understand the secrets of the universe. Olympic runner Usain Bolt became the fastest human in history despite severe curvature of his spine.

But the mystical story of creation helps us understand that such genius did not necessarily come *despite* pain, imperfection, or disability; it may well have derived from it.

On the Jewish New Year, Rosh Hashanah, it is customary to hear the sound of the shofar—an ancient ram's horn. The shofar blast is meant to shake us out of our spiritual slumber, to disturb the status quo. The staccato shofar call, *shevarim*, literally means "broken," and it validates the fractures in our lives, even as it also challenges us to atone, heal, and repair.

Make whole what is broken; shatter what feels whole.

On Rosh Hashanah, the birthday of the world, the shofar invites us to let go of the conventional Garden of Eden creation story with its perfect paradise and instead to embrace the messier, *mystical* story of creation where sparks of God's light get scattered.

The Kabbalists would say that every one of us is an unfinished vessel.

Too often, we see our fissures as flaws.

But as the modern prophet Leonard Cohen sings:

> *Ring the bells that still can ring*
> *Forget your perfect offering*
> *There is a crack, a crack in everything*
> *That's how the light gets in.*

CHAPTER 13

The Boy in the Pink Parka

The first time Jacob proposed to me, he was seventeen. "You should marry me," he said.

My husband loves to tell people he asked me to marry him within days of meeting me on the first morning of our freshman year at Yale. People look skeptical: "Seriously?"

"Well, yes. That is technically true," I explain. "But he wandered into my room at two a.m. and was under the influence of, shall we say, libations. It wasn't exactly *romantic*."

"Don't minimize it," Jacob will jump in. "It may have been impulsive. But I knew. And now you have to admit I was right," he will say with a wry smile, noting our twenty-five-plus years of marriage.

Jacob immediately caught my attention. A blond-haired, blue-eyed Jew from rural Vermont, he was conceived in the back of a Volkswagen van, a detail his self-proclaimed hippie parents still relish recounting. Jacob's father, David, a graduate student at the University of Chicago, was writing his PhD thesis on the American counterculture, so Carol and David traveled to Spokane, Washington, to live in a little A-frame house on a commune for a year of field research. Jacob was born a few months after their return to Chicago.

They moved to Rhode Island when David got his first teaching appointment at Brown University, and Jacob spent his early school years at an Orthodox Jewish day school in Providence. The Buchdahls weren't observant Jews by any stretch, but the public elementary school was intolerably underperforming, and the day school gave them a big break on tuition.

Through second grade, Jacob dressed every morning in a kippah and tzitzit and studied Hebrew and the Bible alongside his secular lessons. But in 1980, when his father didn't get tenure, his parents went searching for the counterculture in Vermont. Their one geographical condition was to be within a thirty-mile radius of Burlington, where there was a Jewish community. When they found a house right at the northern edge of that limit in Georgia, Vermont, the town had 1,800 people, twice as many cows, and exactly one Jewish family: the Buchdahls.

By the time Jacob got to Yale, he didn't fit neatly into any one box, either. He showed up with a hot-pink ski jacket. (To this day he claims it was "faded red," but trust me, it was a neon fuchsia.) His personality was even louder and full of contradictions.

Jacob was a jock and played every intramural sport. But he was also a classical musician who had already performed at Carnegie Recital Hall as Vermont's most accomplished high school pianist. He stood out in his all-male a cappella group, the Baker's Dozen, not because he had the strongest voice but because he was a born entertainer.

Jacob came to college thinking he'd concentrate in physics and minor in piano but ended up in an ambitious new major: ethics, politics, and economics.

He put up posters of basketball players and skiers in his freshman dorm room, but he liked to talk philosophy.

He washed dishes in the dining hall to help cover his tuition and never had more than $20 to withdraw from the newfangled ATMs on campus. But he was the first to treat others to drinks.

He was the funniest person I knew but also one of the most focused students, which I saw firsthand when we studied for a Jewish history class together. Maddeningly, even though I was the one who wanted to be the "professional Jew," he got the better grade.

I couldn't figure him out.

Freshman year, we lived in adjoining suites of six, connected by a fire door that didn't lock. Every night during those first months, a cluster of us talked into the dawn, eating pizza for breakfast, giddy that no sensible parental figure was around to stop us. While I deflected his overtures then and for almost another four years, nevertheless we became very good friends, part of a larger group of inseparable roommates and friends in the same residential college.

One night shortly before spring break of our senior year, Jacob and I went out to dinner together (which was not unusual), and he was mostly silent (which was). I noted his uncommon reserve and asked if something was on his mind, to which he offered a bold profession of love and the admonition that if we didn't try dating before we graduated, we would regret it for the rest of our lives.

I was shocked, even though I'd indulged my own what-ifs about our relationship. But I couldn't admit this to Jacob. He knew I had resumed my long-distance relationship with my high school boyfriend, and in that moment, I demurred again.

Two weeks later, with only a month left before graduation, we were dating.

The relationship got serious fast, but the timing was tough. We had scarcely been together for six weeks when, after graduation, I was on a plane to Northern California to serve as head song leader at Camp Swig for the summer, a longtime dream of mine. In October, after the High Holidays, I had a job lined up teaching English for the year in South Korea. How would this brief relationship endure such long separations of time and geography? Jacob flew to camp in August to try to convince me to forgo Korea. But I felt this was my only chance to spend time learning the Korean language and culture before committing myself to a life in the rabbinate.

Jacob was doggedly persistent, irresistibly charming, and ultimately convincing. In September, as my beloved grandmother Phreda was dying back in Tacoma, and with a year's absence from Jacob weighing on me, I canceled my plans to be abroad. By then, it was late fall and I had no work or place to live, which is how I ended up in the unusual position of living in a wonderful family's empty weekend house in Scarsdale as an unmarried twenty-one-year-old.

Westchester Reform Temple in Scarsdale had first invited me to work there three years before, when I was a college sophomore and they needed a song leader for their annual retreat with Confirmation students. WRT's rabbinic intern at the time had remembered me from Camp Swig and asked if I would take the hour-long Metro-North train to Scarsdale on weekends to lead the Confirmation retreat, Youth Sabbath services, and teen programming.

My admiration for WRT's charismatic new senior rabbi, Rick Jacobs, was instantaneous. I'd never met a rabbi like him before, a former professional modern dancer whose sermons ranged between invitations to spirituality and calls to do justice in the world.

When I canceled my Korea plans to give my relationship with Jacob a real chance, I hoped to stay in the New York area and prepare for rabbinical school. I turned to Rabbi Jacobs for help. He scraped together some last-minute work teaching preschoolers and sixth graders and leading services at WRT and introduced me to the family who was happy to let me live in their Scarsdale "weekend" home on weekdays, rent-free, in exchange for tutoring their son in Hebrew.

Every Friday, I would either travel to New Haven to stay with Jacob, who was then in law school, or bring Jacob with me to crash in Rick's guest bedroom. Rick and his wife, Susie, put me on the "meal plan"—always sharing their Shabbat lunches, family dinners, and kosher pantry—and encouraged me to be part of the bedtime ritual with their young boys, singing lullabies and reciting the Shema. I was at their celebrations and their kitchen table, talking about events in the world, asking every Jewish question churning in my head. They became my family in this family-centered suburb.

Through our many weekends and meals, Jacob and I got a close-up view of the life of a rabbi and a rebbetzin (a rabbinic spouse). We saw how family life could be upended by a death call or synagogue crisis, but also the magical ways their home became the center of the community, with Yom Kippur break-fasts and Sukkot meals. It didn't seem to scare Jacob away; he relished the idea that I could have this respected role in the Jewish community, and that he would have his, too.

When Jacob made his second marriage proposal to me—nearly six years after his first—I said yes.

Kadosh
HOLINESS

The word for "marriage" in Judaism is *kiddushin*, "sanctification."

It shares the same root as more familiar words.

Kaddish: the prayer that sanctifies the dead.

Kiddush: the blessing over wine that sanctifies time.

Kedusha: the liturgy that sanctifies God.

These all stem from the root *kadosh*, which literally means "set apart" but which we translate as "holy." Marriage is the act of making a love *holy*.

In Western culture, holiness is often considered supernatural—endowed from on high, or conferred by some spiritual leader acting as an intermediary with God. But Judaism sees it differently.

In Judaism, each of us has the power to make something, or someone, holy.

It is both remarkably simple and surprisingly challenging: To make something holy, you must set it apart.

When we are told to make the Sabbath holy, we do so by setting the day apart from all other days. There are restrictions on work, technology, cooking, using money. By making this day different from ordinary days, we create sacred time—a moment when the Eternal touches the temporal.

Just as time can be made sacred, so can objects. A kiddush cup. A Bible. A tallis or tablecloth.

When I discuss this idea of *kiddushin*—"sanctification"—with a wedding couple, I use the example of a kiddush cup used for blessing wine on sacred occasions.

I ask, "What makes a kiddush cup holy?"

Even couples well versed in Judaism have a hard time answering. "It needs to be made from silver? It is blessed by a rabbi? It has Hebrew lettering? It is made in Israel?"

In truth, it's a bit of a trick question. A kiddush cup can be made of any material, ornate or simple, created anywhere. The only requirement is that it be a vessel capable of holding an adequate amount of wine—a *revi'it*, or about four ounces.

What makes the kiddush cup *holy* is the way it is used: It is reserved only for sacred occasions, like the Sabbath and festivals. If you purchase a silver goblet studded with gemstones in Israel engraved with the word *Kiddush* on it but then use that cup every day for your morning beverage, it does not remain a kiddush cup. It becomes an impractical coffee mug.

Separating an object or a moment apart makes us savor it, honor it.

Calling marriage *kiddushin* is Judaism's way of saying *Set this relationship apart.*

A wedding is a public declaration to your partner and to the world that this relationship is distinct from all others in your life. In marriage, holiness is made by reserving some emotional and physical intimacies only for the other. By sharing some of life's experiences *only* with that other. By committing to your spouse as your closest chosen family, you have contracted to share sorrows and triumphs as one.

I tell engaged couples that "holiness" is not bestowed by a rabbi. It can only be granted by one partner to the other. It is not a onetime vow but a lifelong pursuit.

I suggest designating special time for each other every week. The oft-cited warning against taking a spouse for granted is no cliché; we tend to give each other what is left over after we have attended to everyone else, expecting our significant others to be there. But if we want these partnerships to be holy for a lifetime, we must continually set them apart.

We also have sacred friendships, sacred family relationships. Every holiness requires thought, sacrifice, generosity, forgiveness, patience, and an intentional differentiation.

Not all relationships are equal. Not all time is the same.

Holiness is not given to us.

It is up to us.

CHAPTER 14

Seminary

If it weren't for Jacob, I would never have become a cantor, but not because he suggested the idea.

It hadn't occurred to me to pursue cantorial studies in addition to my rabbinic track at Hebrew Union College, the seminary for aspiring Reform clergy.

But my courtship with Jacob made me want to stay near him in New York City, which meant opting for the Manhattan campus, which happened to have a cantorial program, as opposed to the LA campus, where I had been assigned.

Since the age of sixteen, my dream was only to become a rabbi. I'd had multiple inspiring rabbinic role models but never a cantorial one. Still, I also embraced my identity as a song leader—forged at Temple Beth El and Camp Swig. Over the years, music had been at the heart of my Judaism—a passion not just to teach a song but to drive it, make it contagious, transporting. So often I could see people's hesitancy to join in loud enough to be heard. My greatest satisfaction was to see every person singing.

But song leaders weren't cantors, and in fact, the two roles often clashed in those days. Cantors often viewed song leaders as glorified folk singers who replaced the historic tradition of liturgical music with "camp ditties." Song leaders often viewed cantors as glorified opera singers who sang *at* you in synagogue, conveying that services were for listening, not participating. These biases, though oversimplified and unjust, were pervasive enough to keep me from any interest in cantorial school. It didn't matter that I had already led music at services for a decade, sang in college, played guitar, and felt, if anyone had asked me, that God felt closest when I was singing. I submitted my application to rabbinical seminary and didn't give cantorial school any real consideration.

Sometimes God has another plan.

Every HUC student spends the first of five years in Jerusalem. My entering clergy class in 1995 was notable for being the first time in HUC's history to have more female students than male. Cantorial and rabbinical students were paired each week to lead services: Cantors steered the music, rabbis delivered the sermons and the kavvanot—spiritual introductions to prayers. My cantorial classmates were generous about letting me sometimes take the musical baton and play guitar, but I could see that I was stuck in one place while they were advancing. They were immersed in Jewish modes, Torah trope, and cantorial melismata, while I had plateaued, leaning on campfire guitar skills and a song leader's repertoire.

Then I learned that, of HUC's three American campuses, I had been placed in Los Angeles for the four years following the first in Israel. I petitioned vigorously to the Jerusalem campus dean, explaining that Jacob was at law school in New Haven and we'd already been long-distance for a full year while I was in Israel. "We can't continue to be a world apart."

I immediately applied for a campus transfer to HUC in New York, but the administration said it was full. "Besides, he is just a boyfriend. Not your fiancé."

That gave us a strategy. We were only twenty-three years old—young, in love, in a hurry—and we knew we were getting married to each other. *Someday.* So Jacob flew to Jerusalem during his law school spring break. In a fanny pack (procured for this sole purpose) was an engagement ring he'd purchased in the Diamond District with a brand-new six-months-zero-interest credit card, and he proposed to me in the courtyard of the Spagettim restaurant in Jerusalem.

I phoned the powers that be at HUC: "Jacob and I are engaged! Now, can you please transfer me to New York?"

"I'm sorry. We are at capacity. Why don't you take a year off, and we promise to put you at the New York campus next year." Despondent, I called my mentor, Rabbi Jacobs, to lament.

"Why don't you apply to cantorial school?" he offered. "The School of Sacred Music exists only on the New York campus. You can do it for a year, learn more Jewish music, and then go back to rabbinical school."

It was brilliant. I loved the idea of studying cantorial music while waiting to resume my rabbinical studies. It would be productive learning, plus a way to start life with Jacob.

That said, my first semester of cantorial school was rough. Most of my classmates were coming off serious vocal training. While I had always been a singer, I had never taken a voice lesson until cantorial school required it.

"You are singing all wrong!" my voice teacher announced. "You project from your chest and have no head voice, no mix between the two. Your range is limited, and you will lose your voice by the time you're thirty-five if you keep singing this way."

But I rather liked my sound. Natural and folksy. And people had always told me they liked it too. I'd never wanted to become an operatic cantor—much as I admired the virtuosos—and the thought of changing this essential part of my religious expression was uncomfortable. But my teacher was right. I didn't want to destroy my vocal cords by singing incorrectly. She had to break down my voice to rebuild it.

The first semester "practicum" performance arrived while I was still in the voice-demolition stage. This end-of-semester mini recital is supposed to display a command of liturgy, delivery, and musicianship. I had been coached weekly all semester to learn a complex range of Shabbat music, which, as required repertoire, everyone else had already mastered. I stepped before the podium and sang in the designated keys that my diaphragm could not support, my sound thin and wavering. I couldn't glide my chest voice into my head voice, and I cracked like a prepubescent boy at his bar mitzvah.

I desperately tried to focus on communicating the spirit of the prayers, but my shakiness betrayed me. I stood at the podium in Milstein Chapel, regretting the whole attempt to combine cantorial and rabbinic ordination. I should have been standing at the podium practicing sermons, not trying to sing "Kol Nidre."

A cantorial student has one main calling card: her voice. What I had thought was a strength now seemed to fail me. I walked off the podium at the end of the practicum and turned away from my classmates so they would not see me crying.

Cantor Benjie Ellen Schiller, a graceful soprano and a new mentor, walked up behind me. "I know that was hard. And not what you want to sound like," she said. "But being a cantor is much more than your instrument. What moves people is an honest, pure kavvanah [intention] in your prayer-leading. This can't be taught. What people compliment me for when I pray is exactly what I see in you."

That encouragement enabled me to get through the next semester. Benjie was the role model I had been missing in the cantorate. Her voice seemed to emit from the purest place, threading itself through the congregation lightly, binding us together. I felt holiness when she led. If she saw something of herself in me during that painful practicum, that was fuel enough.

As the learning continued, I fell in love with the cries and slides of chazzanut—traditional cantorial chanting. I went down the fascinating rabbit hole of *nusach*, the Jewish modalities that dictate how to chant a specific prayer. I was recognized for "Most Improved Vocals" at the end of the year, and it felt like sweet relief. When I received the same honor the year after, it only confirmed how far I had to go. I realized this was no mere way station. I wanted to become a cantor as well as a rabbi.

After a year of cantorial school, which enabled me to be in New York, Jacob and I saw no reason to further delay getting married. The summer following my second year at HUC, just days after Jacob took the bar exam, we were wed in Tacoma by my childhood rabbi, Richard Rosenthal, alongside Rabbi Rick Jacobs and Cantor Benjie Ellen Schiller.

I walked down the aisle in an off-the-shoulder, flower-appliqué white dress I bought off the sample rack at Kleinfeld, my mother and father on each arm, toward a silk canopy that Gina and I had painted and erected on the very spot where I had celebrated my bat mitzvah and led countless services. Benjie composed a new setting from a verse of the Bible's Song of Songs and her lyrical voice made God's presence feel close. I had witnessed the processional choreography before at other people's weddings, but now it was my turn—when I would walk down the aisle with my parents, then symbolically leave them and join my spouse. This was the threshold moment when my "immediate" family would transition from the one I inherited to the one I chose.

Our reception was a modest affair, but since almost every wedding we had attended in Scarsdale had been formal, we made our dress code black-tie optional—which didn't exactly match the ambiance of the synagogue's Formica social hall. We managed to run out of alcohol before the night was over and when we walked excitedly out of the temple with fanfare as a married couple, under a hail of tossed rice, the wedding getaway car hadn't arrived, and we could only stand there, smiling awkwardly while we waited. The wedding had the haphazard, homemade feel of being planned by kids, which we most certainly still were. But it was still the best night of our young lives.

When we finally drove out of the synagogue parking lot, I turned back to catch my parents waving; my heart was full but wistful. I understood in that moment that I was leaving Tacoma for good. It would always be my hometown, but it was no longer my home. We were making a new one.

Shira
SONG

For a cantor, one of the most important Shabbat services of the year is *Shabbat Shirah*, the Sabbath of Song. It falls as the Torah reading cycle reaches the climactic moment of the enslaved Israelites passing through the Red Sea to freedom. The entire congregation rises to hear Moses's Song of the Sea, which has a special cadence unique to these verses. Cantors often go all out and add extra instruments or vocalists for this musical Shabbat.

> *I will sing to God for God has triumphed*
>   *gloriously . . .*
> *God is my strength and song; You have become my*
>   *deliverance* (Exodus 15:1).

It's hard not to be moved by the drama of Moses liberating his people. And that his response to freedom was *song*.

Only as an adult did I learn that Miriam, Moses's sister, was there too, leading the women in her own chant of deliverance. It would be easy to miss Miriam's song; Moses's is nineteen verses long and visually set apart in a special double column in the Torah. Miriam only gets one verse, like a footnote or afterthought, which largely repeats Moses's first line: "Sing to God for God has triumphed gloriously" (Exodus 15:21).

But there is one notable, perplexing difference. When Moses sings first, the Hebrew verb used is the expected *lashir*, "to sing": *Az Ya-shir Moshe* ("then Moses sang"). But when Miriam sings, the Torah uses the Hebrew verb *la'anot*, "to answer": *V'ta'an Miriam*. There is no other usage like it again in the Torah.

Rabbinic commentators over the centuries have seized on this curious word difference and offered their explanations. The twentieth-century Italian scholar Umberto Cassuto deduced that Miriam's verses are a response to Moses's.

Miriam doesn't lead singing so much as *echo*. She has no real song of her own.

Yet I would contend there is something significant in Miriam's song and leadership style: She doesn't sing solo. Instead, she grabs her timbrel, or tambourine, and leads *all* the women in music and dance. Her triumph is collaborative. Moreover, her song does not merely imitate Moses's— she creates a unique anthem of her own. She doesn't sing *to* the people who have just escaped enslavement; rather, she sees their gratitude, optimism, and exhaustion and *answers* their emotion with a communal chorus.

When I was a song leader in training at summer camp, I had one job: Get the kids to sing. This remained true as a cantor as well, but I learned that my principal job was actually more like an energy worker. With guitar, voice, gestures, nodding, call-and-response, my role was to bring a group to exhilarated heights or calm them into focus. Whatever was needed—I used music to answer the moment.

Miriam in the Bible, Ruthie (my childhood music teacher), and Benjie, my cantorial mentor, were the kind of pathfinders I wanted to be. Not a performer but a connector, a responder. Not only a song leader but a spiritual leader, helping people hear their own voices—and maybe even God's—through the making of heavenly sound.

CHAPTER 15

No One Said It Might Be Lonely

As much as I wanted to be a rabbi, I wanted to be a mother even more.

Which is why it was particularly painful to feel both awestruck and incomprehensibly sad when we had our first child.

I was twenty-seven, and I couldn't shake the devastating feeling that I had ruined my life.

Pregnancy had been fairly easy and predictable. I marveled at what my body was capable of, and I had mapped out a natural birth plan based on my self-perceived high tolerance for pain and aversion to medications. But the delivery was just one of many lessons that taught me how little parenthood is within our control.

The day before our first child was born, I woke up and instinctively reached across the bed to Jacob, who was not there. My husband was the youngest law associate on a high-profile case that had just gone to trial. Jacob was in the midst of his third consecutive all-nighter in the office when my water broke—three weeks early. Did I mention it was finals week in rabbinical school? Things were not going according to plan.

I called Jacob, who had only slept a few hours in three days, and told him to take a nap because it might be another very long day. My second call was to Susie, Rabbi Rick Jacob's wife and a dear friend. Right away, she drove me from our home in the suburbs to New York City so I would be closer to the hospital we'd selected before moving to the suburbs. Jacob met me at our friends' apartment and promptly fell asleep on their bed. My doctor instructed me to take it easy for a few hours and see if labor came on naturally. It didn't. After five hours, I stirred Jacob and hobbled the few blocks to the hospital, holding his arm.

Apparently, when the atmosphere's barometric pressure drops quickly, lots of people go into labor. At least this was the hospital's explanation for the overcrowded delivery ward that day. I was finally given a small room and, as many hours had passed, began a regimen of Pitocin to induce labor. An efficient female anesthesiologist came in to ask if I would like some pain relief. I told her stoically *I was doing this naturally.* She shrugged her shoulders—*as you wish*—and walked out the door.

The next ten hours were a blur of pain with me yelling at Jacob, "Don't Speak. DON'T SPEAK!" followed by brief intervals of reprieve. There were no beautiful moments of staring into my husband's eyes as we breathed together, like they'd taught in Lamaze class. I felt like an animal version of myself. When it was nearing midnight and my body was spent, the doctor informed me that in all of that labor, I had not dilated. *Not even one centimeter.*

"GET THAT ANESTHESIOLOGIST IN HERE!" I wasn't polite.

She walked back in and smiled with a satisfaction I tried to ignore. "I thought I would see you again." At this point she had to read me a litany of disclaimers and warnings, to which I quickly responded. *"I DON'T CARE! I'LL SIGN ANYTHING!"*

Epidural in place, within what seemed like a few minutes, I was capable of conversing without screaming at people. Jacob and I actually chatted and laughed. We turned on the music playlist I had prepared for my organic delivery process: Eurythmics, Indigo Girls, Tracy Chapman. Then I fell asleep and my body did all the work. At around two a.m., I was alert, fully dilated, and ready to push.

Gabriel arrived into the world as the most beautiful baby I had ever seen. I could not get over the fact that he was mine. That it was up to me to give him a name. To feed him. To be his *mother*. I didn't feel like I owned or had earned that title yet.

The second night in the hospital, I was nursing rather unsuccessfully, and every time I took a break, Gabriel would cry. When the nurse came in, I shared my concern, and she said my physical lactation machinery needed a few days to gear up. "Just keep feeding him." So that's what I did. For two more hours straight. Until I was weeping and already deciding I was obviously not cut out for this mothering thing.

At that moment a new night nurse came into the room. I told her through tears that I had been nursing for hours and that my newborn would start crying when I stopped. She proclaimed, "That baby is using you as a pacifier! How are you going to survive?" She then whisked Gabriel from my arms, swaddled and dropped him in the bassinet, and wheeled him out of the room. Jacob and I looked at each other, shell-shocked. *How are we going to survive?* That became our refrain. We had no earthly idea.

Those early months of parenting were in many ways an isolating haze. Every day stretched before me without any concrete plans, and in those interminable hours, I seemed to accomplish nothing. It was a victory to shower. I was jealous and resentful that Jacob was able to go back to work. Overwhelmed by everyday tasks, I would lie on the couch, catatonic alongside my crying baby. I pushed the Baby Mozart video, which would sometimes capture my baby's attention, like a drug.

"Here," I said, thrusting a wailing bundle into Jacob's arms when he returned from work. "He has been crying for the last two hours. I am fried with exhaustion."

Within minutes, Jacob managed to quiet Gabriel, which of course only set off my own weeping jag. "How were you able to get him to stop? Why am I failing at this job everyone else does instinctively?"

I remember the first time our son's perfect skin erupted in a rash. "All babies get rashes," my mother-in-law assured me. But I had an irrational certainty that this was the beginning of a much more ominous malady and something was really wrong with him. I felt completely incapable of caring for this tiny life. Where was the manual?

My intense desire to become a mother had been supplanted by guilt and inexplicable sadness. When could I go back to life before motherhood?

In retrospect, I realize I was suffering from a form of postpartum depression, but that diagnosis wasn't in my vernacular at the time. And while I was overwhelmed, anxious, and deeply lonely, I also felt the most visceral love for this infant who was beautiful, growing, and wondrous to me. So how could I be depressed? I spent the first few months thinking I was just not cut out to be a mother.

How am I going to survive? The answer was the loving care of a sisterhood of women who came to my rescue.

First, my mother-in-law, Carol, who swooped in from Vermont the day my water broke and set up the nursery we hadn't yet prepared since we thought we still had plenty of time. She stayed for the first two weeks of Gabriel's life, taking night shifts, changing diapers, and doing countless loads of laundry. Carol's mantra was "The mother is always right," and I was amazed to learn she still believed this even when *I was now the mother.* Carol's only goal was to support me and my competence. She encouraged me to listen to my intuition and she affirmed whatever I did, noting frequently that there is not just one right way to parent. She gave me enough confidence that by the time she left, I no longer feared I would break the baby. I had always loved Carol, but the way she cared for me and Gabriel those first two weeks was a whole other level of generosity.

My mother then took a shift at my side and sang Korean lullabies to Gabriel, which brought me back to my childhood. I cried myself into a nap as she put Gabriel down for his. She taught me how to carry Gabriel, Korean-style, on my back, with a wide blanket wrapped around my middle and tied tight under my chest. When she hoisted my infant son expertly onto her back and proceeded to chop and stir an elaborate Korean dinner, complete with the requisite seaweed soup fed to new mothers, I could picture how she had once carried and cooked with me.

Jacob and I were nearly the first of our friends to have a baby, so I couldn't commiserate with many people. Luckily, two of our dearest college friends had their own first child just seven months before we did. In addition to copious hand-me-downs, a lactation consultant, and generous advice, they also gave us a year of laundry service, as our apartment was a long walk to the laundromat, and loads were frequent. It was the perfect gift.

I still had rabbinic school finals to complete, and my brain was so mushy, I feared it would betray me during the Talmud exam, my most challenging test. I asked for an extension, explaining that caring for a newborn made everything else feel unmanageable. My professor asked compassionately, "Would you prefer to do an oral test? You can answer questions on the phone without writing anything down." It was the greatest kindness. My answers were uninspiring but sufficient; she passed me.

I remember with crystal clarity each person who came to visit in those first few months of Gabriel's life. A congregant and friend who held Gabriel for a couple hours so that I could bathe and eat. An older mom friend who took me out for my birthday and promised it would all get better. The first Scarsdale Mommy and Me group I joined, whose members, to my relief, were completely unfazed by the presence of my screaming infant and just talked louder over the commotion.

They say that it takes a village to raise a child. But it took a village to make me a mother. I was shaped by a sisterhood who had trudged the path before me and lived to tell the tale, sharing their tips and war stories.

I will always remember the first time Gabriel laughed. Not just a smile but a bona fide belly laugh. I found I was able to set him off by tossing his stuffed star toy and making a silly sound. I couldn't get enough of that laugh. I began to feel joy again. The fog was lifting.

By the time Eli arrived two years later, and Rose three years after that, I couldn't understand why I ever thought having a single infant was so onerous. My second two children were born with a mom. Gabriel—and my sisterhood—had taught me how to be one.

Ruach
WIND

One summer, Jacob and I rode our bicycles from Jackson, Wyoming, to Jenny Lake in Grand Teton National Park, a twenty-mile ride that took us almost directly into the wind. Though the road was relatively flat, it was so challenging I almost didn't make it.

But on the return trip, with the wind at my back, there was a sense of someone's hand pushing me along; I was flying.

The experience reminded me of a conversation about God that I'd had with young students in our religious school. Judaism forbids the representation of God in any form, and it can be challenging, especially for children, to believe what they cannot see. They'll often ask how we know that God is real when we can't recognize or touch God.

I said that God may not be a visible, physical being, but that does not mean there is no higher force or presence. "Can you see the wind?" I asked them. "Can you draw it for me? Grab it or touch it?" They could not. They sketched approximations—big fluffy clouds and swirling bubbles. So I asked them, "How do you know that the wind exists, if you can't see it or make it visible?"

They had wonderful answers.

"You can see the leaves blowing."

"Wind can knock down houses in a tornado."

"The wind makes my hair messy."

"Yes," I affirmed. "You can't hold the wind in your hands, but you are sharing with me all the ways that you feel it. The wind is invisible, but you know it exists because of what it changes or leaves behind: the sand dune, the scattered twigs, houses damaged by a storm, tousled hair. It's a good metaphor for thinking about God. "Perhaps," I ventured to the students, "we can understand God not because we can see, touch, or prove God, but because we can see God's impact on the world."

God is evident in what is transformed or pushed forward.

Maybe God is like the wind.

Our ancestors used a wind-like word to describe God: "breath," *ruach*, which also means "spirit."

According to Genesis, we started as clay—"dust of the ground" (2:7)—inert until God blew into our nostrils the breath of life. The idea of God as wind, spirit, or breath—an animating life force—is as old as creation.

I use the *ruach* metaphor with students because it's grasp-able. But I am just one in a long line of rabbis trying to find words or images for a power we can't fathom, for the mystery of having the wind at your back and the realization that there are forces in the universe—friendship, family, or something ineffable—that hold us up, keep us anchored, nudge us ahead.

I try to feel *ruach* at my back when I can't make it up a hill.

I try to be the *ruach* for others when the wind is against them.

Remember, *ruach* is the oxygen already inside you.

CHAPTER 16

Leaving Scarsdale

I surprised myself by deciding with Jacob to start our family in Scarsdale. The community was welcoming and wonderful, but we'd always felt a little outside of it. This wealthy, intellectual, cultured suburb with no sidewalks did not resemble either of our hometowns of Tacoma, Washington, or Georgia, Vermont. But when it came to Jewish life, Scarsdale seemed like nirvana: multiple synagogues, public schools that closed on major Jewish holidays, an aisle full of kosher-for-Passover foods in the grocery stores, and native Yiddish speakers. Still, it took us both a while to admit that Scarsdale might be "home." It was really the temple and its rabbi that anchored us.

Rick, a former modern dancer, knew how to choreograph ritual moments, like drawing out the dramatic sizzle of the Havdalah candle in the wine to symbolize our transition back into the workweek, or demonstrating how to use humor in a eulogy to help transcend grief.

My mother always used to tell me, "Look for your monk; then sit at the feet of your teacher." While she was not thrilled that I was putting down roots in New York, she could see I'd found my monk in Rabbi Rick Jacobs.

When Gabriel was born, Rick accommodated my desire to work part-time as a rabbi, as he did when our other children came along. In my early years as a parent, I wasn't ready to adopt the continually on-call schedule of a full-time congregational rabbi, but I worried that I was pulling myself off the career track. Rick was flexible when most other synagogues were not.

After looking at school districts, we bought our first home with a modest loan the synagogue lent us for the down payment. It was the smallest house in our tony suburb—a 1,600-square-foot stucco Tudor on a tenth of an acre with no air-conditioning. But it was ours, and we fixed it up and began our family.

Over time, this adopted Jewish community felt less and less new. Faces became familiar; friendships took shape. Congregants, who had known me since I was song leading Confirmation retreats during college, watched me graduate, get married, become a cantor and a rabbi, and have three children. I felt like a daughter of the shtetl: They showered me with gifts, hand-me-down clothes, and a crib when my babies were born. They cheered for my successes, and Jacob's too. But the challenge of being a "child" of the community is how hard it can be for them to accept when their girl is all grown up. And how ambivalent one can feel about flying the nest.

Yet here I was, after twelve great years, suddenly thinking about leaving WRT.

It started with a phone call, an invitation to consider applying to be the senior cantor of the historic Central Synagogue in Manhattan. Most Jews in the greater New York area knew the mythology of Central: its exalted Moorish architecture modeled on the Dohány Street Synagogue in Budapest, with vaulted ceilings and stenciled walls; its large congregation with members who come from every borough, diverse economics, differing families, and dozens of mother tongues. They included titans of New York finance, law, and real estate, not to mention leaders of numerous legacy Jewish organizations.

Central's senior rabbi, Peter Rubinstein, was widely esteemed not just for his insightful sermons but for growing Central's membership and stature significantly from when he took the job. He'd held the pulpit since 1991 and shepherded the congregation through the trauma of a horrific fire in 1998 that destroyed its sanctuary.

When I entered the official search process at Central, I didn't seriously think I would leave Scarsdale. But I wanted to explore the opportunity, in part because of some career restlessness. There was already a senior cantor at WRT, whom I admired, who wasn't leaving anytime soon. It seemed that the longer I stayed, the more triangulated I felt between the two senior clergy leaders. The curiosity about Central also came from feeling stuck. I was seen (and perhaps still saw myself) as the kid I'd been when I first arrived, not the professional I aspired to be.

Yet the more I thought about a possible move to Central and New York City, the more nervous I became. The two previous Central cantors had only stayed for four years each, a short tenure not typical of major congregations. I'd be leaving a house with a yard, uprooting three kids into a New York City apartment with little green outside the windows. And with Jacob working as an assistant US attorney at the time, it was unclear whether we could afford to live in the costly city on our salaries. Leaving WRT for Central felt like a giant, imprudent risk.

But then I was offered the job. And not only was it immensely flattering, I felt instantly energized, full of ideas, excited by the prospect of meeting new colleagues, challenged to make a new start. I couldn't stop thinking about it.

Everyone in my life had an opinion. Jacob wanted to stay in Scarsdale, though he assured me that he would support my decision either way. WRT offered very generous terms if I remained. Rick Jacobs, who had been so accommodating of the part-time schedule I'd requested since becoming a mother and was invested in my staying, warned that New York City would not be so friendly. "I protected you from so much," he reminded me, with a caring but unmistakable paternalism that also affirmed it might be time to graduate.

I called my mother to talk through the decision, weighing all the virtues of Scarsdale—how wonderful its public schools were, how good the rabbi's family and congregation had been to me.

"I know if I stay I would be so comfortable here," I said to her.

My mother replied with her trademark incisive bluntness. "Angela. The goal of life is not to be comfortable. The goal of life is to pursue your purpose." Her maxim was a soft rebuke.

In the end, the most important professional decision of my life was decided by a coin toss.

I called my friend and then dean of the Hebrew Union College, Rabbi Aaron Panken of blessed memory, for advice. Aaron admitted that, as a WRT congregant, he wasn't completely objective in his leanings but he wanted what was best for me. He listened patiently to my back-and-forth, toggling between the obvious benefits of staying and the unknowable risks of going. Finally, he said, "Toss a coin to decide."

"WHAT?" I retorted. "I'm not making the most important professional decision of my life with a coin flip!"

Aaron insisted that I was going to keep flip-flopping, but if I left this to fate, it would resolve everything.

"Go on," he said. "Do it while I'm on the phone. Heads, you're staying. Tails, you leave."

I put the phone on speaker, flipped the coin in my little WRT office, and it landed on heads.

"Wonderful!" Aaron responded. "I'm so glad you're staying!"

I let that verdict sink in; the coin had decided I was to stay. That's when I knew for sure, in my gut, that I had to go.

The stretch and discomfort of a new experience would teach me things I could not learn by staying still.

Mitzvah
COMMANDMENT

Bat mitzvah is appropriately understood as "coming of age," but people often forget its literal meaning: "daughter of the commandments."

At thirteen, one becomes responsible for *all the mitzvot,* "commandments" of Judaism—613, to be precise.

But of all the obligations, there is only one that makes the top ten and also promises longevity: "Honor your father and your mother as God has commanded you, so that your days will be long upon the earth that the Lord your God is giving you" (Exodus 20:12).

Why does the Torah offer such a big reward—perhaps the greatest—of a long and prosperous life in return for doing this commandment? Because it's hard to do. If it just came naturally, we wouldn't need the directive.

The difficulty lies in a fundamental and intractable tension between parents and children: We are hardwired to replicate ourselves (parenting, as the author Andrew Solomon wrote, is not called "reproduction" for nothing). But children have a different impulse—not to imitate but to individuate.

As we grow older, many of us expend a good deal of effort making sure we do not become our parents. Maybe the word "offspring" is no accident; we want to *spring off* the path our parents charted for us, sometimes venturing far afield.

A midrash teaches that Abraham's father worshipped and sold idols. When Abraham was entrusted to mind the idol shop, he smashed the idols to prove the impotence of his father's "gods." Abraham's first act of adulthood was to break from his father's path of faith. This individuation is not just rebellion—one can honor parents by departing from them.

To understand this paradox, look at the obligations in the Talmud regarding what parents must do for their children: instruct them in Torah, teach them a trade, find them a life partner, teach them to swim. Or applied metaphorically: raise children who can think critically, support themselves, find love, and ride the currents of life. In other words, successful parenting means raising an independent child who will no longer need you.

When we are young and reliant on our parents, our attention and deference to them comes naturally. Ironically, it is precisely at the moment when parents have succeeded at their task—when offspring become grown and self-sufficient—that children need most to be reminded to honor those who endowed them with that independence.

While thirteen is clearly not the age of adulthood today, it is the starting point of this vital separation. I love that Judaism has chosen to give awkward teenagers the platform at this pivotal moment, permitting them to give a public speech from the bimah interpreting Torah and its relevance and lessons.

Independence can coexist with respecting your parents. Individuation can be compatible with attachment.

Choosing to become a rabbi didn't seem like an act of rebellion. But it was an act of separation.

It's sometimes hard to live across the country in a different time zone, when my hometown and parents feel far away. But I believe they see how regularly I credit them, how I aspire to live out the values they instilled. They have often said they consider my life in New York to be their success.

We honor our parents by walking with them—and also by walking away.

After smashing his father's idols, Abraham leaves his family's home, heeding God's call to go forth—*lech l'cha*. His father, Terach, who was also traveling to Canaan, stopped in Haran and settled there instead. It is only when Abraham left his parents' house and wandered to a place he "did not know" that he ends up completing the journey his parents could not.

CHAPTER 17

Building a New Music

During my first Shabbat as the new cantor in Central Synagogue's ornate, majestic sanctuary, all I felt was dread.

The summer services were typically sparsely attended, but even as I looked out at the "regulars," they were strangers to me. It was a stark contrast from the extended family I had just left in Scarsdale, where I came of age and built my family. In that suburb, where streets were leafy and lovely, where I knew people in every coffee shop, market, and baseball field, life felt manageable and intimate. New York City felt alien—rougher, louder, coarser.

Now, at thirty-three, I had moved to that tougher town to join a historic pulpit, my first full-time position, knowing almost no one. Moreover, I had stepped into the big shoes of a gifted cantor, an exquisite soprano who floated out high A's effortlessly. I still carried the insecurity, seeded in cantorial school, that I was not a "real" singer. At Central, I inherited an organist, a choir of six professional singers, and a fat binder of formal choral music. Did I dare pull out my acoustic guitar?

In the interview process for the job, I'd shared my vision that music can be the greatest vehicle for building Jewish community and identity.

I expressed my hope that our worship would represent the soul of the congregation and convey who we are, embody what we value. I asked the search committee if I had the mandate to make changes in Shabbat worship.

"Yes, of course," said the incoming president, "but just know that we had a bongo experiment many years ago that didn't go well."

My insecurities leaked from my head to my body. Those first months, my stomach churned so much acid that it burned my throat while I slept. As I began rehearsals for the High Holidays, my first big introduction to the congregation, I could barely sing. In this state of nervousness, I reverted back to some of my old singing habits, relying on my chest voice, which severely limited my range. A folk voice is not well suited to the formal, grand music of Rosh Hashanah and Yom Kippur. In singing "Kol Nidre" before a thousand worshipers my first year, I jumped down an octave for many sections of the piece because I was so afraid of not hitting the notes. In the middle of services, I silently signaled to my music director—who sat high in the temple's organ loft at the far end of the sanctuary, nearly a city block away—to lower the key for all of my remaining pieces. Somehow I managed to refocus on trying to convey the liturgy just as I'd practiced it, despite a voice that threatened to betray me. I knew I needed to pray the words of this crucial service, even if the sound wasn't what it should be.

Central's beloved Cantor Emeritus Dick Botton then walked onto the bimah and sang "Retzey" with his beautiful, sonorous baritone and the congregation burst into applause. I felt so small, certain that everyone wanted to return to his heyday and that sound. My self-doubt was confirmed by several congregants who said after the service, "You have a lovely tone, but 'Kol Nidre' is meant to be sung by a male voice." I was grateful to have made it through my first New York City High Holidays, but I had barely passed muster.

In my first year, I was the only cantor among the clergy and I needed collaborators. My music director, David Strickland, hired only months before I arrived, though immensely talented, had never worked in a synagogue before. I asked Ivan Barenboim, a young clarinetist from Argentina, to play every Friday night; his klezmer wail injected Yiddishkeit into the music and was as close to a plaintive human voice as you could get from a reed.

The three of us started to develop a "Central sound," which combined ancient melodies that were at least a thousand years old, nineteenth-century chazzanut or cantorial chants, twentieth-century folk melodies of Shlomo Carlebach and Debbie Friedman, and more contemporary twenty-first-century compositions. I invited additional musicians—including, yes, even a bongo player!—for special services only, aiming for a musical evolution rather than a revolution.

These modest changes nevertheless unsettled those congregants most comfortable with the sounds of their past. Contrary to many assumptions, there is not a set musical canon for synagogue worship; melodies vary by denomination, region, and synagogue. But each person has their own definition of "traditional," which typically means "the music that I grew up with."

I knew that I was making changes, but I was still unprepared for the negative response of some of the congregants at first. One woman publicly challenged me at a "Welcome the Cantor" cocktail party, "Why have you stopped playing the organ at services? I don't come to Central to hear all this happy-clappy music!"

I drew strength from the mandate in Psalm 96: "Sing to the Lord a new song," words written by the biblical David, the musician turned king whom I have to imagine also encountered resistance when he tried to change familiar melodies.

I pressed forward, secure in the belief that we had two choices: sing a new song or find ourselves frozen in place. I had seen it happen before.

On my first trip to Israel as a teenager, I'd been electrified by a young and inventive Jerusalem synagogue that borrowed melodies from subversive sources like a French monastery and Native American chant.

In 1989, the fledgling congregation didn't even have a building, but we all piled into a basement room and the walls vibrated with vitality. When I returned several years later to this community, it had a beautiful new building and tour buses brought worshipers there by the hundreds from around the world. It was my Shabbat service of choice when I lived in Jerusalem for my first year of rabbinical school. A decade would pass before I was able to return again, and as I sat in the congregation, whose members had aged alongside the rabbi, I was both comforted and disappointed to hear the community singing the *exact same melodies* from my first visit eighteen years earlier. The energy was gone—I saw how what was once thrilling innovation had become calcified tradition. I resolved to reimagine worship whenever possible, even as it meant leaving the familiar, because this musical boundary-crossing was how we would reinvigorate ancient words.

To be Reform Jews, after all, is to literally *re-form Judaism*. I learned that it did not take long for a new tune to become a favorite, and then quickly become "tradition." We are always making new musical memories; borrowing melodies, pairing unlikely sounds, adapting the music of the moment to make a distant vocabulary accessible—this is what Jews have been doing throughout history. The evolution at Central took time, but I was privileged to have the encouragement of my Senior Rabbi as well as growing support from the congregation. Over the years, not only did the number of worshipers increase each Friday night, but we became more of a singing congregation. I felt grateful to have found a home that embodied that charge from Psalms to "sing to God a new song."

Krechtz
THE SIGH

The *krechtz* is the Jewish wail.

It's a mournful sigh, essential to Jewish inheritance.

In a poignant book about the destruction of Eastern European Jewry, *The Earth Is the Lord's*, the twentieth-century philosopher and theologian Rabbi Abraham Joshua Heschel devotes an entire chapter to what he calls "the sigh": "There were many who did not trust words, and their deepest thoughts would find expression in a sigh. Sorrow was their second soul, and the vocabulary of their heart consisted of one sound: 'Oy!' And when there was more than the heart could say, their eyes would silently bear witness" (16).

If sorrow has been our people's "second soul," the *krechtz* has become the expression that transcends words, or replaces them. That unmistakable, well-earned exclamation is heard and felt in our story, our music, our prayers.

In cantorial school, I was expected to learn the Hebrew language, liturgy, and melodies. But the most important thing to master as a real chazzan—the Hebrew word for cantor—was the *krechtz*.

It sits somewhere between a howl and a hiccup. It is the sometimes-pleading, sometimes-weeping, often-wistful sound that emanates from deep in your kishkes. It's raw, a little jagged.

The person hearing it should feel something breaking, entreating, lamenting.

The singer should worry less about the musical notes and more about the emotional ones; this is the sound of pain, passion, and heartache—the fullness of Jewish experience.

The *krechtz* is not found in any Italian opera. It's a quintessentially Jewish sound—the way our people have expressed sorrow and the way we've survived it. Jews are not a people who repress pain; we let it out.

Science now confirms the importance of this release. The average person sighs every five minutes. Without these exhalations the billions of tiny air sacs in our lungs don't get enough oxygen. The fastest way to keep breathing is to let your breath go. Somehow Jews knew that suppressing emotion is to choke on it. We have to vent.

When we physically express an "oy"—a *krechtz*, the sigh of our innermost heart—we renew the breath within us. Regeneration is built into the sigh itself.

Rabbi Nachman of Breslov in his magnum opus, *Likutei Moharan*, speaks of the spiritual practice of the *krechtz*. "See how precious is the sigh and groan of a Jewish person. It provides wholeness [in place] of the lack. For through the breath, which is the *ruach*-of-life, the world was created."

When you express a sincere *krechtz*, expelling the sound from deep within, the emptied body will automatically fill up again.

Just like that first *ruach* (breath) that God sighed into our clay form to give us life, we are re-souled when we sigh our deepest longings and worries.

Don't hold it inside. Let the sigh go.

Let your *krechtz* empty you; notice your breath replenished.

Perhaps it was the *krechtz* that saved a people through millennia of pain. Today, it might just save us again.

CHAPTER 18

Royalty and Refugees

New York lived up to my most outsized expectations of a robust, unapologetic, spiritual, intellectual Jewish Promised Land. We enrolled our children in a pluralistic Jewish day school named after the theologian Rabbi Abraham Joshua Heschel. The school taught them Hebrew and Jewish studies and made it easy to live according to the Jewish calendar with holidays off and early dismissal every Friday afternoon to prepare for Shabbat. My children developed two Jewish hubs in their lives—Heschel and Central. Their closest friends were in school, but they also collected a crew of fellow congregants, thanks to Shabbat services and several Central trips to Israel.

But I could not escape how starkly, by contrast, I neglected to connect my children to their Korean heritage. I felt inadequate to provide it. While it was the family joke to excuse my frequent malapropisms with "English is Mom's second language," the reality was that my Korean language had almost vanished. I could barely communicate with my Korean aunties beyond indicating which foods I wanted to eat. We didn't celebrate Korean holidays to anchor our year. We had no Korean community to speak of, even though New York has the second-largest Korean population in the United States.

I had always felt guilty for not passing on a stronger Korean identity. Whenever someone asked me how I conveyed Korean culture to my children, I cringed hearing myself describe it: "They enjoy Korean food and folktales, and we will make a pilgrimage soon to my birth place." My answer reminded me of many cultural Jews who transmitted a Jewish identity based on bagels, a few Bible stories, and perhaps a trip to "the homeland." When people asked my children if they were Korean, they would answer, "Our mother is Korean." They did not identify themselves that way.

An invitation to participate in a television series provided an unexpected step toward more connection.

In January 2012 I sat across from Harvard professor Dr. Henry Louis Gates Jr. at a card table that his production team had set up in my living room. Over four hours, he unearthed pages and pages of news clippings, immigration records, and genetic information about my ancestors, while his crew filmed my reactions for his new PBS television series "Finding Your Roots." My parents, at Gates's invitation, listened in from the next room.

I wasn't sure how I had been selected for this fifth episode in the first season of the show. Usually Gates featured movie stars, professional athletes, politicians, and other celebrities. But the Pew Foundation had sponsored a segment featuring religious leaders. So along with Pastor Rick Warren, leader of the Baptist evangelical megachurch Saddleback Church, and Muslim theologian Yasir Qadhi, dean of the Islamic Seminary of America, Gates had decided to talk to me.

In advance of our sit-down, the PBS team had scoured archives I didn't know existed, from Romania to Korea, to help me trace my lineage and story. As we settled into my living room, Gates began to reveal his research, showing me the birth certificate of my paternal Romanian great-grandfather Srul Hirsch Soss, born in 1871.

A ship manifest revealed that when my Jewish grandmother Phreda Soss's parents and older brother landed at Ellis Island in 1902, their first home was on East 47th Street in New York City, just blocks away from where I then lived. Phreda was not yet alive when they arrived, and would be the first in her family to be born in America. Dad's grandfather H. S. Soss then followed his brother to the Pacific Northwest and ran a local pawn shop in Spokane, Washington.

Gates showed me the antisemitic newspaper clippings of the time ("Romanians don't sell to Kikes")—evidence of why the Sosses fled to America

"Does knowing about how your family was persecuted affect your understanding of your own commitment to religion?" Gates asked.

I admitted that the Jewish side of my family, having been in America for a hundred years already, felt so distant from their immigration story; I had not focused on the religious persecution that prompted them to leave. Suddenly I grasped more starkly what it took to hold on to Judaism, how much anti-Jewish hate they'd seen and how determined they were to give future generations safety and freedom.

Finally, it was time for the big reveal, that climax in the show when Gates startles his guest with some unexpected blood connection or buried family secret that almost invariably brings his guests to tears.

As I sat with bright lights and cameras fixed on my face, Gates unfurled a long scroll, my maternal family tree. There in print was confirmation of a long-held piece of family lore: that Mom's family was descended directly from kings, part of a royal line dating back to the fourteenth-century King Taejo, founder of the Joseon dynasty, his son, King Taejong, and grandson, King Sejong the Great.

King Sejong earned his title as "the Great," having created the first portable sundial, rain gauge, and *Chongganbo*, the first East Asian musical notation, which made it possible to record pitch and length of notes. Most importantly, King Sejong was the author of Hangul, the Korean phonetic alphabet. Before Hangul, Koreans adopted Chinese characters for reading, which required years of learning to achieve literacy. Sejong wanted all his subjects to have access to knowledge. He created a simple alphabet with only fourteen consonants and ten vowels so that even a child, in a few weeks, could learn to sound out words. Korea's noble class did not agree to democratize learning for the common people, so it would be nearly five hundred years, after the end of World War II and the Japanese occupation, before Hangul was widely taught and accepted.

Sejong was Korea's most important and influential king. I could not get over the sight of my name on the immense family tree connecting me directly to that king, through my mother, Yi Sulja, her father, Yi Samdal, his father and grandfather and beyond in a long all-male thread stretching back nineteen generations. I absorbed this amazing piece of family history and dropped my composure to yell to my mother listening in the next room, "Mom! The rumor is true! I'm a Jewish Korean princess!"

By happy coincidence, my *Finding Your Roots* episode was filmed just months before our family trip to Korea in April 2012. It was my first return since high school and my first-ever trip with Jacob and our kids.

Eleven of us, including my parents and Gina's family, piled into what we called the Party Van, traveling the peninsula from the streets of Seoul to the beaches of Gangmun to the temples of Seoraksan mountain to my mother's village of HyunPoong.

My mom made use of the many hours on the road, intent on getting all of her grandchildren to read Hangul, in part to prove the genius of her ancestor's alphabet and in part to bolster my children's tenuous Korean connection. When the kids started decoding Korean shop names and street signs, she was triumphant. "King Sejong's descendants will read Hangul!"

Our newfound connection to Korean history changed how my children experienced Korea, how they viewed their heritage. When we went to the magnificent Gyeongbok Palace—the original home of the Chosun dynasty, spread out over nearly one hundred acres with more than seven thousand rooms, they joked that, had they been born five hundred years earlier, the palace grounds would have been their backyard. When we passed by the thirty-foot golden King Sejong statue in the heart of Seoul, my children proudly hollered, "Hey, Grandpa!"

In truth, there is very little of King Sejong's DNA in them. And five hundred years after his death, Sejong's ancestors now number in the hundreds of thousands, so we're certainly far from unique. Apparently, there is a big family reunion in Korea from time to time, though we've never been invited. But learning that we were related to this Korean icon made us feel part of a grand story. It made a greater claim on us. I am also a descendent of Abraham and Sarah, as is every Jew. How differently would I walk through the world if I could see the family tree laid out before me to prove it?

Our intuitive identity can be fortified, however belatedly, by finding our roots.

Tikkun
REPAIR

The practice of capturing members of Korea's cultural elite and bringing them to Japan, which is how my grandmother's family ended up there in the 1920s, began as far back as the late sixteenth century. Imperial minister Toyotomi Hideyoshi enslaved up to two hundred thousand Korean farmers, scholars, and artists, including many potters who had been trained during the Koryo dynasty in beautiful celadon and porcelain. Hideyoshi kidnapped the famed Yi Sam-pyeong, who discovered a white clay that would become Japan's famous porcelain.

The Japanese appropriated Korean artistry as their own, even as they tried to erase Korean culture. When my mother was born, she was not allowed to have a Korean name, so her parents gave her the Japanese name Yukiko. Koreans were taught only Japanese in school and not allowed to even speak their own language at home. So my mother's first tongue was the language of her captor.

After World War II, with the occupation over, my mother's family finally moved back to their homeland. Once my mother earned her first income as a tour guide, she began collecting antique Korean pottery—bowls and vases that dated back before the Japanese invasion of the twentieth century. These were not just elegant objects; they were links to a proud Korean heritage. The Japanese could steal the art form but not the art itself.

When I moved into a new apartment, my mother gave me a few of her prized pieces: a seventh-century Shilla dynasty black urn, a twelfth-century Koryo dynasty celadon dish, and a fifteenth-century Chosun dynasty white vase. I placed the white vase on the most prominent windowsill in my living room.

Everything in our new home was electronically wired, and as I was going to bed after just moving in, I was excited to push the "all off" button on my nightstand, which would turn out all the lights in the apartment.

Then I heard the crash.

The tech installer had programmed the switch so that not only did it turn off all the lights in the apartment, it brought down all of the shades, one of which knocked over the vase as it descended.

The antique vessel lay in shards on the ground. I dropped to the floor with tears in my eyes.

My architect suggested a way to salvage it: a Japanese method of repairing cracks in ceramic vessels with a mixture of lacquer and gold. It's called *kintsugi*, which literally means "golden repair" and dates back to the fifteenth century.

My first thought was, *Does it have to be a Japanese method?*

He sent me the contact information for a master *kintsugi* artisan in Brooklyn. Her name was Yuko, which was, wondrously, almost the same as my mother's given Japanese name of Yukiko.

I wrote to Yuko and told her a little bit about my mother's story and what this vase represented to my family and heritage. She wrote back:

I will be emotional when I will fix your vase. I know the past history. It makes me sad and want to close my eyes. As a Japanese, I am grateful to be able to fix a broken Korean vase. I would like to restore it with the utmost respect for your mother.

Three months later, I went to Yuko's studio in Brooklyn to pick up the reconstructed vase. It had golden veining throughout the vessel like a spider's web and looked exquisite—the scars now holding a new story. She also presented me with a gift wrapped inside a wooden box tied with string: a five-hundred-year-old Arita ware teacup, made with the renowned porcelain craft brought to Japan by a Korean potter. She had purchased the broken cup in Japan, repaired it with silver, and now gave it to me as a present, an ancient restoration.

When I returned home, I placed the vase and the teacup on a shelf—far away from the electric blinds. Of course, the vase will never be the same. But now the golden cracks have rendered the vessel stronger than it was before. The scars have become its beauty marks. And a Japanese woman named Yuko restored this piece of Korean culture to me.

It felt like my own small yet cosmic *tikkun*. A golden "repair."

CHAPTER 19

The Mother in
the Emergency Room

P eter is not going to be senior rabbi forever."

These words were dropped in my lap by one of Central's past presidents, Kenny Heitner, over lunch in the fall of 2012. He advised me that any responsible lay leadership needed to think ahead to succession, and even if there was no specified timeline for Peter's retirement, I should start considering whether I might aspire to his job.

Rabbi Rubinstein had sometimes shared his thoughts with me about his own "graduation," as he so aptly put it, but that transition felt like an abstract thought, not at all imminent. Kenny urged me, "Big decisions sometimes get thrust upon us when we would have done well to mull them over ahead of time."

I don't know if Kenny was prescient or all-knowing, but just five months after that conversation, Peter announced that he had decided to step down in the summer of 2014 after what would be twenty-three years of leading Central Synagogue. The news was an earthquake for our community and even for the larger Jewish world. "Forget the Pope," blared a headline in *Tablet Magazine*. "Peter Rubinstein to retire."

Peter was not just beloved and revered; he was the emotional heartbeat of this historic congregation, steering a shaken community through 9/11, financial crises, and reckonings over interfaith marriage and Zionism. Most importantly, he shepherded Central through its hardest chapter in 1998, when a spark from a workman's blowtorch set off a devastating fire that gutted the stunning sanctuary, leaving only a smoldering skeleton. Peter kept a displaced community together during the years of reconstruction. He demonstrated that the congregation's soul resided not in its bricks but in its people, no matter how makeshift the pulpit. Just as all the Israelites contributed to building the Tabernacle, Peter invited all members to contribute to renovating the sanctuary, down to children stenciling the walls. Central embodied God's directive in Exodus: "Build me a sanctuary that I may dwell among them."

To say Peter would be a hard act to follow was an understatement. He would leave the footprints of a giant. I knew whoever succeeded him would have to be attuned to what congregants would be missing and mourning without him.

Yet they also knew me. I had been part of the proverbial family for seven years as their senior cantor, leading Shabbat services and officiating at their bar and bat mitzvah ceremonies, baby namings, and funerals. I had sat at their sickbeds and stood under their chuppahs. When Peter went on his months-long sabbatical, he left me in charge of running the congregation, a humbling signal of his trust in me, trust I hoped the congregation also shared.

But as I contemplated what it would mean to apply for the top position, it was not lost on me that I'd never been employed as a full-time rabbi. Yes, I'd had a front-row seat to watch how Peter did the senior rabbi's job, but that was as daunting as it was inspiring. Peter's attentiveness and unremitting commitment to his flock seemed impossible for me to duplicate. With grown children out of the house, he didn't just pastor to members during office hours but went out to dinner with congregants virtually every weeknight, along with his devoted wife, Kerry. Peter taught students late into the evening and was always first on call for life-cycle emergencies. When I actually tried to picture myself in his role, I couldn't see how to square it with my obligations as a parent. I wasn't willing to miss every weekday dinner with my children, their baseball and basketball games, their piano recitals. And because my husband also had a demanding job, he could not be a traditional, full-time rebbetzin.

So my initial response to Kenny at lunch was that it was not the right time for me. When he asserted that I was up to the task, I thanked him but explained that it was impossible to imagine how I'd manage it at this stage of my life.

"You understand that if you miss this opportunity, someone else will take the job and likely keep it for the next twenty or twenty-five years, and you will have lost your shot," Kenny said. "Will you be happy with that?"

I wasn't sure how to answer. For the whole of its 175 years, Central Synagogue had only been led by men. Of course, women had only been ordained as rabbis since 1972. But I could count on one hand the number of female rabbis who helmed large congregations, and there were none in New York. I could only assume this was not just a vestige of sex discrimination but at least in part because the job requirements were viewed as incompatible with motherhood.

My husband and a few close friends pushed back with a different lens, urging me to think about "leaning in"—a phrase that had been popularized by Sheryl Sandberg in her viral 2010 TED Talk about the lack of female CEOs in America. Sandberg encouraged women, who have often underestimated their own leadership capacities, to reach for the promotion, the top job.

Sandberg ignited an overdue national conversation about how women often internalize a sense of inadequacy or self-doubt, how we can let the pulls of parenthood and career feel like a zero-sum game. She asserted that gender equity would never happen until more women occupied the highest positions of business, government, education, and other fields of influence, and that therefore women should be more unapologetically ambitious.

In a provocative and controversial rejoinder to Sandberg's campaign for more courage and self-confidence, the political scientist Anne-Marie Slaughter wrote a 2012 *Atlantic* article entitled "Why Women Still Can't Have It All." She disputed the feminist notion she had been raised to believe—and which she embodied for a long time—that she could have a high-powered job and simultaneously raise her children at full tilt.

The debate between these two impressive women was roiling in my head as Jacob and I discussed whether I should throw my hat in the ring at Central. I had already slowed my career path by working part-time for my first six years in Scarsdale as an assistant rabbi and cantor while I raised three babies. Becoming Central's senior cantor was my first full-time position and it had been an adjustment—learning to manage a staff team, more meetings than I had ever imagined, late-night and weekend responsibilities, life-cycle demands that could come at any time and require upending my calendar completely.

But there was no denying that the more involved I'd become, the more gratifying the work became. I felt genuinely privileged to be with our members during their sweetest high points and darkest grief. Whether they were seeking solace or celebration, finding the right ritual or piece of Jewish wisdom could transform the way they traveled through heartache or celebration. I had loved the chance to reimagine the energy of Friday-night Shabbat services over the years with new instrumentation, unfiltered joy, and permission to bring vulnerability and sorrow into the room. Nothing gave me more jubilation or inspiration than seeing the sanctuary fill up with people who found a renewed sense of spirituality and connectedness.

Rabbi Rubinstein and I sat down for a private meeting about his news and what it might or might not mean for my next chapter, a conversation he has permitted me to share.

He was my closest colleague, not just my teacher but my champion. He'd insisted that I be included in every major decision about Central's worship and programming. He'd given me a seat on the board of trustees' highest governing body, the executive committee, a role not often given to cantorial colleagues. He had consulted me on personnel dilemmas and sensitive grievances from congregants. I had come to rely on his frank counsel, and this was a moment when I really needed to know: Did he think I could do this job?

I will never forget sitting together in his booklined, stately office, a room in which we'd had so many collaborative meetings and shared confidences, only to hear him ask me, "You're so spiritual, Angela. Are you sure you want to do all that development and management work?"

And then:

"You're such a good mother. How are you going to handle this job with your three young kids?"

Even though I was grappling with those very doubts, the question still rankled, because I knew it was never asked of my male colleagues.

His final, ultimate litmus test felt the most unfair: "The issue with working mothers is that when their child has to go to the emergency room, the mom feels she has to be there," Peter cautioned.

"That's not necessarily true," I sputtered. I would be that mother who could balance competing demands and trust my husband or babysitter for some emergencies if I couldn't show up immediately. The only way I could do the job I already was doing was because my husband is an equal partner. Jacob had, in fact, become "Parent 1" for the children's schools because he more reliably answered his cell phone, filled out their medical forms, and volunteered for school activities.

I left Peter's office spinning; it was not the vote of confidence I had sought or expected. It took me two weeks to summon the courage to return to the subject: "Peter, you've been my mentor and advocate, but you have stopped short of saying I could be senior rabbi, and I think it's only because I'm a woman and mother." I then repeated the comments he'd made in our conversation two weeks prior.

Peter listened thoughtfully and responded, "I didn't mean to imply you couldn't do it. I think you can do anything. I guess I just come from a different generation."

On March 13, 2013, Central sent out an email informing the entire congregation that Peter was retiring, that there would be a national search for a replacement, and that I was choosing to be a candidate. My inbox was flooded with notes of surprise and support from congregants, colleagues, and friends. But I could sense—not just from Peter but from others—that merely floating the notion that I sought the senior job was considered *chutzpadik*; my confidence was hubris, my ambition unseemly. It's amazing how, for so many women I know, simply thinking oneself ready to be considered for the chief role can be regarded as a demerit.

Some were not subtle about their doubts. A longtime, powerful Jewish leader in the congregation took me to lunch in order to say, "This is an Ashkenazi Jewish congregation, and it should be led by an Ashkenazi rabbi." No matter that my father was an Ashkenazi Jew. What he meant was that Central's senior rabbi should be "white."

A former board member expressed the views of others: "People who know you, love you, Angela. But there are others concerned you might not have the *gravitas* for the position." I knew that this was a coded way of saying, *You don't look or talk like a sixty-year-old man.*

I was surprised that so much of the judgment and disapproval came from other women, of many ages, who clearly saw my opportunity through the lens of the sacrifices they'd made in their own parenting or professional lives. They seemed to view my interest in the job as an implicit critique or rebuke. I started to understand that being a female senior rabbi might not be celebrated by everyone. That realization not only stung but deflated me. Expecting to feel more encouragement and partnership than skepticism and detraction, I felt more lonely than I could admit.

The timing of Peter's March 13 retirement announcement was ironic: That same evening I was scheduled to appear at a women's salon with Anne-Marie Slaughter to discuss the challenges of balancing leadership roles with motherhood.

And then the call came from my daughter's school nurse at three p.m.: "Rose fell on the playground today, and while she's no longer crying, it's possible she broke her arm. I think you need to take her to the emergency room."

You can't make this up, I thought. *God is testing me.*

Of course this would happen on *this* day, when the congregation was first learning of my desire to become senior rabbi; when Jacob, who rarely traveled for work, was on a plane to California for business; when I was scheduled to speak about work-life balance to a group of ambitious women alongside Anne-Marie Slaughter, who was probably right that we couldn't "have it all."

I girded myself and called our pediatrician, who confirmed she could do an X-ray at her office. Rose sounded fine when we spoke by phone, and I breathed a sigh of relief; I was committed to disproving Peter's litmus test *on this of all days.* My nanny picked Rose up from school and brought her to the doctor. But two hours later, she called back: "The doctor couldn't do her X-ray. We are heading to the ER. And you have to be there to sign her in."

As I raced in the cab to the hospital, I told myself I could sign forms, give Rose a tight hug, and still make it out in time to preach the virtues of work-life balance. But when Rose saw me as the sliding doors opened, her eyes suddenly filled with tears. "Will you stay with me, Mommy?"

I instantly knew the answer. There wasn't even a moment's hesitation. I wanted to be there with my daughter, and I couldn't take a job that would demand otherwise.

After an hour's wait and an X-ray that showed Rose had not broken her arm, my eight-year-old looked up at me, smiling. "It doesn't even hurt anymore!" I kissed Rose on the head and my nanny took her home. I'd missed the salon dinner but still made it to the discussion. And when Anne-Marie asked me about work-life balance, I started by telling the gathering of women about my day, insisting that we *can* have the job and the family, as long as we accept the inevitable messiness.

After eight months of Central's careful search process, which included a written personal statement and two seven-hour interviews in front of a search committee of ten congregants asking me about my vision for the synagogue's membership growth, worship experience, staff management, and education programming, I got that phone call: "You are the nominee to be Central's next senior rabbi." I could not actually absorb that it was true. I saw instant flashbacks to my Jewish childhood—my first time on the Temple Beth El bimah singing with Ruthie, lighting the menorah in my public high school, guitar practice in my Jewish camp bunk, all the classmates who had looked askance at my Jewish star necklace, the friends in Israel who had gently told me I wasn't actually a Jew. I don't cry easily, but the tears came.

Still, the selection process was not over because the board required a vote from the entire congregation. Ballots could be mailed to the synagogue by proxy, but over two hundred people chose to come to the congregational meeting to vote in person. While Michael Gould, the chair of the search committee, spoke to the crowd about my candidacy, Peter waited alone with me in my office. As I walked into the sanctuary to hear the vote results and they announced that I would be Central's sixteenth senior rabbi, the first woman to hold this title in its 175-year history, the congregation rose to its feet. I was overwhelmed. After an endless line of hugs, Peter and Kerry took me and Jacob out to a beautiful dinner to celebrate. They presented me with a silver heart necklace, which felt like a symbol of Peter passing the torch, turning over this community—which had his heart—to me.

I felt the weight of both immense honor and daunting expectations, of breaking a stained glass ceiling. I also appreciated that the path to every position I'd held before was paved for me by another woman who had managed to make the first crack. I was mindful of how many eyes would be on me, and I knew that if I failed in this job, it would have ramifications for every woman who followed.

Looking back now, over a decade into my senior rabbinate, I don't sugarcoat reality for any rabbi who wants to be a parent. I've missed more baseball games and taekwondo tournaments than I can bear to count. I have had to cut summer weekends short or arrive late because of a wedding or a funeral. My kids have witnessed me spend hours on the phone calling members to whom I owe a check-in or talking through a synagogue issue with my executive director and board president. But to this day, my children have never questioned that the most important role in my life is being their mother. Since I was rarely home in time to cook dinner, I relished cooking a hot breakfast for my kids every single day in my pajamas, serving them healthy waffles (yes, there is such a thing), and hearing about their friends and their worries. Most of all, Shabbat shaped our family. Even as I worked almost every Sabbath—leading Friday-night services at six p.m. and often nine thirty a.m. and eleven thirty a.m. services the next morning—we protected Friday-night dinners, where we would share our favorite parts of the week. And Saturday afternoons after services, we gathered with our Shabbat crew from my children's day school and had the kind of leisurely, long lunch that stretched until sundown. To paraphrase nineteenth-century essayist Ahad Ha'am, more than we kept the Sabbath, the Sabbath kept us. It's still the glue that binds our family together.

True, I sometimes felt embarrassed that my husband knew our kids' schedules better than I did. My kids poked fun that by the time Jacob and I had our third child, Rose, she seemed to be raising herself, just as they joked that without my career, I would have been an overbearing helicopter parent. But as my children grew, I would practice sermons with them and incorporate their insightful feedback. They began to see the benefits of getting communal support and appreciation for being a rabbi's kid, not just the scrutiny. In a big synagogue there were always so many people who recognized and looked out for Gabe, Eli, and Rose, whether it was at services, around town, or at summer camp.

As they got older my kids frequently and spontaneously shared their admiration and respect for my work. When my middle child told me that he, too, was interested in becoming a rabbi, I felt overwhelmed with pride and some relief that I hadn't scared him away. My children had seen the joy and meaning in this sacred pursuit.

At the end of that momentous day back in March 2013, when Central announced the opening of its senior rabbi position and my interest in the job, when I had to be at the ER with my daughter just as Peter had predicted but still made it to my evening event, I thought about the fallacy and oversimplification of trying to "have it all." I slipped into Rose's room when I came home, watched her sleeping peacefully under her colorful comforter, and wondered if she'd inherit my same ambivalence. I knew at that moment that I could never hope to be a senior rabbi like Peter Rubinstein. Just a senior rabbi like me.

Tisomet Lev
ATTENTION

It was not always easy for my daughter to have her voice heard in our house, given that her garrulous older brothers tended to dominate conversations. It didn't help to have two working parents who were frequently preoccupied by text messages, or the news, or by those much larger (and louder) brothers.

When Rose was small and she really wanted to say something important, she would walk over to me, take both my cheeks into her little hands, and turn my face to look directly at hers.

It's always hard to give anything your complete concentration, even one's child. But it's especially difficult these days, and not just for overextended people like me.

We have undergone a cultural shift, in great part due to new technologies that bombard us with content, lure us to focus on our screens rather than each other. Full attention is no longer given priority as an American value. We exercise while streaming Netflix. Take a walk while listening to podcasts. Check email during meetings. Shop online while talking to our parents.

Doing only one thing at a time feels like an old luxury at best. At worst, we see it as inefficiency, a waste. *Low productivity.*

We have also made being available at all times a priority. We rarely permit ourselves to be off the grid or even temporarily unavailable.

If someone picks up their phone because it buzzes in a meeting, somehow this is no longer considered impolite, even though we are obviously all less attentive to one another. This is just how our culture understands, and has come to normalize, the idea that anyone is reachable at all times. We expect prompt responses to emails and texts within minutes.

Those little pings, however, sabotage our sense of being present. I can be working on a sermon or a speech that requires real concentration, but I don't turn my ringer off in case of a personal or professional emergency. Every email or text that comes in is a subtle demand for attention.

We have made our flexibility a priority over our focus. We can now live anywhere, take our meetings from anywhere, in any time zone, at any hour. The trade-off here is that most of us have lost our ability—maybe even our will—to give anything *everything*. This is a shame, because attention is perhaps our highest form of care, excellence, and love. Our most precious commodity.

The Hebrew word for attention, *tisomet lev*, literally means to "place your heart." When you give something your full regard, you direct not just your eyes, ears, or mind but also your heart.

When Rose grabbed my face in her hands, she didn't just want me to listen to her story; she wanted my heart in it.

I am pained when I think about the things that have consumed my attention over recent years: polarizing online diatribes, mindless dance videos, gossipy group chats, and countless, countless emails.

Ultimately, our lives will be the sum of what we've given our attention to.

So, as you set your priorities, think hard about where you are placing your heart.

CHAPTER 20

Female Posse

My parents didn't have close friends. They had family. Mom often repeated the cliché she wholly believed in: "Blood is thicker than water." From my earliest memory, she urged me always to take care of my sister, pronouncing, "Gina will be your best friend for life."

That was certainly true of her three sisters, who were her strongest allies and soulmates. I can picture them still: sitting at the kitchen table pinching meat filling into hundreds of mandu wrappers, making batches of kimchi together, laughing over childhood stories, bragging about their kids' grades, comparing cosmetic creams, sharing wild greens or mushrooms they'd harvested from Mount Rainier. But I noticed my mother never seemed to do any of that with girlfriends. She wasn't willing to risk the vulnerability that intimacy required. Or maybe she never learned how.

My father was similarly close with his brothers, Al and Jack, eight and nine years his senior. Tall and athletic, their status as cooler and wiser was cemented when they were already in college and out of the house when my father was only ten. My dad found it almost too painful to talk about losing Al, who died in his fifties of leukemia. But he had a standing weekly lunch with his surviving brother, Jack, which they kept until Jack's death at ninety-one in 2023.

My father did occasionally see some of his childhood friends. They would go to a Tacoma Tigers minor league baseball game together or meet for bar food at Katie Downs along the waterfront. But those occasions were notable. I remember my father saying in passing that his ten years away in Korea made him lose touch with "the gang," who seemed to move on without him. He never confessed it, but I also suspect that my mother, with her strong accent and foreign manner, didn't exactly mesh with all their American wives for couples nights either.

It wasn't that my parents were antisocial. Dad was a regular at Sabbath services and at Sunday Torah study at synagogue; Mom was well known through her volunteer work with the Korean Women's Association. But these were their extended communities, not close friends. I can hardly remember a time when anyone from synagogue or the KWA visited our house on 21st Street.

When it came to cultivating my own deep friendships, I felt like I was charting new territory.

I navigated the typical childhood dramas of declaring a "best friend" and then switching to a different one, the painful betrayals teenage girls often visit upon each other. I had a best friend in high school named Jeff who lived down the block and wanted to be a rocket scientist when he grew up (he actually became one). Jeff and I managed to have our own separate romantic relationships while keeping our friendship close and uncomplicated. I was friendly with several cliques in high school without being in one of my own, comfortable moving in and out of groups but preferring to spend individual time with a few good friends. My younger sister would sometimes feel hurt when I went out with my class-mates, since she was my best friend above all; wasn't family the clos-est tie?

Female friendship became important to me only in adulthood, when I started to see how anchoring it could be. I am fortunate to have found a small circle of kick-ass women, some friends since college, whom I love fiercely, admire immensely, and rely upon when I'm feeling vulnerable. We discuss our jobs, kids, partners, stresses, anxieties, and triumphs. We share meals and practical tips, do yoga, hike, and bike with lots of ferocity and conversation. I couldn't exhale or relax without these women; they have seen me grow up and I can be silly and mindless with them, talk too loudly, and laugh too hard. I wear athleisure around them, which never looks right on me. I am unworried about whether my words are rabbinic or even politically correct, and when one of us is struggling, we learn from watching each other navigate the slings and arrows.

For example, my friend Ruby, who has a public profile as a prominent researcher and physician, was suddenly trolled in the most ugly way dur-ing the pandemic. Her response was novel and ingenious: She posted a picture of an adorable otter, a cultural mascot where she lives: It's hard to spew bile when you're faced with a disarming aquatic mammal.

This started a bit of a movement in her female doctors' group, which took to posting otter pictures to anyone who would attack one of their own. One of Ruby's colleagues noted that female otters, also known as "bitches," will lock arms with each other when they need to sleep, form-ing a raft so that no one gets left behind or lost. Contrary to the image in the wild of "eat or be eaten," here was a model of females protecting, propping up, and literally keeping one another from going under.

I know I would be out to sea without my own raft of bitches.

One particular lifeboat has been my Upper West Side Shabbat crew. For more than fifteen years, we have had Sabbath meals together with our children almost every week. We met through the Abraham Joshua Heschel Jewish Day School, where our children were enrolled. Most of the other families had grown up more ritually observant than Jacob or I did; during Shabbat, they didn't drive, use electronics, or cook. This meant that Saturday afternoon, after I had officiated services at Central, one of them would host lunch around one p.m. for a gang of fifteen to twenty people. With no place to go, no work we could do, no birthday parties or soccer practices planned (by mandate of the school), we would just sit around the table, discussing current events, swapping parenting challenges and funny stories. Our children, all unplugged, would find analog ways to pass the time, playing Ping-Pong, board games, or bedroom hoops and just shooting the breeze with no distractions.

In the summer, it was even lazier: The entire crew moved to a beach house on Long Island for Shabbat. It was a taste of kibbutz living, where parents took turns cooking big meals, watched each other's kids, shared cleanup duties, and enjoyed the long days while a gaggle of children entertained themselves on the lawn.

It was there, more than a decade ago, while sitting on some porch chairs, that one of these dear friends, Ilana Ruskay-Kidd, then the head of the Manhattan Jewish Community Center Preschool, confessed that she was contemplating her next professional chapter. "I think the Jewish community needs a day school for kids with special needs," Ilana said to me and Ariela Dubler, then a law professor at Columbia Law School.

Ilana's vision seemed to come out of nowhere. None of her own children had special needs, nor had she pursued that educational specialty.

But she ran an early-childhood school and saw up close what was missing. "It doesn't feel right that children with special needs have to choose between a deep Jewish education or one that addresses their learning differences."

As it happened, within months, I, too, began considering a major career shift—what it would mean to apply for the senior rabbi role at Central Synagogue instead of continuing very happily as senior cantor. And by coincidence (or maybe not), Ariela was approached to consider leaving her tenured chair at Columbia Law School to apply for Heschel's opening as head of school.

Each of these moves felt radical and risky. Over many intense months of discussion, questioning, and examination, we served as each other's sounding boards, confidantes, and brain trust. When I felt myself unmoored, these two women buoyed and anchored me. We supported each other, and within a year, all three of us had made significant career changes that I don't think we could have managed as well alone.

By sheer luck, divine hand, or perhaps the oddities of the Jewish professional calendar, all three of us began our new jobs—senior rabbi of Central Synagogue, head of the Heschel School, and founder and head of the Shefa School, the first Jewish day school for children with learning differences, on the very same day: July 1, 2014.

These transitions were not just professional shifts, but a response to an ineffable call for each of us. I suggested that we mark the milestone by going to the mikvah—the ritual bath that sanctifies transitions of many kinds—together. Sitting in our towels at the edge of the reservoir of warm water, we began by sharing some highs and lows from the previous year. I expressed how grateful I felt to have these friends, how essential they were in helping me make it to this moment. As I took my turn dipping into the living waters, I thanked God for my raft, my female posse who keeps me afloat. Blood may be thicker than water, but we need both to live.

Chaver
FRIEND

The fourth-century BCE philosopher Aristotle said, "No one would want to live without friends, even if he possessed all other goods." In other words, human connections are more essential to our existence than any worldly belongings.

But Aristotle understood that not all relationships answer the same yearnings, and he distinguishes three degrees of friendship: need-based, pleasure-based, and character-based. These categories reflect the most important aspects of friendship: usefulness, company, and moral character.

Over a thousand years later, Maimonides, the Medieval scholar, offered a Jewish spin on Aristotle's three categories of friendship. The first is a *chaver to'elet*, a "friend of utility." This is like your friendly neighbors who will lend you a couple of eggs, the parent who carpools for soccer practice, the colleague who brings you a meal when you're sick. You like each other, help each other, feel responsible for each other. While this is considered the "lowest" level of friendship, it should not be denigrated. These ties form the crucial basis for a caring community.

The next level is a *chaver nachat*, a "friend of satisfaction and joy." That's the friend who makes you laugh until you're doubled over. The one who makes walking in the park or shopping for clothes a celebratory occasion. The friend you would call to share a particularly triumphant moment, a tender hurt, or a book you loved. These friends give our lives color, taste, radiance.

But there is one more level of friendship, which Maimonides considers the highest: a *chaver ma'alah*, a "friend for higher purpose." This kind of friendship is rare—candid, clarifying, and precious. It's a friend whom you trust completely and know will always act with your best interests at heart. It's a friend with whom you can reveal all aspects of yourself, including the soft, self-doubting parts, and know that she will protect and advise you, lift you up. It's the friend who not only shares your core values on the deepest level but who becomes a partner in your projects—to make those values manifest in concrete ways.

It has been a singular gift to work with a *chaver ma'alah*, Abby Pogrebin, on my first book. This memoir would not have happened without her steadfast belief that my story was worth telling, and she put in countless hours to help bring it to life. I met Abby in 2006 because she contacted me after attending a bat mitzvah I helped officiate. Her email described feeling deeply affected, that perhaps she'd found her Jewish home. We met for lunch at Alice's Teacup, she joined Central the next day, and we have been talking ever since.

One year after I became senior rabbi, Abby was selected to be synagogue president. At first I worried that our easy, unfailingly candid friendship would be complicated by the daily static and stresses of synagogue stewardship: unhappy congregants, HR decisions, budget woes, or bedbugs (yes, we once had them). Not to mention she was now head of the board of trustees, which is effectively my boss. But rather than becoming awkward, our bond grew stronger as we aligned (most of the time) on solutions, had each other's back, and challenged each other when necessary. We shared a goal of ensuring that our growing synagogue would remain as intimate as possible, an extended family of community, responsibility, and care. Abby helped create the blueprint and has never left the project. And all the while, our shorthand still seamlessly moves from the professional to the personal—from discussing Central's membership policies to practicing yoga together to arguing over the best smoothie ingredients.

When you find a *chaver ma'alah* who makes you better, smarter, who urges you forward when you falter and places your step stool for better vision, the impossible tasks feel doable. You are not only transformed, but together you get to impact your small corner of the world. Most of us are fortunate if we find one or two friends of higher purpose in our lives.

Pirkei Avot, the Ethics of our Fathers (1:6), teaches that Jewish tradition compels: "Find yourself a rabbi, acquire for yourself a friend." The verb in Hebrew for "acquiring" a friend is the same as "to purchase," which of course doesn't mean that you are to literally buy your friends. Rather, this teaching reminds us that friendships cost something—our time, compassion, vulnerability, generosity. We are not meant to go through life alone, nor are we able to discover our highest purpose by ourselves; friendships are our engines, our oxygen, our lighthouse in the harbor; they deserve tending.

CHAPTER 21

The Biennial

On December 6, 2013, my mother flew from Tacoma to San Diego to watch me lead Reform Judaism's largest Shabbat service.

Before the pandemic called a halt to large convenings, every two years, six thousand people from every Reform synagogue in the country—rabbis, cantors, educators, temple presidents, student leaders, and the Reform faithful—gathered for five days of seminars, conversations, music, and worship. Shabbat services on Friday night and Saturday morning were the peak communal moments of these Reform Biennials.

My mother, who no longer clears five feet, arrived dressed in her Tacoma winter clothes. As she left the airport taxi in front of the convention center, she rolled her suitcase up to its front doors and was greeted by an official with a lanyard and clipboard who took one look at her and offered, "Ma'am, I think you are at the wrong convention."

"Is this the Jewish Convention?" my mother asked.

"Yes, it is," the gatekeeper responded.

"Well, then, this is where I belong. My daughter is leading services for everybody tomorrow. She is the rabbi!" she proclaimed, beaming.

Once inside, Mom called my cell phone to let me know she'd arrived and had already made her usual stop in the ladies room.

"Angela, they were talking about you in the stalls!"

"In the bathroom, Mom?"

"They were excited about your new job. They said, 'She used to be the cantor, but she's going to be the head rabbi now. Top rabbi. Leading the largest synagogue in the whole world.'"

"Well, maybe not the *world*—"

"Angela. They said you were 'a first.' They sounded proud. You are a symbol. So I walked out of my bathroom stall and told them, 'That is my daughter!' I told them all."

I flashed back to my mother's anxious reaction when I admitted, at age sixteen, that I wanted to be a rabbi: "You could do anything, Angela! Why set yourself up for this?" She'd fretted that I would always be viewed as "not Jewish enough." That I might not ever get a job. That a life in Judaism might create an unbreachable distance between us if I embraced a world that would always be fundamentally foreign to her. But in reality she never discouraged me and has been emboldening me every step of the way.

That Shabbat morning in San Diego, I walked onto the pulpit erected in the cavernous convention center. At my side was Rabbi Rick Jacobs, with whom I'd led hundreds of services at WRT in Scarsdale. Now he was appearing in his new role as president of Reform Judaism's umbrella organization, the Union for Reform Judaism, representing more than 1.5 million Jews in North America. And I was wearing my new title as well: the newly nominated senior rabbi of the historic Central Synagogue in Manhattan. Even though it had been seven years since Rick and I worked together, we fell back easily into the joyful teamwork of weaving liturgy and song. I looked out at an ocean of faces filling countless rows of folding chairs. The words of one of the first pieces of the service, *Shiru L'Adonai*—"Sing unto God"—sent me back again to childhood and Debbie Friedman's anthem:

Sing unto God, sing a new song.

Rick opened the service and introduced me:

"Before Rabbi/Cantor Angela Buchdahl was called to serve *another synagogue*'—he smiled mischievously—"I had the joy of leading services with her for years in Scarsdale. After every service, someone would come up and ask me, 'Now . . . *where is she from?*'

"I would answer, 'Tacoma, Washington.' But that was not what they wanted to know. And I knew that. I would tell them, 'She is a fully trained cantor and rabbi. She went to thousands of years of school for that!'

"'That's interesting,' they'd always respond. 'But . . . *is she Jewish?*'"

The Biennial congregation, who already knew me as the first Asian American cantor, erupted in laughter. The laughter didn't bother me. Or I should say, it *no longer* bothered me. I had come far enough to be able to laugh along.

"No more shallow definitions of Jewishness, please," Rick continued, addressing the leadership of the Reform Movement. He then urged his audience to hear his more serious point: "Can we move beyond the tribe? Beyond ethnicity, to the very heart of Jewish life?"

This is what Reform Judaism has been doing since its start—transforming our understanding of Jewish ritual, identity, and engagement. Reform Judaism is often misunderstood, maligned, as "Judaism lite," the "easy option" defined by what Reform Jews "don't do," rather than the true challenge of "informed choice" when it comes to religious observance.

But Reform Judaism was founded on a noble—many believe necessary—goal of bringing Judaism into modernity, so that the core principles of ethical living, pursuit of justice, equality, scientific inquiry, and academic truth would not be in conflict with Jewish practice. Reform clergy innovated their services with more accessible liturgy, mixed seating so families could sit together, and the addition of instruments to elevate worship. Reform was the first major denomination to ordain women (1972) and HUC started admitting openly gay students in 1989. The Jewish ethos of human partnership with God in healing what is broken—*tikkun olam*, "repair of the world"—became a central orientation to ethical Jewish living.

A core proof text for Reform Judaism could be the verses read in synagogue on the holiest day of the year, from the prophet Isaiah, who rails against a ritually observant community of Israelites who fast and pray on Yom Kippur but who are ignoring the needy, the captive, the oppressed right outside their door:

"This is not the fast I seek," decries Isaiah. "No, this is the fast I desire:

"To let the oppressed go free;

"To break off every yoke.

"It is to share your bread with the hungry,

"And to take the wretched poor into your home;

"When you see the naked, to clothe them,

"And not to ignore your own kin."

Reform Judaism saw itself as a prophetic Judaism rooted in moral action, human dignity, and informed choice. In the beginning, any observance that didn't have an immediate ethical rationale was seen as superfluous, perhaps even distracting from true religiosity as defined by Isaiah. Many early Reform Jews purposely shucked the Mosaic dietary or clothing laws they saw as archaic and irrational. More than a century later, many Reform Jews have reembraced some of these ritual laws as they realized that the particularism of the customs carries some of the depth, power, and cohesion of Judaism.

This continued evolution is why we call ourselves Reform Jews; "reform" is an active verb. We are not "reformed," in the past tense. In every generation, Reform Judaism has helped American Jews "sing a new song" while living fully in the modern world.

Sing unto God, all the earth . . .

That cavernous auditorium was perhaps not "*all* the earth," but it gave me a glimpse of my corner of it. Central congregants were out there cheering. My former WRT family from Scarsdale was in the crowd too. As were peers and friends from cantorial and rabbinical school and from my summer learning programs. But most meaningfully, there was my mother, quietly bursting with pride in the front row.

I responded to Rick's generous introduction by gesturing toward my "Korean Buddhist mother" as her face appeared on the jumbotron. I thanked her for selflessly and steadily raising me and my sister as Jews, even though it meant she'd be set apart from the tribe that her family inhabited, and that she would not pass on her own religious tradition. I acknowledged her sacrifice and that of the countless other non-Jews in the wider community who have done the same. When the crowd of six thousand rose to their feet and erupted in an ovation, I could see Mom's eyes twinkle with tears. She had always felt like an outsider in the Jewish community—right down to a few moments ago when she rolled her suitcase up to the conference door—and now she was being honored and acknowledged by multitudes. It was, she said later, one of the most important moments in her life.

It was for me, too. I stood on that temporary bimah as a Jewish Korean American woman without having to choose one identity, one box, one story. For so long, I had carried the heart of the stranger, but I now saw that every moment of outsiderness had been a teaching. My welcome in that convention hall was like a voice from above, confirming I had taken exactly the path I was meant to. I scanned the many faces and hoped they could feel that wondrous, inexplicable, bone-deep sense of belonging, coming home to a people, an inheritance, and themselves.

Anavah
HUMILITY

In 2014, when asked to offer the blessings at the White House Hanukkah party for President Barack Obama, my initial response was, "I'm honored, but no thanks."

Jacob looked at me incredulously. "Are you nuts?"

"I'm just being invited because I'm a Korean female rabbi," I argued.

"Exactly," he pushed back. "That's why you have to do it."

I'm not sure where I learned that humility was about self-effacement or making myself smaller, but I have come to understand that this is not true humility but its own form of hubris; it's still making something about you rather than what or whom you serve.

Moses is described by God as "more humble than any other person on the face of the earth" (Numbers 12:3), but he was hardly timid or reserved. He stood up to Pharaoh, demanding that the Israelites be freed. He smashed God's stone tablets in the face of his people's idolatry. He put down his people's rebellion and exacted their punishment. The Bible makes clear that Moses's humility is not about meekness but about how much he is willing to subjugate his own self-doubt, fears, anxieties, and personal interest in service of a higher purpose.

Musar, a Jewish spiritual practice dating back to the tenth century, teaches that humility—*anavah* in Hebrew—is the foundational trait necessary for leadership. Alan Morinis, in his book *Everyday Holiness*, offers a useful *anavah* affirmation: "No more than my space, no less than my place." Humility requires a clear-eyed self-assessment of our role, abilities, and gifts, and the ongoing discernment to assume our rightful place in order to fulfill our purpose—no more but no less.

Anavah can be a challenging spiritual practice, especially for female leaders. Taking up our appropriate space often requires us to be proactive: claim our seat at the table,

work to change policies, assert our voice. This can be per-
ceived as arrogance, bossiness, or overt ambition. But
anavah demands we take this initiative; false modesty can
be irresponsible—even a betrayal.

Queen Esther, one of the rare female heroines in the Bible,
initially receded from her role as leader. Selected as queen
for her beauty, Esther kept her Jewish identity hidden from
her Persian husband, the king. When Haman, the king's
adviser, plotted to kill all the Jews in the land, Esther's
cousin Mordechai pleaded with her to intervene. But Esther demurred, citing the law that anyone who approached
the king without being summoned would be put to death.
Mordechai rejected her misplaced and mistaken humility:
"If you keep utterly silent in this moment, relief and deliverance will come for the Jews from somewhere else, while
you and your father's house will perish. And who knows if
you have come to your position for just such a time as
this?" (Esther 4:14).

How often do we shrink ourselves in the name of humility—
avoid speaking up, duck important decisions, decline special honors? Who are we to veil our God-given light behind
reticence, lowliness, and self-doubt? Each one of us must
take up our proper place in order to be agents of holiness
and justice in our world.

I did eventually say yes to leading blessings at the White
House Hanukkah party. As I kindled the flames on the
menorah before hundreds of Jews in a room filled with
Christmas trees and wreaths, I spoke of what it meant to be

the first female Korean rabbi invited to represent the Jewish community in the People's House. And I was honored to address the first Black president of the United States, who himself had the appropriate *anavah* to take his place in the White House when the moment called him.

CHAPTER 22

Is That a Rabbi on the Stage?

O n a cold December night in Manhattan, I was sweating. I'd been invited to join a panel one Friday in 2016 at one of the most influential Orthodox synagogues in the country, Kehilath Jeshurun (KJ), on the Upper East Side. I would be one of three rabbis joining in a conversation about the state of Jewish life. This dinner program was a clear Rubicon crossed—the very first time that a Reform rabbi had ever been invited to speak from their pulpit. I was a female mixed-race Reform rabbi, a trifecta that would make many Orthodox Jews shake their heads in disapproval or even reject my Judaism wholesale.

There would be no microphones to amplify our voices in the sanctuary; Orthodox Judaism prohibits turning on electricity during the Sabbath. As is typical of most Jewish events, we'd eat first, gathering in the social hall for a festive supper.

My fellow panelist was Rabbi Elliot Cosgrove, senior rabbi at Park Avenue Synagogue. He is widely considered one of the brightest lights in the Conservative movement, and had become a good friend, especially since we came to our respective Manhattan congregations just one year (and thirty city blocks) apart.

Our KJ host was Rabbi Chaim Steinmetz, a wise, warm Canadian transplant who had recently been named to the top job, the first time this synagogue would be led by someone outside of one rabbinic dynasty—the Lookstein family line—in more than one hundred years.

Chaim's strict observance included a renegade streak; he was determined to shake things up a bit—namely, being in public conversation with more progressive voices than his predecessors had ever done.

I knew that Chaim's invitation was entirely well intentioned, but I wasn't so sure how his congregation felt about me being there. On that December evening as I looked out at KJ's pews and up at its balcony, where the women sit separately for services, I noticed my heart starting to race. This was not just a first for KJ to have a female Reform rabbi on their pulpit; it was also a first for me, speaking before a large crowd of Orthodox Jews. Even though people seemed friendly, I started imagining silent accusations of illegitimacy. My brain had delusions that the audience would grill me on Talmudic questions just to stump me and prove that I shouldn't carry the title "Rabbi."

Pull yourself together, I scolded myself.

I could hear my dad's reliable pep talk in my head, but every affirmation had a counterargument.

"Angela, you were just featured on the *Today* show with Cardinal Dolan."

"Dad, I talked about interfaith unions. Orthodox Jews don't permit marrying outside Judaism."

"Honey, you were just at the White House, leading Hanukkah blessings with the president."

"The Orthodox clergy at that White House Hanukkah party did not consider me a real rabbi."

"And yet you were named head rabbi of a historic synagogue in New York City."

I hadn't had the heart to show my dad *The Jewish Press* headline when I got the job: "It's Official: You Can Be a Non-Jewish Rabbi."

I'd like to say that I didn't need anyone else's approval and could generate my own internal sense of identity. I had been doing that for most of my life. But I still wanted to be acknowledged for my position. I didn't see myself as a rabbi only for my congregation but a rabbi for the Jewish people. The more my leadership expanded, the more my sense of communal responsibility did as well, but that meant I kept butting up against the boundaries of belonging.

It didn't make much sense that despite being invited to this bimah by its senior rabbi, I was suddenly sinking in the quicksand of self-doubt. But this was one of those visceral episodes where being introduced as "Rabbi" in a community who defined this title differently triggered all the demons in my head.

In 2015, just one year earlier, the Rabbinical Council of America—the nation's Orthodox leadership—reaffirmed its prohibition of women's ordination, calling it a "violation" of tradition: "We cannot accept either the ordination of women or the recognition of women as members of the Orthodox rabbinate," the Council stated, "regardless of the title."

It wasn't until 1972, the year of my birth, that the first female Reform rabbi was ordained in America. The year 1985 saw the first female Conservative rabbi. And now the Orthodox movement was trying mightily to hold the line, especially since the trailblazing Rabba Sara Hurwitz had been ordained in 2009 and started a yeshiva for Orthodox women's leadership.

In addition to my being a woman, in this Orthodox crowd at KJ it could unsettle just as much that I was of interracial and interfaith parentage. Children born of a non-Jewish mother were not considered halachically (legally) Jewish.

Reform Judaism rejected this absolute in 1978 when I was six years old and Rabbi Alexander Schindler, the president of the Reform movement, gave his landmark "outreach" sermon. He called upon the liberal Jewish community to open its doors to interfaith families and to accept Jewish children of these unions as Jews, whether they had a Jewish mother or a Jewish father.

This visionary, controversial call for acceptance upended the Jewish identity landscape. It allowed my own family to join Judaism with full welcome. But it also caused some Conservative and Orthodox circles to view Reform Jews with suspicion, as potentially illegitimate.

Sitting on the KJ bimah, I glanced at Rabbi Chaim Steinmetz, who had thoughtfully conceived the event despite knowing that my presence could be contentious. He smiled with a reassurance that slowed my pulse. I turned to Rabbi Cosgrove, with whom I'd long shared sermon ideas, management woes, and Shabbat lunches. I listened to the moderator, my friend, journalist Abby Pogrebin, whose first question to all of us was "Why is this evening by itself so unprecedented?"

My panic began to ebb. Somehow I found my footing. I heard myself answering questions about pluralism, prayer, pastoral care, and the rise in antisemitism. I saw the audience listening, nodding, even applauding the spontaneity and candor of three very different rabbis in one conversation. But when I walked off that stage, it hit me as hard as it ever has: I can still be derailed by the doubters. No matter how far I've come. No matter how deeply invested I am. I still longed to belong.

Chesed
KINDNESS

For as long as there has been Judaism, there has been distrust among Jewish sects. In the time of Temple Judaism in the first century CE, there were at least four major warring factions: the Pharisees, Sadducees, Essenes, and Zealots. And when the Temple was destroyed in 70 CE, the rabbis blamed it on the destructive infighting between Jews, which they called *sinat chinam*, "baseless hatred."

The fall of the Temple spelled the end of Judaism as it had been practiced for centuries. Until then, Jews had only communicated with God through priests who made animal sacrifices. Without the Temple, Jews lost their focal point for worship, and priests lost their leadership. But the new rabbis of the first century radically reenvisioned Judaism, replacing sacrificial offerings with prayers of the heart.

After the destruction of the Temple, Yochanan ben Zakkai, the patriarch of Rabbinic Judaism, was walking through the rubble with his student Rabbi Yehoshua. "Woe is us!" Yehoshua cried out. "The altar where we atoned for our sins is in ruins!" Yochanan comforted him, saying, "Don't grieve, my son. God has given us another path to atonement rather than animal sacrifices: through acts of loving kindness" (Avot d'Rabbi Natan 11a).

No longer would a high priest mediate our relationship with God through smoke signals from an altar. Now every Jew would directly serve God through *gemilut chasadim*—actual, human-to-human decency.

It was a radical claim for its era: The offerings you brought to God were not physical, but sacrifices of time, compassion, and care.

The rabbis understood that a world destroyed by senseless hate could only be rebuilt with acts of love.

As it says in Psalm 89, *Olam Chesed Yibaneh*, "The world is built on kindness."

There is a difference between tzedakah, charity, and *gemilut chasadim*—acts of loving-kindness. Tzedakah is a gift of resources, whereas *gemilut chasadim* are gifts of oneself. Giving your time, presence, and attention is a lot to ask. But that is the point.

Performing acts of *gemilut chasadim* can be even more challenging when it comes to compassion for people we dislike or disagree with, especially in a time of polarization. This requires us to give something up: comfort, insularity, certainty.

But acts of kindness replaced ritual sacrifices; they *should* demand something of us.

Gemilut chasadim became the rabbinic blueprint for rebuilding a world that had been demolished by hostility.

So, let's make the sacrifice for each other in order to rebuild the world.

CHAPTER 23

Births, Burials, and Bedbugs

To be a rabbi is to be in the awe business. I have the privilege of accompanying people through momentous transitions: a child's birth, a parent's final breath, welcoming in the Jewish New Year with thousands singing around you. I am equally awed by the courageous acts of human progress I get to witness: The nervous thirteen-year-old stepping up to her bat mitzvah pulpit to lead the congregation. The child of Holocaust survivors returning to his ancestral home to learn the stories his parents were unable to tell. The new widow learning to live alone for the first time in decades.

While I have often helped people across a difficult boundary, more often they have guided me.

In my first months as senior rabbi, I was faced with the sudden brain death of my nine-year-old congregant Riley on the night before she was to return home from summer camp. Riley was joyful—always dancing and full of music. She had an easy way of turning classmates into friends, including my own nine-year-old daughter, Rose, who had loved her since nursery school. It was impossible to believe that a girl so full of life could be gone so unexpectedly. Riley's body was still hooked up to breathing machines when I called her parents, not knowing what to say. Never had my training felt so inadequate.

Riley's dad spoke to me from the hospital in Albany, forty-five excruciating minutes from the Maine camp, where Riley had been transported after a sudden heart seizure. "I am lying here in bed next to my daughter, my beautiful daughter, and she is here, but she is no longer here. We are just keeping her alive now so we can donate her organs, so her heart can beat inside someone else and give them life," he told me.

Even in their anguish, Riley's parents had the presence of mind to want to share her with the world, knowing that her tragic death could maybe save others. Riley's father showed me where God was and restored my sense of faith just when I might have lost it.

Awe can be inspiring, startling, or frightening, sometimes all at once. My job description is to help people appreciate the wonder of the world we often rush through, to remind them that each of us is unfathomably complex, inescapably mortal. Every rite, prayer, holiday, memorial, sermon, Torah learning, protest, blessing, and celebration is in service of helping us make sense of it all—where we fit in, how to respond to what we see or experience. My own belief is reinforced by the fortitude and selflessness I witness every day in others, kindnesses that take my breath away.

And yet. The bulk of a rabbinic week is not about epiphanies, walking people through life-altering moments, or pondering the meaning of existence. Ever since the Bronfman program at age sixteen inspired my call to the rabbinate, I had pictured a rabbi's routine as parsing texts, translating big ideas, teaching eager students—every day heady and mind-altering. Once I started my internship in rabbinical school, reality set in.

The job description of a senior rabbi is, yes, spiritual leader, teacher, listener, comforter, and moral guide. But it also includes fundraiser, human resources manager, security officer, antisemitism responder, welcome usher, long-term strategist, interfaith representative, diplomat, and budget planner. The spiritual doesn't happen without the practical. There is a Talmudic phrase: *Im ein kemach, ein Torah.* "If there is no flour, there is no Torah."

For many clergy, we are expected to run the business of an institution often with little training. I've learned from two exceptional executive directors who have taught me what I was never taught in seminary, who are always thinking twelve steps ahead, anticipating strategic questions, managing multiple departments, often wisely reining in my overenthusiastic ideas.

It is thanks to these tireless partners that I came to realize that changing Central's family-leave policy to include all parents, implementing a $15 minimum wage for our employees before the state required it, and fundraising to upgrade our synagogue's metal detectors was not just stewardship but an expression of Torah. Similarly, the direct service and social justice programs we've conceived or sustained—whether our volunteers are serving breakfast to hundreds of homeless New Yorkers every week, mentoring students, or helping the formerly incarcerated find internships—these, too, are an expression of Torah. Sacred texts are not only preoccupied with how we relate to God or our fellow Jews; they inform how we treat every fellow human being in the everyday tasks of living—paying fair wages, treating strangers with empathy, paying attention to our neighbors in trouble, offering second chances. I learned that a rabbi's countless behind-the-scenes meetings about HR policy, security, strategic planning, volunteerism, and budgeting are some of the ways that we live our Jewish values in the world.

I am so lucky to have an extraordinary clergy team at my side who carry so much of the pastoral, ritual, and educational load for our congregants, and who inspire me every day with their devotion and passion. And yet I am still so often aware of all the needs we are not meeting.

I can't count the instances when I have let people down, been distracted, missed an event I shouldn't have. With so many congregants—more than thirty-five hundred households as I write this—I have daily anxiety over whom I neglected to call back, write, or visit. How much is enough when it comes to praying at the bedside of someone holding on to life, or comforting congregants who have just buried a parent, spouse, or—heaven forbid—a child? There is simply no limit. I have been grateful for the congregants who tell me when I've failed them, much as it stings. I go home and replay the mistakes. But their honesty gives me the chance to ask for forgiveness and learn to do better.

Humility is its own kind of awe. I was taught that in an unconventional way, early in rabbinical school. I was twenty-four, sitting in a plain conference room at the Eden Roc Hotel in Miami, as my Wexner Graduate Fellowship class anxiously awaited our first workshop with the leadership guru Ronald Heifetz. Heifetz had recently written a bestselling book, *Leadership Without Easy Answers*, which had become required reading at Harvard Business School, where he taught. Heifetz was known for leading transformative, emotionally charged sessions that not infrequently made people cry or seek therapy.

He walked in, a narrow face atop his narrow build, and quickly set to arranging the eighteen of us in a large semicircle of banquet chairs. My class was made up of aspiring Jewish professionals: rabbinic students from different denominations, Jewish studies PhD candidates, Jewish communal and education students. Heifetz assessed us with a quick glance before choosing his first victim.

"You." He pointed to me. "Come stand in front of this group."

My nose instantly beaded with sweat.

"I want you to address this gathering and to sing their song," he instructed. "Not with words—use the syllable 'la.' La, la, la. Just see what comes out."

His use of "their" utterly confused me. What was *their* song? I knew my class intimately by now; we didn't have an anthem.

It was clear he wasn't offering more clarification and I couldn't stall. "La, la, la," I began, haltingly at first, willing a melody. I had always been a comfortable singer, but this was obviously not a singing exercise, rather some opaque leadership test, and I had no idea what success looked like.

After ten interminable seconds of awkward warbling, I closed my eyes, and then, inexplicably, a tune began to flow.

"Stop. STOP," Heifetz called, interrupting my reverie.

"You are singing *your* song. That's not what I asked for. I want you to sing *theirs*." He gestured to my class, who looked back at me sympathetically.

I started again, keeping my eyes open and looking left—to a classmate who smiled back at me, encouraging a few notes. I looked to the next one in the circle, who held my gaze long enough that I could discern her silent communication, sparking more sounds. As I focused on each person around the circle, an instinctive melody ultimately emerged.

When I finished, the room was hushed. Something had unfolded that I didn't quite have language for. I was feeling pretty proud of myself, and after catching my breath, I started chattering about how revelatory that exercise had been. "I felt it—did you feel it?"

"STOP," interrupted Heifetz once again. "Stop talking," he chastised. "You just *held* this group. You know it. But you can't then turn around and ask for applause. If you need love and praise for what you just did, you need to get it from somewhere else. Not from the people you're leading."

I never forgot that lesson: You will ultimately succeed if you tune into your people, help them sing their song. But be aware of what you are actually needing when you do. Everyone wants affirmation. But if we rely on approval from the people we serve, we fail at leadership; we will make decisions based on whether or not we'll be popular and loved.

Congregants can ascribe a great deal of power and godliness to their rabbis—and nothing is more dangerous than when we actually believe all the hype. At our best, we create the conditions for noticing and being present to the sacred in life. But there is a seductive danger in presuming, or hoping, that a congregant is experiencing awe in response to you. Rabbis are not "sacred vessels" but human beings, fallible and imperfect. And one of the greatest lessons a rabbi can impart is that one's spirituality comes through each other.

In ancient times, only the priests had the authority to bless others, but the Torah later charged us to be a nation of priests. This was not just about democratizing leadership but about spreading it around.

We are all in this awe business together.

Yirah
AWE

In ancient times, there was no higher standard than to be "God-fearing."

When Moses speaks to the Israelites near the end of his life, he instructs them, "What does God demand of you? Only this: that you fear Adonai your God" (Deuteronomy 10 12).

The quintessential examples of God-fearers were the Hebrew midwives. When they were commanded by Pharaoh to kill all male Hebrews, the midwives refused because, the text says, "they feared God." Had they acted out of their fear of Pharaoh, they would have followed *his* command. Instead, they risked their lives to spare the babies, understanding that they were answerable to a higher moral authority.

One might dismiss the midwives' act as self-preservation, assuming these women simply dreaded God's punishment more than Pharaoh's. But God-fearing doesn't mean being afraid. There is a different Hebrew word for that: *pachad*. Rather, the Hebrew word used here is *yirah*, which is more like "trembling reverence." *Yirah* means both "fear" and "awe"; they are deeply connected.

Maimonides reinforces this understanding of God-fearing as awe: "And what is the way of fearing God? When a man reflects upon God's wondrous great works and creatures and perceives from them God's inestimable and infinite wisdom."

Yirah is the awe we feel when we take in the vastness and beauty of nature, human striving, or the quiet but important ways God shows up in our interactions, or the acts of kindness we receive and offer.

More recently, Rabbi Abraham Joshua Heschel designated awe as our primary religious stance. "Our goal should be to live life in radical amazement," he wrote. "Get up in the morning and look at the world in a way that takes nothing for granted . . . Never treat life casually. To be spiritual is to be amazed."

Why is awe so integral to spiritual life? What does awe do?

For one thing, awe puts us in our place.

During a trip to Lake Powell some years ago, a guide took us on a boat to a spectacular spot encircled by high red rock cliffs. He explained that below us lay an ancient Navajo burial ground. When asked by a member of our group "What are we doing here?" the guide looked around for a moment and quietly said, "We are feeling small."

This kind of humility does not render us insignificant. Rather, it makes clear that we are just passing through, that the flow of life preceded us and will outlast us. Feeling small inspires us to serve something bigger than ourselves. As it did for those midwives.

Awe can be terrifying and destabilizing. That is why our ancestors were wise to choose the same word for fear and awe. *Yirah*. It's hard but useful to feel humbled sometimes.

The Proverbs echo this: "The beginning of wisdom is *yirat haShem*—fear and awe of the Lord" (Proverbs 9:10).

Awe tempers our ego, takes us out of ourselves, connects us to others and maybe even to a larger power. When we realize we're insignificant, just a speck in the universe instead of the whole, it puts our concerns into perspective, stretches our empathy beyond narrow self-interest, leads us to wonder.

God demands one thing chiefly—*yirah*, that wondrous, uplifting, daunting, ennobling experience that leads us to the big gift of sometimes feeling small.

CHAPTER 24

A House Divided

It was a Monday morning, January 30, 2017, and I was watching the country convulse on the TV news in my airport hotel room. I had come to Dallas with my synagogue president and executive director for the annual meeting of large congregations of the Reform Movement. We could not have expected to land smack at ground zero of President Trump's travel ban on people from predominantly Muslim countries.

"We want to ensure that we are not admitting into our country the very threats our soldiers are fighting overseas," he said. "We only want to admit those into our country who will support our country and love deeply our people."

Protests were roiling the airports, and as we arrived at the Dallas terminal, hundreds were holding signs and chanting, "America for all!" and "Shame!"

Over one hundred attorneys from the Dallas–Fort Worth area had set up a makeshift war room in our hotel basement, welcoming four thousand lawyers nationwide who had traveled to offer legal counsel to those caught in limbo at the airport.

We could see a queue of concerned family members and activists right outside the conference room where Los Angeles Rabbi Yoshi Zweiback and I had been asked to lead a prayer service.

What is the point of communal prayer, I thought, if it does not respond to the most urgent issues of our time? If it cannot enlarge our compassion for those most vulnerable? Fortify our resolve to do what might be uncomfortable?

Yoshi had stayed up late into the night writing a new song for morning services that would speak to this moment, invoking the words we recite on Yom Kippur about opening the gates of mercy. He invited me to add harmonies and an additional lyric and now overgenerously asserts we "co-wrote" it.

Pitchu b'hesed, pitchu b'ahava, pitchu b'tzedek. "Open us to kindness, open us to love, open us to justice."

After a quick rehearsal, we began our weekday service with this liturgy. I could sense sadness and disquiet in this group of rabbis, lay volunteers, and temple directors. The outrage at the airport—seven days after Trump took office—was just the latest flashpoint in how splintered the country had become, and the Jewish community along with it. Every one of us struggled with how to lead in this moment.

I thought of the difficult conversation that I'd had with my congregant Beverly just days earlier.

"Rabbi, you know I love Central. I travel forty-five minutes from Brooklyn to come to Friday-night services each week. This congregation inspired me after nineteen years of partnership with my wife, Nina, to convert to Judaism. But last Friday night, the Shabbat after Trump's inauguration, I looked around the pews and I thought, *These are not my people.* This congregation didn't organize buses to the Women's March. You didn't publicize a message of indignation to Trump's ugly rhetoric. I don't feel I belong here and wanted to tell you personally that I am leaving."

I loved Beverly and was not willing to let her go so easily. I understood her discomfort and acknowledged that Central was not a congregation filled with people who all think, or vote, alike, but this diversity was precisely our strength. I told her that one of the root problems in our country right now was that people were intentionally siloed. That there are so few places left in America where people can talk, eat, and sing alongside people with politics and priorities different from our own. I understood that she might be more comfortable in a congregation filled with people who were all ideologically aligned. But I argued that the spiritual curriculum of our lives is enriched by seeing the humanity in those with whom we disagree.

She stayed at Central. And she helped lead a small discussion group of politically diverse congregants who learned to listen to each other while studying Jewish texts.

I also heard from Andrew, a congregant at the other end of the ideological spectrum. He chastised the Reform Movement's social justice arm for invoking the Torah in criticizing the administration's immigration crackdown. "You're not leaving room for those of us who consider immigration to be out of control, that measures are needed to stem the tide. Our Jewish texts don't prescribe just one policy. That's not only simplistic; it's alienating to Reform Jews who believe or vote differently."

Holding together a large, multifaceted congregation and making it feel like a united community is a daily challenge. I don't always see eye to eye with my members, but I feel compelled to hear their views and try to understand them. I often learn the most from people with whom I deeply disagree. Judaism emphasizes that there is more than one way to look at an argument.

Some people are surprised that the Torah—Judaism's foundational book—does not legislate theological belief. Unlike Catholicism, for example, which has 255 "infallible declared dogmas," covering topics from immaculate conception to resurrection, Jews have a wide range of possibilities when it comes to God, heaven, and the nature of evil. The Torah provides a litany of upstanding actions that are the litmus tests for being ethical and faithful: respect for parents and elders; tzedakah (giving) to the less fortunate; visiting the sick; caring for the stranger, the widow, the orphan; not exploiting workers, including paying wages on time. These mitzvot legislate actions, not creeds. Judaism stands by the idea that there can be more than one truth and there's no greater proof of that than the Talmud, which includes reams of rabbinic disputation around what each line of Torah means.

A famous story of the Talmud details a long-standing argument between two leading rabbis of the first century, Hillel and Shammai. A voice from heaven finally comes down and proclaims, *"Eilu v' Eilu!"* "These [the words of Hillel] and those [the words of Shammai] are both the word of the living God."

There is more than one way to read a text. More than one way to chart a life of piety and responsibility. More than one way to think about immigration policy.

And yet, the Torah does provide a moral compass, a set of primary directives. Welcoming the stranger is one of them. This mandate is born not just out of our sacred values but our own historical experience.

I had reminded my congregants of this at the High Holidays just two months earlier—in October 2016. In my sermon, I cited a Gallup survey about whether America should open its doors to ten thousand refugee children, innocents caught in the crossfires of war.

"Ask yourself: Would you let them in?" I challenged my community.

"More than two-thirds of Americans polled by Gallup said, 'No, we should keep them out.'

"But this was not a recent poll regarding the Syrian refugee crisis," I continued. "Gallup took this poll in 1939, right after the highly publicized events of Kristallnacht, the violent pogrom in which Jewish businesses and synagogues were shattered or burned to the ground all over Germany. Those ten thousand children seeking refuge on our shores were mostly Jews. *Those strangers were us.*"

It's so easy to forget what it was like to be at the bottom of the ladder once we've climbed it. But the Jewish people have always insisted on memory—revisiting our hardship and redemption. We recall this, in part, so as not to repeat the mistakes of our oppressors.

Some congregants came up to me after that sermon and admonished me: "Politics have no place on the bimah. I want my synagogue to be my sanctuary."

If by "sanctuary," they meant free of challenge or self-examination, that was no sanctuary I could promise or provide. I was reminded of the Talmud's instruction: "A person should only pray in a house with windows" (Berachot 34b). Surely, windows offer light and allow us to appreciate the miracle of God's creation. They bring serenity to our house of worship. But windows also summon us to see the world beyond our walls and allow others to see what we are doing.

Our Jewish texts describe the difference between the priestly and prophetic role of a rabbi. Clergy are trained to assume a priestly responsibility—guiding and supporting people through their milestones and misfortunes. Priests must go outside the camp to bring in the marginalized and struggling, to help them find community. They counsel and heal. But there is also a prophetic role of a rabbi, which requires delivering uneasy truths, however hard to hear. The biblical prophets weren't popular in their time, but it was their blunt rebukes—Isaiah's admonitions and Jeremiah's warnings—that forced society to reckon with its moral failings and try to do better.

I don't think any of us rabbis in that Dallas hotel room felt like we were priests or prophets, but I was personally grappling with how to use my pulpit to reject America's barring of a people based on religion. We prayed in that airport for the strength to carry out the values of our prophets.

> *Learn to do good.*
> *Seek out justice;*
> *Help the oppressed.*
> *—Isaiah 1:17*

> *If you do not oppress the stranger, the orphan, and the*
> *widow . . . then I will dwell among you in this place, in this*
> *land that I gave to your ancestors forever and ever.*
> *—Jeremiah 7:5–7*

Yoshi and I draped our guitar straps over our prayer shawls and sang the lyrics he adapted: "Open us to kindness, open us to love, open us to justice."

I inserted Emma Lazarus's words, inscribed on the stone base of Lady Liberty, which have become their own liturgy:

"Give me your tired, your poor, your huddled masses yearning to breathe free . . . Bring the homeless tempest tossed to me, I lift my lamp beside the golden door."

Even in a windowless airport hotel, we had to look outside the window. Sometimes a conference room becomes a sanctuary. Perhaps even a protest of its own.

Hevruta
SPARRING PARTNER

Jews are famously opinionated, argumentative, and stubborn, a cultural disposition that goes back millennia.

After the destruction of the Temple in Jerusalem in 70 CE, when Jews could no longer commune with God through animal sacrifice, they found a new pathway: debating Torah with a partner. Modern Judaism, as we know it, was created in a noisy, crowded *beit midrash*—study hall—where debate became a divine calling. Jews learned in pairs, called *hevruta*. The most legendary *hevruta* of the Talmudic period was between the learned Rabbi Yochanan ben Zakkai, head of the academy, and Resh Lakish, who was once a bandit and had no formal training in Judaism but possessed an insatiable curiosity and street smarts. Imagine Albert Einstein sitting down to study with Al Capone. They were an odd couple.

But odd as the pairing might be, they were ideal sparring partners, because Lakish was unafraid to challenge Yochanan. They shared a mutual respect.

On one occasion, however, Yochanan mentioned Lakish's sordid past as an outlaw, making Lakish so humiliated and upset that he fell ill and died.

Yohanan was inconsolable. So the community brought him a brilliant new *hevruta*. This one seemed like a perfect match; every time Rabbi Yochanan made an argument, his *hevruta* would find the text that confirmed it. But after only a few days, Yochanan became exasperated: "I don't need you to tell me I'm right. I already think I'm right," he complained. "When I used to argue a point, Resh Lakish would challenge me twenty-four times over, until the matter became clear to both of us."

Yochanan cried in anguish over his lost study partner, "Where are you, Resh Lakish?" Yochanan loses his mind. And then he dies too.

When I heard this story, I finally understood the famous expression "Two Jews, three opinions."

The saying always perplexed me. If the joke is supposed to highlight that Jews never agree, it would suffice to say "Two Jews, *two opinions*."

Where did that third opinion come from?

The story of Yochanan and Resh Lakish's *hevruta* provides an answer: It says that each would argue his points until the matter *became clear to both of them*. In other words: Together, they came to a third opinion. Only by listening to opposing views could they arrive at a conclusion that transcended either of their original positions.

We sometimes lament that "Two Jews, three opinions" hurts the community, splinters us. But it is most definitely a feature, not a bug.

In valuing robust debate as a path to truth, rabbinic Judaism sought to define itself as distinct from Christianity. In 325 CE, a group of Christian bishops, at Emperor Constantine's request, wrote the Nicene Creed to establish a uniform consensus on beliefs and rituals within the Christian world.

Contrast that with the Jewish law of the Talmud, also codified in the fourth century, which decidedly does *not* establish uniform Jewish practices or beliefs but instead presents different sides of an argument and often answers one question with another.

Over time, the queries and commentaries of subsequent rabbinic giants were written into the margins so that in studying Talmud today, you can even argue with the sages across centuries.

The Talmud doesn't proffer or require religious creeds. It offers a *process* for how one should deliberate, refine, and ultimately arrive at one's own beliefs. This search for knowledge is holy in itself.

Our world has become starkly binary: You're either with me or against me, on the left or the right, Democrat or Republican.

But there should always be more than just two opinions.

In order to find the third way, consider committing to this core intellectual practice:

Seek out a *hevruta* in your own life.

Not just the friend who always agrees with you, but a real sparring partner—a Lakish. Remember that the goal is not to win the battle but to expand and deepen your understanding. The baseline is decent discourse and open-minded debate. Ask yourself why someone with an opposing view might be coming at an issue so differently. See if it alters your lens.

Rabbi Yochanan and Resh Lakish were willing to sit in the discomfort of dissent and even doubt because they knew that their arguments were in service of something bigger than themselves: *getting closer to truth.*

CHAPTER 25

Does the Artist Taint the Art?

Sometimes rabbis have to address an injustice that happened decades in the past, one that we assumed was long buried.

Composer and singer Rabbi Shlomo Carlebach could bring Jews to tears or a kind of rapture. There might be no more ubiquitous musical canon than Carlebach's; his compositions have become such classics that most Jews mistakenly believe they come from the "Old Country," or even "from Sinai"—a metaphorical designation for music that is *ancient*—traced to the ninth century, if not earlier.

Bearded, burly, and emotional in his delivery, Carlebach descended from rabbinic dynasties in pre-Holocaust Germany and was himself born in Berlin in 1925. When his family immigrated to New York, Carlebach studied in an Orthodox yeshiva in Williamsburg, Brooklyn, and went on to become an ordained rabbi, a teacher for the Lubavitch sect, and a famous defier of convention. He played his guitar in West Village clubs, where he befriended folk legends such as Pete Seeger and Bob Dylan. Unlike most Orthodox rabbis, he talked freely about God and went on to start a commune-like synagogue called the House of Love and Prayer. He would often open his services by saying, "Holy brothers and sisters, I have something really deep to tell you," and according to a 1998 *Lilith* magazine article, "he was known for his frequent hugs of men and women alike, and often said his hope was to hug every Jew—perhaps every person—on earth." Carlebach was also unafraid to collaborate across denominations and advocate for women's leadership. In 1989, when Women of the Wall challenged the men-only prayer space at Jerusalem's *kotel*, Carlebach was the only male rabbi present to support it. He was the first Orthodox rabbi to ordain women and encourage us to sing out loud in services, despite the traditional prohibition on female voices as potentially arousing. Carlebach was, in short, a charismatic spiritual leader with an avid following who, more than any other Orthodox rabbi of the twentieth century, championed feminist causes.

He was also accused of sexually molesting women and girls for decades, some as young as twelve years old.

I had heard whispers about Carlebach's behavior by the time I was a teenager, already at this point steeped in his music. There were rumors that he would end concerts by kissing everyone on the mouth or that his hugging might include unnecessary (and unwanted) rubbing. In 1998, a few years after Carlebach's death from a heart attack, *Lilith* published a well-sourced report with testimonials from dozens of women who alleged that Carlebach harassed and abused them. These women told stories of late-night inappropriate phone calls, fondling of breasts and genitalia, and rubbing and thrusting his body on theirs. I was horrified.

But I kept singing the music he'd composed.

I justified it by telling myself that great art often comes from complicated, flawed people, and I could separate the art from the artist. Rabbi Carlebach, whom I saw perform at Yale when I was a college student, would always correct the audience if they sang even *one note* of his melodies incorrectly. "If it were *my* melody, I wouldn't mind," he intoned, "but that is not how I received it from God."

Some might have heard those words as the declaration of an enlightened prophet or a pretentious narcissist. But I agreed with his fundamental point that he was merely the messenger. Carlebach had a divine gift for musical spirituality, which seemed to flow through him. So I continued singing his songs for decades, even as I learned more about his past. His music was bigger than the man.

But the reckoning of the #MeToo sexual abuse awareness movement, which took hold in 2017, shook me. There was renewed scrutiny about Carlebach's sins, including testimony from a woman whose mother described being molested by Carlebach in her youth. This woman, prompted by #MeToo to come forward decades after the assault, recounted what it felt like to walk into any synagogue, any Jewish camp, and to always hear the music of the man who victimized her mother. Carlebach's misconduct was widely known in the Jewish world, and through indifference and inaction, our community conveyed that it didn't care. I realized that I, too, was responsible—not only complicit by being silent but by continuing to perform his work.

And yet I still believe we should maintain a distinction between a work and its author; our culture would be impoverished if we banned the masterpieces of a Wagner or Picasso, despite their egregious personal flaws. Can't we condemn their actions even as we acknowledge their contribution?

In 2018, I brought this question to my synagogue's clergy team and board of trustees. The discussion went beyond Carlebach, as we studied Jewish and secular texts that explore whether positive works can be disconnected from problematic actors and how to respond to a religious leader who commits grievous sins.

I reached out to Neshama Carlebach, Shlomo Carlebach's daughter, whose career as a musician has been intimately connected with her father's legacy. Just one year earlier, Central had hosted Neshama for a Shabbat service, and she had become a friend. She'd wrestled personally with her father's legacy in a candid *Times of Israel* essay in January 2018, writing: "Our tradition teaches us that silence is consent, and I cannot remain silent in the face of so much pain. . . . I accept the fullness of who my father was, flaws and all. I am angry with him. And I refuse to see his faults as the totality of who he was."

In the end, my Central team and I determined that our responsibility was to educate, not erase. We decided to take a one-year moratorium on singing any Carlebach melodies, while making sure to speak and teach about why. This was not to punish Carlebach or make amends for him; it was not our place to do either. We concluded that the survivors of his abuse deserved some response, a signal that we'd heard them. One year was not a magic number, but it marked a traditional mourning period. One year took us through an entire cycle of holidays and seasons without Carlebach.

That winter, I spoke about Central's decision in a sermon, then was asked to describe our thinking more fully in the Jewish publication *The Forward*. Soon after, many congregations reached out and said that they, too, had decided to shelve Carlebach music temporarily or indefinitely. I heard from the American Conference of Cantors, who asked me to discuss with them a possible movement-wide hiatus on Carlebach music.

One of the painful things I came to realize is that even measured, just decisions can create hurtful, unjust consequences. Neshama, whose career centered around singing her father's music across the country, was soon disinvited from a signature event at the Union for Reform Judaism

Biennial. Many synagogues and Jewish community centers canceled her appearances.

It troubled me that Rabbi Shlomo Carlebach's sins, which were finally being recognized by the Jewish community, would hurt yet another victim: his daughter—more collateral damage from his original abuse. While the Jewish world was grappling with its overdue reckoning, the wrong Carlebach was paying the price.

When the yearlong moratorium was up, we gradually reintroduced Carlebach's song "*Shiru L'Adonai*" into the Friday-night service. I received an agitated letter from a sexual abuse survivor (though not of Carlebach), who said that we should never allow his music to return, and I responded that a year without his melodies had changed us. We had discovered or written new songs and introduced young composers to our repertoire. Our services had been transformed because of this suspension. But we would not completely discard the music of the past. Judaism's charge to "renew our days as of old" means finding a path forward that remembers but does not delete or whitewash our history.

I received an email from Neshama soon after we brought back her father's music. "Can we talk?" she asked. We met in my office and she told me that this year of enforced "silence" from the stage had spurred her to find her own voice, separate from that of her father. She'd produced an album of music that was entirely new, rather than rooted in her father's work. She asked if she could sing a piece for me.

I close my eyes so I can see all that can be
We will rise, I do believe

By the time she'd finished her song, we were both crying. I committed to help bring her voice back into the Jewish world. While I had led the way on a break from Rabbi Carlebach's music in the past, I also wanted to lead the way in supporting Neshama's music in the future. I invited Neshama to return to our bimah to speak and to sing.

"A year and a half ago," I addressed the congregation, "Central Synagogue made the decision to take a one-year moratorium on singing the music of Shlomo Carlebach. We did it to send a message to those many women who had come forward, to say that we'd heard them and they deserved a response from the Jewish community. What we never intended was the harm that this brought to Rabbi Carlebach's daughter, Neshama. And this is why I wanted to invite Neshama back to Central Synagogue tonight. Neshama, you stand on your own."

She sang gorgeously, soulfully. It wasn't closure, but it felt like a *tikkun*, a repair.

Some people have asked, "Why would we ever bring back Rabbi Carlebach's music?" I answer that we do it because I think his music has a life and a memory that is far beyond him. We still sing Carlebach because I believe we can restore the divine sparks that reside in broken vessels.

Gibor
HERO

When I was a kid in religious school, we glorified King David—a simple shepherd and gifted musician turned king of Israel. Young David vanquished the giant Goliath with courage and wit. He brought the divided Northern Kingdom and the Kingdom of Judah into one united monarchy and established Jerusalem as our Holy Capitol. I grew up loving a King David ditty with accompanying hand jive that ended: *Chai, chai, v'kayam!* "Long, long may he live!"

But then I studied the Hebrew Bible—the parts they don't include in the children's illustrated versions—and the perfect story took a terrible turn. I learned that this icon of the Jewish people lusted after a married woman, Bathsheba, abused his power in order to sleep with her, and then deliberately sent her husband, Uriah, to the front lines to be killed.

How many times have our heroes turned out to be deeply flawed human beings? How many times have we had to wake up to the hard lesson that no story is just one story—that there can be those who do incredible good and also monstrous harm? Both can reside within a single person.

I saw this firsthand in 2021, when a past congregant accused a former Central rabbi—beloved and brilliant—of "taking advantage of me sexually." Because these allegations concerned events that were forty years old, because there had been *some* redress by the Central Conference of American Rabbis twenty years earlier, my first response, I'm not proud to say, was somewhat dismissive, protective of the synagogue. Then the former member introduced me to another survivor of his abuse, who revealed that her romantic relationship with the rabbi began when she was only fifteen years old. I knew then that any worries for the synagogue's reputation paled in comparison to the moral breach of ignoring these transgressions.

With the support of my board president and executive director, the only others who knew of the conversations, we embarked on a thorough, independent investigation, and indeed the law firm we hired delivered a disturbing verdict: The rabbi had engaged in multiple counts of predatory sexual behavior, including sexual contact with a minor. I knew we needed to tell the congregation, despite those who insisted the rabbi was too old and infirm to weather the inevitable storm. Staying silent would only retraumatize his survivors.

Our tradition is clear about teshuvah: If you harm someone, you must apologize to them directly; it is not enough to ask forgiveness of God. The victims made it clear this rabbi never made teshuvah with them, even though he claimed he did his repentance. And they felt an exhalation when we finally aired the truth. We chose to leave his photograph on the wall among those of Central's other past Senior Rabbis, so as not to erase him from our history, but underneath the frame, a plaque explains that he was expelled from the Reform Movement's rabbinic body and what our outside investigation found.

Time and again, towering figures who exemplify compelling leadership also commit moral crimes. But do we take down every statue and painting? Erase them from our history books? Expunge whatever they taught or built in light of the sins we've discovered?

Even King David was not excused. In the Psalms, David reckons with the gravity of his transgressions—we learn of his self-loathing, remorse, and humility. He repents, but God nevertheless metes out punishment: David is not granted a chance to build the Temple in Jerusalem, his most desired legacy. He has too much blood on his hands. Our tradition's message is unequivocal: There must be a price for harm.

In a later Talmudic text (Sanhedrin 107a), King David bargains with God for forgiveness, first asking for atonement over unintentional sins, then for sins done in private, and finally for his transgressions of adultery and murder. In verse after verse, David owns up to his offense, repents, and repeatedly begs, "Please forgive me."

For each of David's sins, including the worst of them, God responds, "These are forgiven." Our tradition offers us a merciful God.

But then David asks God to leave out his gravest sins from the history books, essentially saying, "Can you please just not put that part in the Bible?"

God draws the line. "*That* I cannot do." In our tradition, we may forgive, but there is no forgetting.

It's not enough just to apologize. But once a person repents, we should not erase or discard that human being forever. Despite the current movement to tear down any traces of leaders who bear the stain of past sins, our tradition says it

is incumbent upon us to remember all of their actions—
not just their worst.

We call a hero a *gibor* in Hebrew, but Judaism does not
offer us the flawless heroes we crave. *Gibor* derives from
the root *gever,* which simply means "man," affirming that
even the heroes we elevate are merely human.

CHAPTER 26

Pandemic 2020

I was scheduled to begin my four-month sabbatical on March 22, 2020.

The concept of sabbatical was born in the Hebrew Bible—Leviticus 25—where God insists on a *shmita* year, a "year of release" for the land and its workers, every seven years. Given its religious origin, many rabbis earn and receive sabbaticals. I had taken one leave of absence in 2010, two months long. I was giddy with what I had planned for this time: to explore and learn *lishmah*—"for its own sake"—which included learning with a cohort of rabbis at the Hartman Institute in Jerusalem, joining an improv comedy class, training for a triathlon, and traveling.

But a week before my respite was scheduled to begin, the global Covid quarantine plunged the whole world into an involuntary sabbatical, an unplanned cessation of normal life. Of course, I no longer felt comfortable taking a work recess. My college-aged son moved back home, we pivoted at Central to virtual engagement for everything, and I tried to figure out how to maintain a cohesive community from an unprecedented distance.

I will never forget the first time I tried to create "Sabbath" in lockdown.

My family had temporarily escaped the city to a Connecticut home graciously offered by a congregant, and I set up a makeshift Zoom "sanctuary" in the peaceful wood-beamed living room. Built in 1786, the house had great charm but few electrical outlets. I positioned myself at a card table near the window and stretched two extension cords to the far end of the room in order to plug everything in.

The Zoom viewers saw a serene Sabbath tableau. Little did they know that behind me was a green screen projecting a picture of the living room window, a ring light shining brightly in my face, a table jerry-rigged with three large artbooks to raise my laptop, seven more artbooks to construct a platform for my Shabbat candles and challah plate—all crowded together to put every ritual object in view and approximate a tranquil atmosphere.

Even with all the comforting signposts of the weekly holiday, I felt lonely during that first Friday service. My family was in the house but not in the same room, in order to cut down on extraneous noise and the chance that they might mischievously make me laugh. They watched and prayed via livestream on a large television in the basement den. I interacted with my fellow clergy in their boxes on my screen, but they were miles away in their own makeshift "studios," striving to connect through technology to our scattered congregants, each in their own quarantine bubble. Never had leading services felt so challenging. I hadn't realized how much I'd relied on the energy that comes back from the people in the pews each Friday night. But my body knew it immediately, as I sweated through a service held together with Scotch tape.

As we made our way to the Kaddish prayer, which always marks the end, I reached for the challah to make a final blessing and started to feel strangely warm. This heat wasn't just sweat. My tallis was on fire. The candles had ignited its fringes. Of course this was all streamed live as I yelped, yanked off my prayer shawl, and put out the flames with an art-book. *Shabbat Shalom!*

So much for my first peaceful Sabbath in quarantine.

Despite that clumsy start, we began to get the hang of virtual Shabbat and were soon broadcasting from the sanctuary, where a trio of clergy—all safely distanced on the bimah—streamed services from an empty synagogue out to the world. Our online Shabbat community grew exponentially as newcomers became "regulars" and word of mouth led Jews around the world to our livestream. This resulted in a reimagined congregation that had never really existed in Jewish history, one that spanned time zones, denominations, and native languages. In a strange, poignant way, the pandemic served as a unifier and equalizer; suddenly, the Jewish people not only had a common history and text but a global shared experience in real time.

Offering our usual pastoral attention was more challenging. When we faced our first Covid death—a relatively young father died alone in a hospital—his family was anguished at being prohibited from visiting their loved one. They could only say goodbye via FaceTime as he took his last breath. Judaism provides a road map for death that includes bedside confessional, immediate funeral, burial, and shiva gathering. But how could the family mourn when all of this was now impossible in person?

While this man's wife and children were dealing with a delayed autopsy and their inability to gather with their community to mourn, I suggested we meet on Zoom to pay tribute and share memories. The family initially resisted, but after gentle encouragement, Central created its first virtual funeral.

Awkward as it initially felt, the gathering proved to have an unexpected, powerful intimacy: seeing the faces of mourners and friends up close on the computer or iPad; reading the chat function in real time as it filled with expressions of affection and support; creating an online guestbook of condolence and remembrance. The assembly was larger than it would have been in person, given how immediate burials often prevent out-of-town friends and family from attending.

Throughout April and May 2020, we saw three times the number of deaths in a typical two-month period. And while not all were clearly Covid-related, many were connected to the pandemic, including deaths of those who delayed medical attention because the hospital felt risky, or of solitary elderly members who could not survive the isolation.

Despite the grim lockdown climate, there was also a spirit of resilience in our synagogue community and our city, along with a strong impulse to connect. Volunteers signed up to call homebound congregants. Our director of youth education, Rabbi Rebecca Rosenthal, reimagined online learning in a way that preserved the content and the fun. My colleague Cantor Dan Mutlu, a magnificent talent, joined with his wife, Nina, an accomplished violinist, and their three musical children to perform song-filled skits on Facebook Live, Rabbi Ari Lorge taught pickling—a passion of his—on a humorous Zoom talk show called *What's the Dill?*, and Rabbi Mo Salth led Shabbat worshipers in New York City's seven p.m. tribute to essential workers, banging pots out his window. Social media was full of cantors singing elaborate Zoom tributes, inventive virtual seders, and sermons from around the world, lifting up scared, disconnected people.

I took comfort in connecting virtually with as many members as possible, but that attentiveness was now taxing me differently than usual. The need was simply greater, and the pressure not to leave anyone untouched was keeping me awake at night. I had to find a way to refuel if I was going to keep ministering remotely.

Meditation had been my on-again, off-again discipline for the last decade; I'd studied with teachers through the Institute for Jewish Spirituality years before, but never made daily practice a priority. During Covid, it occurred to me that I could stay tethered to my community while staying accountable to my own practice by leading a morning meditation every day during lockdown. If others were waiting to join me on a scheduled morning call, I wouldn't be able to skip it.

Many years earlier, I had offered a three-part meditation series at Central. I was skeptical that type-A New Yorkers would make "doing nothing" a priority. Indeed, only eight people attended the first session, and by the last, a mere three remained. So I did not have high expectations for how many would call in for an eight thirty a.m. phone meditation during the pandemic, but felt committed nonetheless.

To my surprise, more than 150 people showed up for the first morning. Within a few weeks, more than four hundred people joined me every single day for ten minutes of spiritual reflection, storytelling, or Jewish textual teaching, followed by twenty minutes of sitting together in silence. People wanted to be together, even virtually. I could not believe the instant community that took hold.

Since the format was audio only and early in the morning, I often led meditation in my pajamas with a cup of coffee in hand. I was more candid in my prepared reflections than I'd ever been from the bimah. This daily "meditation circle" began to feel like a close group of friends—my confessional space for the daily struggles, vulnerabilities, and small triumphs of spirit.

This six-month experiment changed my spiritual practice. I started out insecure about my own ability to offer "mindfulness" guidance, feeling like an imposter, and in the first weeks quoted heavily from the words of my own teachers, Rabbi Sheila Petz Weinberg, Sharon Salzberg, and

Sylvia Boorstein. But as the weeks progressed, the daily silence helped me find a more personal voice. When it came to our ancient texts, they showed themselves more than capable of meeting this modern moment, offering wisdom for living in exile and displacement, for noticing and slowing down, for finding big blessings in tiny miracles.

Our daily meditation group counted the Omer together—the traditional practice of marking the forty-nine days between Passover and Shavuot. Numbering our days during the quarantine felt newly significant: Even if the days seemed monotonous, blurred together, we were charged to make each one count. We appreciated the opening of buds in April and expressed gratitude for the simple chance to notice them when so many others could not. We mourned the death of George Floyd after his murder in May 2020, and I spoke of teshuvah—"repentance"—and how we reckon with the ongoing work of addressing the scourge of racism that our society had not overcome.

Ironically, my postponed sabbatical helped teach me the lessons of the biblical *shmita*: how this pause from normal life's productivity allows for growth, as I stumbled to find a meditation teacher's voice, tried to maintain a regular writing practice, and forged a greater nearness to so many congregants. This fallow field of the quarantine was still bearing fruit, and I realized I could feel nourished and anchored in a period of relative scarcity and uncertainty.

Eight months after the original start date, I did finally reschedule my sabbatical. I took it in the middle of November 2021, still deep in the days of masks, virtual classes, and limited travel. My four sabbatical months, originally scheduled with abundant activity, now stretched before me with a gaping vacancy that filled me with a little dread. But our communal, pandemic-induced "sabbatical" had taught me to trust in the possibility of quiet, space, release, and unexpected connection.

Shabbat
REST

As a child on a family road trip down the Pacific Coast Highway, I visited the bizarre Winchester Mystery House in San Jose, California. In building this home, Sarah Winchester aimed to create a sanctuary away from the demons that had haunted her since the deaths of her infant daughter and husband. So in 1886, she began obsessively building without an architect, hiring carpenters to work in shifts every hour around the clock for thirty-eight years, until the day she died. Her original eight-room home grew and grew, haphazardly, until it was a sprawling palace covering six acres, with 160 rooms, two thousand doors, and forty-seven staircases, many leading nowhere.

Winchester never paused long enough to enjoy being in what she created, nor to ponder its purpose. Without a plan, she ended up with a monstrous, outlandish tourist attraction rather than the sanctuary she'd envisioned.

Obviously, most would never build a home that way. Yet the Winchester House could serve as a metaphor for how we build our lives these days. We're relentlessly adding, striving, renovating, and improving our careers, our bodies, our minds. We do this work continuously, obsessively, often haphazardly.

But if you have no blueprint, if you do not stop to reflect on the ultimate purpose of all the construction, you can wake up one day and realize you've built a life without a soul.

Rabbi Abraham Joshua Heschel in his seminal book *The Sabbath* articulates how the Sabbath serves as this map within Judaism's architecture of time.

Instead of measuring hours by productivity ("Time is money!"), Judaism maintains that not all time is created equal. Instead, time is divided into two distinct categories: *kodesh* and *chol*, "sacred" and "ordinary."

In ordinary time, you build your homes, your careers, your families, your communities.

But on the Sabbath, you build your palace *in time*—your structure for sanctifying moments. Shabbat is a radical and beautiful innovation that our ancestors protected and handed down. We are not meant to strive day in and day out. Sacred time is designed to help you see yourself and the world around you as whole, enough, perfect as is. Not focusing on the deficits and fractures but the gifts and blessings. Sacred time is set aside to just *be*.

Neither Jacob nor I grew up keeping a traditional Sabbath with the suspension of electronics, travel, or shopping. But when we started a family, we decided to follow these Shabbat rules and found them surprisingly liberating. Without television, phones, computers, or the ability to pretty much do anything "useful," we spent—and continue to spend—Saturday afternoons at leisurely lunches with friends or playing board games, reading on the couch, or taking the time-honored Shabbos *schluff* (nap).

On one particularly lazy Saturday afternoon, I was lying on the bed reading Harry Potter to my son Eli, then six. As I finished a chapter and put the book down, he nestled his head into my shoulder, looked up at me, and sighed. "Mom, this is the point of life."

It took my breath away. *Yes, Eli, this is the point of life.*

It's those sacred moments when you're not reaching for anything else. When you allow yourself to feel there is absolutely nothing missing. When you feel so full, so present, that the moment is entirely self-contained, timeless, good enough. Complete.

You don't have to believe in God to know that this state of being is holy. But Shabbat doesn't just happen. Ironically, rest requires effort—a conscious letting go of productivity and self-improvement, of noise and drive. We must release the desire for more.

It's important to create, build, renovate, and improve. But one day a week it's also important to stop. Pause. Rest. Reboot. Be together with loved ones or be quiet with yourself. Try to feel at peace with where you are *in this very moment*, without trying to alter or improve a thing.

Construct your sanctuary in time.

It is the point of life.

CHAPTER 27

Reckoning with Race

After the murder of George Floyd in the summer of 2020, I was highly attuned to the racial reckoning happening not just in America but also in my own Jewish community. For the first time, I decided to share my own story in a sermon; it began with an anecdote from decades ago.

Are you Jewish?

Are you Jewish?

Are you Jewish?

When I was in college, the Chabad Lubavitchers, an ultra-Orthodox religious sect, would park their Mitzvah Tank, a portable outreach center made from a retrofitted U-Haul truck, at the corner of High and Elm Streets, outside the post office, and pose this question repeatedly, like a jingle, to many students passing by. In the early nineties, Yale was about 25 percent Jewish, so asking "Are you Jewish?" was like spotting fish at an aquarium. Most of my Jewish friends were accosted multiple times a day.

But *not one time* in four years did they ever ask me.

I would have liked the free Shabbat candles they were handing out.

Or to sit in their makeshift sukkah in the back of their Mitzvah Tank. Or to have been acknowledged, even once, as a member of the Tribe.

Maybe I should have been relieved that they didn't approach me. Because growing up, whenever I entered a new Jewish setting, I could hardly escape the question "YOU'RE Jewish?"

My grandmother Phreda, knowing the challenges I felt to my Jewish identity, bought me a sterling-silver necklace with a *Chai*—two Hebrew letters that spell the word for "life"—when I was ten. Anytime I walked into a new Jewish community, I'd put the chain around my neck to announce myself as a Jew. I wore it like a talisman to ward off questions, but it only seemed to elicit them.

"Who gave you her necklace?" a boy asked me at Jewish summer camp.

"Do you know what *Chai* means?" another inquired at a youth group convention.

"Why are you wearing that?" queried an Israeli student I met during my high school summer program.

It was exhausting.

Over the decades, the questions finally stopped coming. I had reached a level of visibility that if I walked into a Jewish community, people recognized me as a rabbi. Younger Jews of color would tell me that I had helped them find their place; I felt so grateful and relieved. Twenty years earlier I had joined the board of the Multiracial Jewish Network, an affinity space for Jews of color who felt marginalized elsewhere. Our goal was to transform the mainstream Jewish community so that our existence as an organization would become unnecessary. I thought that moment had arrived.

But as I entered my seventh year as senior rabbi, in the midst of a surreal global pandemic and widespread racial protests, I began hearing from Jews of Color at Central.

An email from a Black congregant, Robert, was both disturbing and arresting. "On a weekly basis," he wrote, "this Jewish community makes me feel like an outsider."

The first time he stepped into our synagogue, Robert added, he had been followed inside and tracked by a security guard. He almost didn't return after that.

He described how regulars would approach him every single Sabbath service, asking:

"How did you come to be here?"

"What neighborhood are you from?"

"*Are you Jewish?*"

Robert's email reopened an old wound.

How could I, as a Jewish woman of color, be leading a synagogue that was perpetuating some of the same narrow thinking and behavior that had almost driven me from the Jewish community? I'd expected to give a High Holiday sermon that year about the national discourse on race, but I realized that I had to clean my own house first.

So I wrote what was perhaps my most personal Yom Kippur address, in which I shared what it was like to be assumed a stranger in Jewish settings all my life. And I was determined to debunk the notion of Judaism as a race.

First I wanted to convey that the notion of Judaism as a "race" originated from those who used it to oppress us. The earliest reference to the Israelite people as akin to a race is made by the biblical Pharaoh in Egypt, who spoke in racialized language to justify the enslavement of the Hebrews and the killing of their firstborns.

The first historical articulation of Judaism as a race was during the fifteenth-century Spanish Inquisition. The Inquisitors insisted that even those Jews who converted to Christianity still possessed a polluted, impure Jewish bloodline. Later, in an effort to dehumanize Jews, the Nazis used pseudoscience to claim that Jews had identifiable racial features and an innate propensity toward certain behaviors and beliefs. This idea of Judaism as a "race" is a construct—created by our enemies—to help justify and fuel countless antisemitic tropes used against us throughout our history. And yet we Jews still hold tight to this idea of race: that we have immutable characteristics—a bloodline, "a look," a type—that make us what we are.

But Jews have never been just one color or cluster of chromosomes. When the Torah first calls us a "Nation"—when we come out of Egypt— we are described as an *erev rav*, a "mixed multitude." When we were exiled from Israel over two thousand years ago, we spread out to every imaginable corner of the world, from India to Ethiopia. The majority of Jews in Israel today are not Ashkenazi Jews of European descent but Jews of Color from Middle Eastern, African, and Asian countries.

And even in America, the assumption of Jews as "white people" is increasingly outdated. In 2019, the first Jewish population study to measure Jews of Color in America found that they represent at least 12 to 15 percent of American Jews. That means that out of approximately 7.5 million Jews, about a million are Jews of Color. Some descend from ancient Jewish communities in Iraq, Morocco, and Libya; some were born of interracial unions; some entered through transracial adoption; and some became Jews by Choice. But until the American Jewish community rethinks our tribal, racial notion of Jewish peoplehood, most will remain invisible to the affiliated Jewish community, avoiding synagogues, JCCs, and other Jewish cohort groups. They, too, often feel their Jewishness questioned or diminished in these settings.

Heredity is important and meaningful. It is powerful to imagine oneself in an ancestral line of Jews that goes all the way back to Sinai. But it is time, once and for all, to stop seeing Jewish Peoplehood as a race.

Instead, we need to see each other as part of the same family—one that can come through birth, yes, but also adoption, conversion, or sacred pledge, like a wedding couple who becomes family through vows. We Jews are a family connected by something stronger than blood; we are bound by our covenant with God, by an ancient call to help repair the world. Every Jew who feels responsible to this covenantal relationship should be counted as an equal.

I concluded my sermon with a final anecdote of hope. "A few years ago, as I was walking on the Upper West Side, on Broadway, there was a mitzvah tank parked on the corner. I saw a boy, not yet bar mitzvah age, in a black hat and suit. But as I hurried past, he stepped right in front of me, looked me straight in the eye, and asked, 'Are you Jewish?'

"I stopped in my tracks. *He was seriously asking me.* I had to hold myself back from my urge to embrace the boy.

"'YES!' I said excitedly. 'Yes, I AM JEWISH! Thank you *very much!*'

"The young boy, confused by my passionate response, shrugged his shoulders and offered me a box of candles. 'Happy Hanukkah,' he said as he walked away.

"The boy thought nothing of it, but I've replayed that moment many times since. It was my Hanukkah miracle. He gave me a taste of a Jewish Peoplehood that was beyond race, where the color of my skin and the shape of my features were no longer the markers of my authenticity. In that young Chasid's question was a revolutionary assumption, one that could truly change the world: He could see me and imagine that we were part of the same family."

The overwhelming response to my Yom Kippur sermon surprised me. It went viral—by sermon standards, anyway. I received hundreds of emails and calls from Jews of Color saying that Robert's story and mine captured their own.

The sermon was graciously commended by the Jewish press; *The Forward* described it as "one of the year's important primary texts." Several college professors added it to their Jewish studies syllabi. I was even stopped by a saleswoman at Nordstrom who recognized me; her manager had asked their entire team to view the sermon as part of their racial sensitivity training. It was clear that the feeling of being the stranger was not just true for Jews of Color. There were many Ashkenazi Jews for whom the message also struck a chord. An older gay man said he felt marginalized in the Jewish community. A young Jew spoke in a quivering voice about her lack of faith in God, fearing this put her outside the tent. Another woman described how her family could not afford synagogue dues and felt unwelcome. And a woman without children felt that Judaism didn't value her presence without kids.

The intermittent isolation that makes us feel "the stranger" was widely shared. I knew this was how I'd experienced the Jewish community for much of my life, but I could not have imagined how many Jews, even those with two Jewish parents, felt like a stranger for one reason or another. So many of them were navigating multiple, seemingly competing identities: Black and Jewish, Orthodox and feminist, gay and observant. Speaking truthfully out loud for the first time about the realities of being a Korean Jewish female rabbi, I had clearly touched a nerve: We can be made to feel like an interloper even in the places we consider "home."

In the crucial American race conversation, I have seen that this feeling of separateness and exclusion extends far beyond the Jewish community. Every minority group can talk about how they have felt ignored, judged, or diminished. We all watched how the Black community and its allies organized after George Floyd's murder. How the Asian community, culturally trained to keep our heads down, began speaking up after the pandemic stoked virulent anti-Asian hate. I understand for the first time how even white men in America are feeling abandoned, denigrated, and disregarded, shamed for the sins of the nation's forefathers, disadvantaged in the job market, assumed to have the worst traits of "privilege."

I wonder how, in this time of unprecedented loneliness and fracture, our own feelings of *outsiderness* could spur empathy rather than anger, to bring us nearer to each other rather than drive us further to our corners. If we recognize that *every one of us* carries the heart of the stranger, maybe we'll finally grasp that our need for belonging is the starting point for a common humanity.

Erev Rav
MIXED MULTITUDE

The word "race" only came into modern usage in the nineteenth century. But the practice of categorizing groups in order to subjugate them is an ancient practice.

In fact, this is exactly what the Pharaoh did in Exodus, when he is the first to call the Hebrews *Am B'nei Yisrael*—the nation of the children of Israel—a designation that casts the Israelites as a racial bloodline. Threatened by how numerous the Israelites had become, he stoked their fears, railing, "Those people will outnumber Egyptians and rise against us!" Pharaoh's message has been repeated by Israel's enemies through the centuries: "Jews will not replace us."

Race is a construct, but *racism*, on the other hand, is all too real. And yet many Jews still cling to this idea of Jewishness as a race, that there is a genetic blueprint, "a look," that makes us what we are.

In response to my sermon on race, I received variations of this retort: "Rabbi, you say Judaism is not a race, but I took a 23andMe ancestry test and it says my DNA is 99.9 percent Ashkenazi."

Maybe so. But "Ashkenazi" only represents *one strand* of the Jewish people. It would not match the genetics of Jews who came from thousand-year-old communities in Iraq or Yemen. Our diversity is not only a product of centuries of exile but originates with our birth as a nation coming out of Egypt.

After God inflicts the worst plagues on Egypt, Pharaoh finally relents and lets the Israelites go. The text says that six hundred thousand of them left. But then the next verse says *"V'gam erev rav alah."* "Moreover, a mixed multitude went up with them."

Who is this *erev rav*, this mixed multitude who joined the Israelites escaping oppression?

Rashi, the prominent medieval commentator, says that the *erev rav* was comprised of converts from different nations.

Ibn Ezra, a Spanish commentator of the Middle Ages, says something more radical: that the mixed multitude actually included Egyptians—the purported enemy—who fled alongside the Hebrew slaves.

In this pivotal origin story of the birth of our nation, the Torah makes clear that the Jews are not only a lineage of Israelites but rather an ethnic patchwork—including converts of all nations, even Egyptians!—who deeply suffered under Pharaoh's harsh and selfish leadership and who yearned for a new chapter and homeland.

Pharaoh wanted to cast our people as a racial tribe to subjugate us. But *Am Yisrael*, the nation of Israel, rejected that description and openly welcomed anyone who had the courage to flee oppression and seek liberation. We left enslavement as an *erev rav*, a beautiful mixed multitude: Israelites, converts, and anyone who reached for God's outstretched arm, or that of their neighbor, to walk hand in hand out of that narrow place into the Promised Land. Today as ever, we are Black, Brown, Asian, white, converted, adopted, and every combination of each. There is no such thing as purity or homogeneity. But we all share the memory of our enslavement and the yearning for freedom.

I think of America too as a mixed multitude. A country whose citizens do not share a single cultural or ethnic origin but are bound by a striving for liberty, justice, and the pursuit of happiness for all its citizens. Nationhood should not be about race, a contrived hierarchy of value based on skin color, but rather on a pledge of allegiance to our highest ideals.

CHAPTER 28

"He Has a Gun"

I prefer not to use the phone on Shabbat, but my father had contracted Covid and my mother was worried for his health; I needed to check in on them.

While listening to my father describe his ailments and how my seventy-nine-year-old mom was taking breaks from caretaking by sledding at warp speed down their snowy, steep Tacoma hill (she actually does this), I received an incoming call from a Texas number I didn't recognize. At first I decided to ignore it.

My phone transcribes the first part of any voice message, and the words I saw unspooling were hard to believe: *Rabbi. Gunman. Says he has bombs.*

Now distracted, I quickly signed off with my parents and listened to the full voicemail message. A mature voice spoke calmly: "This is Rabbi Charlie Cytron-Walker. I am the rabbi of Beth Israel in Colleyville, Texas. This is not a joke. There is an actual gunman here and he wants to speak to you. Will you please call us back at this number? This is not a joke."

I did not know the rabbi, but a quick Google search revealed that he had graduated from HUC's seminary just five years after I did and was indeed leading a congregation in Colleyville. I checked the news, but there was nothing about trouble at a Dallas-area synagogue.

I called Central Synagogue's head of security and he instructed me to call the number to find out more. My husband stood beside me as a second set of ears.

On the third try, someone picked up. "Hello, this is Rabbi Charlie Cytron-Walker."

"This is Angela Buchdahl. *Are you okay?*" I asked, feeling somewhat stupid for even asking the question.

"*Not really*," he said in measured tones. "There is a gunman here holding four of us hostage. He wants to talk to you. Would you please speak with him?"

I would learn later that this man, a forty-four-year-old British citizen, had arrived at the temple on a chilly Saturday morning and knocked on the locked glass door. Rabbi Cytron-Walker let him in and offered him a cup of tea and a seat in the sanctuary. When the rabbi started the Shabbat service and turned his back to the pews, he heard the click of a gun behind him.

Now this gunman was on the phone with me. In an agitated voice, he explained that he was originally from Pakistan. He had traveled from England all the way to Texas, on a mission he was convinced I alone could help him fulfill.

"You are an influential rabbi. I know you run a large synagogue in New York, so that gives you connections. You have a lot of power; I saw you in a picture with President Obama. I see you also play guitar and sing." He added, "What I need requires a woman's touch."

I looked at my husband, unnerved by the random collection of facts this dangerous stranger had researched.

He continued, "I need you to use your influence and do as I say. And you should know: *I love death more than you love life*. Do you hear that?" I recoiled at this nihilistic declaration, which he repeated several more times throughout the conversation.

"I have a backpack with bombs that could blow up the synagogue," he warned me. "There are many more bombs in Brooklyn and New York City that I could detonate and hurt a lot of people." By this point my husband had dialed 911 on his own phone to have them listen in on our call. "But if you do exactly as I say, no one needs to get hurt," he said. "Do you understand?" I answered yes, hoping I could do what he was about to ask of me.

"There is a federal facility about twenty minutes from here," he said. "There is a prisoner there, Dr. Aafia Siddiqui. She is my sister, and she was unfairly framed. She has been sitting in federal prison for eighteen years—suffering, raped. You, as a woman, can understand why she needs to get out. You need to use your connections, make some phone calls, and get her out of that prison and bring her here to the synagogue. It's only twenty minutes away. You have one hour to get this done. Do you understand?"

"Yes. I will do this right away," I lied, my heart sinking. I knew there was absolutely no way a federal prison would release anyone. I would not be able to deliver on his singular demand, but I wanted him to believe that I could.

"You don't want any of these nice people to be hurt, right?" he continued. "They have children. Jeff, do you have kids?" he called out. I heard a voice in the background say, "Yes, I have children." My eyes filled with tears as I started imagining the panic and devastation of the children and families of these four men, captive to this madman's delusions of Jewish power.

He turned his attention back to me. "You bring my sister here to the synagogue, then nobody has to get hurt. You have one hour."

Blood pounded in my head and I found it hard to breathe. After hanging up, I turned my attention to the 911 dispatcher, whom Jacob had kept on the line. At some point Jacob had been transferred from New York's 911 control center to one in Colleyville.

The 911 representative in Colleyville sounded a little overwhelmed, admitting there were only four dispatchers at their local site—needless to say, "hostage-taking-by-terrorist" was not part of their usual protocol. Since the Shabbat service at the Colleyville synagogue had been livestreamed, people from the community had already flooded the line with frantic calls about a gunman. But this dispatcher had heard the terrorist's demands through my speakerphone—the only outside call he made—and she asked that I stay on the line and wait for the FBI hostage negotiation team to get on the line. Never had soothing hold music felt more incongruous.

While I waited, I learned that Aafia Siddiqui was one of the most notorious female terrorists on American soil, known to prosecutors as "Lady Al-Qaeda." She had become a radical cause célèbre in Islamic extremist circles; both the Islamic State and the Taliban had offered to trade American prisoners in exchange for Siddiqui's release. Siddiqui was indeed being held in a federal facility just a few miles from the Texas synagogue, but she was not really the gunman's sister. In fact, when the FBI called her in the midst of this crisis, she refused to speak with him at all.

While I was still on hold, another call came in from the gunman in Texas.

It had been almost an hour. I was terrified to explain to him that I had not been successful. I told the 911 dispatcher that the terrorist had called me again. "Why don't you call him back?" she suggested in a cheery Texas accent. "All four of us here know what's going on, so you can just call any one of us when you're done." I was pretty certain that this was not what the FBI would have suggested. I'd seen the movies: Where was the phalanx of federal agents with headsets and a roomful of audio equipment? But I dialed the number back. The gunman didn't waste any time: "What progress have you made?"

I tried to assure him that I had called all of the right people, that we were taking concrete steps, and that he should not do anything rash. I desperately wanted to buy more time, so I confided that I didn't have as much influence as he thought. "Nonsense," he countered. "Every Jew has influence, and *you* definitely do."

Every Jew has influence. Assertions about Jews running the world have long been a hallmark of antisemitic conspiracy theory. Now this ugly trope was being hurled at me while four lives hung in the balance.

"I am running out of patience," he snapped. "And you are running out of time." He hung up.

I have never simultaneously felt so responsible and so powerless. I could not bear the thought that my own misstep might trigger the worst. I called the dispatcher back and relayed the second call with the gunman. By now it was one p.m. When I hung up, I sobbed.

I was planning to spend Shabbat lunch with friends as we usually do, and while this was a most unusual morning, remaining at home felt too claustrophobic. So I decided to stick to my plans and head across town with Jacob, knowing I could stay in touch with law enforcement on my cell phone. I also felt, maybe irrationally, that it was a small way to defy this dangerous terrorist: We would maintain our Jewish ritual even as he tried to stop us.

When I arrived at my friends' table they could see immediately that something was wrong. As I told them of my surreal conversations, everyone was stunned and supportive. It wasn't until three-thirty that the FBI called me back and wanted to know my whereabouts. Eight grim-faced officers from the FBI and NYPD descended on my friends' apartment. I replayed the original voicemail messages and shared the two conversations with as much detail as I could recall.

They were satisfied with how I had answered the calls but ordered me not to pick up the phone if the gunman called again. The law enforcement team said they would stay with me until the situation was resolved, and together we returned to my apartment across town. The night wore on with no word about the status of the hostages. I kept imagining their families' terror and could already envision the heartbreaking headlines.

But then, miraculously, at around ten thirty p.m., we learned from Texas governor Greg Abbott's Twitter account that the hostages were free. The gunman was dead.

I cried again—my entire body shaking with relief.

In the days after the hostage standoff, I listened to Rabbi Cytron-Walker's many media interviews and was impressed and inspired by his unflagging equilibrium, clarity, and generosity of heart. He explained the rudimentary but crucial method he and his congregants had used to escape: when the gunman took his finger off the trigger, the rabbi threw a chair at him and yelled for the hostages to run—and they all did.

But as admiring as I was of the rabbi, I felt sickened by what he'd had to face. Angry that one person with a firearm could jeopardize a synagogue and four congregants who had simply come to worship. Scared, for the first time, for all clergy's safety, including my own. Protective of my synagogue. Outraged at the explosion of antisemitic attacks all over the world.

Rabbi Cytron-Walker urged Jewish institutions to seek the training he and his congregation had received only months before, which had made all the difference. He rejected any suggestion that he should have refused to welcome the unknown visitor, citing the Jewish mandate to "welcome the stranger because we were once strangers" ourselves. He insisted that we not use this incident to justify demonizing the outsider. But he was saddened and angry that the gunman took advantage of his hospitality and that now synagogues would have to increase security and prepare for the worst.

My own team at Central was understandably shaken. The lay leadership insisted I be escorted home by a guard as I walked the six blocks from the sanctuary to my apartment building. I felt silly but also reassured.

I kept hearing the gunman's voice in my head at night and asking myself whether I could have done more to speed the hostages' release and end their terrifying ordeal. I kept returning to the chilling realization that the gunman had been prepared to die: *"I love death more than you love life."*

He was right that Jews *do* prize life over all else. *Pikuach nefesh* is also translated as "saving a soul." Jewish law's highest priority is the preservation of human life, and this trumps any other religious rule.

It might sound obvious that nothing is more sacred than life, until you hear the voice of someone who does not believe that. How do you persuade, or even reason with, someone who does not value his next breath?

I thought about Rabbi Cytron-Walker's courage, what it must have been like to call his kids during the standoff and hear the fear in their young voices, how he had to hold up his Colleyville congregation, a small community without resources for extra security. He had literally put his life on the line to save his fellow congregants, and now there were rabbis all over the country wondering if they would manage to do the same.

Rabbi Cytron-Walker was asked in an interview if he would ever go back to his synagogue. "Of course I am going back in the building," he replied. "This is what Jews do."

That is what Jews do. Have done. Will always do. *Choose life.*

Tikvah
HOPE

Taken from a sermon delivered on
January 21, 2022

When I sat down to write this sermon, I could not even begin.

And then I realized I simply needed to start with something that Jews have done for centuries, which is to offer a blessing:

Baruch atah, Adonai Eloheinu Melech HaOlam, Matir Asurim.

Blessed are You, Eternal God, who *frees the captive.*

You freed the captives.

Thank God.

The alternative was unimaginable.

And of course, it is not only God who deserves gratitude and praise for the freeing of the four held captive for eleven hours in a synagogue in Colleyville, Texas, last Saturday.

I am thanking and blessing Rabbi Charlie Cytron-Walker, who showed unearthly calm, unflagging humanity, and heroic courage in unthinkable circumstances.

And I bless the three other congregants, who are also my heroes—models of strength and selflessness when they were facing the possible end of their lives.

I am also grateful to Central's head of security, the NY Jewish community's security expert, law enforcement, and the FBI, for how seriously they took this crisis. And the many Jewish organizations who work to keep our community safe in ways we don't always see or acknowledge.

I wanted to begin with gratitude because that was the overwhelming emotion I felt when the siege was over.

But after that initial relief, I could not find words.

Because my secondary rush of feelings has been much harder to digest.

More ominous.

I knew I would be addressing you, my beloved community, and you would want and need words of comfort and hope from your rabbi.

But I do not have those words for you. Not yet.

I cannot assure you that this will not happen again.

And I do not have some neat pronouncement for how we will fight back the alarming, ugly surge of antisemitism.

I cannot tell you that I'm not replaying Rabbi Cytron-Walker's unfaltering voice on my cell.

"We have an actual gunman who is claiming to have bombs, and he wants to talk to you. This is not a joke."

Thank God this terrifying episode ended safely. But not simply.

And I remain deeply unsettled.

And if you are a Jew in America today and you are not feeling unsettled, you are not paying enough attention.

I am unsettled because the world has only the most simplistic understanding of antisemitism. And we saw how dangerous this age-old conspiracy theory can be.

I am unsettled because I saw firsthand that you cannot negotiate with a terrorist. And more and more people in our country and around the globe are captivated by terrifying, hateful ideologies, which they value more than their very lives.

I am unsettled because Rabbi Cytron-Walker's kindness and generosity was used against him. He opened his door to this man and gave him tea.

This rabbi welcomes the stranger, and this is his reward?

We have to protect ourselves and we cannot be naive.

But I also know that if we only build fortresses around our sanctuaries and our hearts, then hate wins.

I am unsettled because I heard the terrifying voice of radical extremism, filtered through the mind of a deranged person. Who was able to get a gun. And to hold four people—and an entire Jewish community—hostage to his terror.

And I think of the ripple effects, the countless resources we will spend to prevent it from happening again.

When the gunman called me the second time, he said, "I'm running out of patience. And you're running out of time."

I had already talked to the authorities. I knew there was nothing else I could do. But wait. And pray.

I mean *I really prayed*: a trembling, pleading prayer—the same words we sang tonight, and the same words I learned the rabbi uttered while being held captive:

Hashkiveinu Adonai Eloheinu, l'shalom.

V'haamideinu Malkeinu l'Chayyim.

"Help us lie down in peace, Adonai.

And to rise up again to life renewed."

You could say my prayer—all of our prayers—were answered.

The prayers of those four families and the congregation.

The prayers of a breathless worldwide Jewish community.

But we've emerged and now we are anxious. Angry. Frightened.

And I cannot tell you not to feel those things.

I am feeling them myself. And I don't quite know what to do next.

But I knew this is not where I could end this sermon. So I looked to our Torah portion for the week, *Parshat Yitro,* Jethro, and the message was just so pertinent it felt like God was winking at me.

Right there, the line jumped out: *Lo tu-chal a–seh–hu levadecha—* "You cannot do it alone."

This was Jethro's line to Moses, who was consumed under the weight of leading. But this message is for all of us.

Of course. None of us can do this alone.

I know that I could not have been on those calls on Saturday without my husband, Jacob, next to me and Rabbi Cytron-Walker's steady voice on the other side.

I know I felt lifted by all the notes and the love and care I felt from this community, my Central colleagues, my Hartman Institute rabbis, my friends.

I could not do this without all of you, showing up tonight, whether in this space or online.

You are showing up not just for Central but for Judaism.

You've shown up for fearlessness in the face of fear.

None of us can do this alone. Even as this pandemic has tested us and forced so many of us to be more alone than we ever thought we would be—our tradition keeps pushing us back into community and tells us we are not meant to do this only with other Jews.

It is important that the person who shares this essential wisdom—Jethro, Moses's father-in-law, is not Jewish. I saw every faith community show up for us last weekend. And I want to thank our interfaith clergy colleagues who showed up for us tonight—it is deeply meaningful and reassuring to us that you are here. We need to partner with people of every faith, and good faith, in the fight against antisemitism, racism, extremism, and hatred of every kind.

We cannot do it alone. And thank goodness we do not have to.

I began with one blessing, and I end with another, taken from Zechariah. The Reform Movement incorporated these prophetic words into the service on *Tisha B'av*—the day that commemorates some of the most tragic episodes in Jewish history.

Baruch Atah Adonai, Eloheinu Melech HaOlam Asher Asanu Asirei Tikvah.

Blessed are you, Adonai, who makes us captives—*of hope.*

I am not yet ready to muster a message of optimism tonight.

But I cannot escape it . . . eventually.

Because we, as a Jewish people, are unshakably, doggedly, eternally *captives of hope.*

CHAPTER 29

October 7

E *in Milim.*

There are no words.

I heard this refrain over and over from my Israeli family and friends in the days following October 7, 2023: the day of the largest, most vicious massacre of Jews since the Holocaust.

Early on that fall morning, I was visiting my son's college campus for family weekend and went to breakfast in the hotel lobby. Someone I hardly knew came over to my table. "Rabbi, I think you need to look at the news that is coming out of southern Israel." When I saw the chilling pictures on social media of Hamas militants perched on the back of pickup trucks with machine guns, rushing through bulldozed fences into Israeli kibbutzim and towns, I knew this was different than any other attack. The surreal reports came out in dribbles: text messages from terrified children hiding in their homes; video of a young woman dragged out of a jeep in bloodied sweatpants; footage of young people running for their lives in a vast dirt field; death tolls of twenty, then sixty, then four hundred, then twelve hundred. Only after several days did we understand that everything had changed.

Ein Milim.

How can mere words describe the ruthlessness of hundreds of terrorists streaming into Israel to set entire families on fire, rape and mutilate women, seize elderly Holocaust survivors, and shoot babies where they slept? What words could be said to a father witnessing a video of his twenty-year-old daughter, petrified, screaming, as Hamas dragged her off into the tunnels below Gaza?

Ein Milim. There are no words.

As this murderous rampage unfolded on Shabbat, Jews in Israel, not yet knowing exactly what was happening, unfurled the Torah scroll for Simchat Torah, which celebrates the completion of the annual Torah reading cycle. Every Jewish community in Israel and throughout the world reads from the last verses of Deuteronomy, *Devarim*, which describes the death of Moses and begins again in Genesis, *Bereshit*, with the story of creation.

In a cosmic, haunting echo of what was happening to our family in Israel, the Torah cycle moved from *Devarim*, which literally means "words," to a world that was *tohu vavohu*—"formless and void."

Israel and the entire Jewish world passed from *Devarim* to *Ein Milim*.

But then Genesis describes how God initiates creation: "God said, 'Let there be light.' And there was light."

God creates light—creates the entire world—*with words.*

As a Jewish people, we understand the power of words to create a reality. Words bolster nations, build bridges, bring healing. But words can also become curses and weapons. Jews have never affirmed the childhood rhyme that "words will never hurt us." We know how very lethal they can be. And we also know how silence—the absence of words—can enable evil and chaos.

As I sat heartsick and devastated by the deadly violence in Israel, I was shocked by the words I heard immediately following the October 7th attack. Words like "resistance," "decolonizing," or "freedom fighters," words that valorized, even celebrated, Hamas's brutality. Words that perversely found a way to blame Israel for these monstrous attacks. The contortions people engaged in to blame defenseless children, teenagers at a music festival, or Holocaust survivors for their own murder betrayed a moral bankruptcy I could not believe possible.

Also upsetting were the muted or ethically opaque statements from the people we look to for moral leadership, like university presidents who could not bring themselves to state clearly the simple truths of these attacks: The perpetrators were murderers, and they targeted Jews.

Central belongs to an organization of interfaith leaders representing many of the major churches, synagogues, and mosques in New York City. In the days following October 7, the group attempted to issue a statement in response to the Hamas attack, but the draft was limited to vague platitudes: "We stand in solidarity with the people of the region." After some back-and-forth, the group never issued a statement at all.

This interfaith community in New York, home to the largest population of Jews in America, was unable to unequivocally condemn the horrors of October 7.

Academic and faith leaders know the power of words, and instead of taking principled stands, again and again, I saw them choose language that made false equivalencies, blamed Jewish victims, and implied moral ambiguity in a savage act against civilians. It was chilling to realize how many people, often those who generally have the most compassion for victims of oppression and violence, simply have a blind spot when the victims are Jews.

Never before had I felt how important words were for shaping realities. And how deafening silence can feel in the face of barbarity. When I heard President Biden in the days following the October 7th massacre deliver his emotional, unequivocal condemnation of Hamas as a terrorist organization, when he named the atrocities as unadulterated evil, and when he clearly affirmed "We stand with Israel," I started crying. I didn't even realize how much I needed to hear the president of the United States say it. But words matter because the truth matters.

I was unsure of what consolation I could offer the congregation when I was reeling emotionally myself.

I found my grounding by going to Israel.

UJA-Federation invited me on a small clergy mission, and I took my seat on one of the few EL AL flights still flying to Tel Aviv in those early days when other carriers had stopped. That was where I knew I needed to be, to signal to an anguished country that I, and our Central Synagogue community, stood with Israelis and to remind myself of how our people respond to trauma.

We landed in what felt like an abandoned airport. I'd never seen Ben Gurion so barren, quiet. Our Jerusalem hotel, normally bustling with tourists, was now so empty that it echoed. Many other hotels in town had been repurposed as temporary housing for the more than two hundred thousand Israelis who had to flee their homes from the southern and northern cities still at risk since the outbreak of war.

We traveled to the Dead Sea, usually a sleepy tourist area of about one thousand residents, which was converted almost overnight into a temporary city for fifteen thousand evacuees who sought refuge from their torched and bullet-ridden houses near the Gaza perimeter.

The lobby of a large hotel housed nine hundred survivors from Kibbutz Be'eri, one of the communities most devastated by the October 7th attack. Residents transformed the foyer into a memorial; a table filled with candles served as a makeshift altar to the 108 members of the community who had been massacred. A wall was filled with posters depicting abducted babies, grandmothers, and all ages in between.

We heard sickening stories from people who had witnessed the torture of their family members and neighbors, who survived that black day by cowering in their bomb shelters, gripping the door handle for ten hours to keep the door closed. It was agonizing to listen to descriptions of survivors who had waited for the IDF to come to their rescue, a deliverance that never arrived.

Amid rivers of grief, we also encountered breathtaking resilience among those who had lost too much and heard deep gratitude for the thousands of volunteers helping around the clock: social workers, trauma specialists, yoga teachers, and therapists, all offering their services daily to thousands. One educator moved to the Dead Sea to set up seventeen makeshift schools, one for each ransacked kibbutz, with principals from around the country volunteering to take the helm. In Jerusalem, which had thirty-five thousand evacuees, and in Eilat, which had sixty thousand, we observed a similarly impressive army of volunteers coordinating cooking and babysitting with inspiring efficiency. The selflessness and urgency of this response from Israeli civil society was astounding and restoring. I felt myself start to breathe again. *This is what Israel does*, I thought to myself. *It's a nation that refuses to crumble, refuses to abandon its own, refuses to be a victim.*

We drove to Har Hertzl, the military cemetery with its rows of tombstones, to attend the funeral of Lavi Lipshitz, one of the first soldiers to die in Gaza. Hundreds of people crowded the gravesite, where the coffin was wrapped tightly in the nation's flag. Like us, many did not know the soldier personally but had come to honor the fallen in this latest war for Israel's survival. I could not see the family from where I was standing but heard their broken voices over a microphone sobbing through Kaddish. When the skies opened up with a torrential thunderstorm, it was as if the angels themselves were weeping.

We visited the home of Doron Perez outside Jerusalem. Doron's son Daniel, twenty-two, had been commanding a tank and taken hostage. His other son, Yonatan, also a soldier, had survived a shot in the leg on October 7. Yonatan was set to be married the week after the attack and the family could not decide whether to postpone the wedding while Daniel remained in captivity. Believing that there is no stronger defiance of the enemy than to keep living, they proceeded with the celebration: a commitment to the future.

After the wedding, we sat with Doron and his son and daughter in their yard. Yonatan was dressed in his army uniform with his gun on his back, about to return to his base. His father explained that Yonatan was now exempt from serving because his brother was in captivity; the IDF doesn't want to add to a family's emotional strain and risk. Through tears, Doron said proudly, "My son asked me to sign the waiver declining the exemption, to let him return to the front. I wouldn't sign; I didn't want him to go. And he said, 'You're responding like a father, but this is the son you raised me to be—to protect our country.'"

There wasn't much concrete help we could offer in the face of so much tragedy. But Israelis kept thanking us for coming. Just as with my rabbinic duties at home, I was reminded of how important it is just to be present. I visited with an Israeli rabbi whose reserve duty assignment was "casualty informer," which meant he had the excruciating and sacred task of knocking on doors to tell a family about the loss of a loved one.

He said he had not been sleeping, but it strengthened him to see twenty rabbis fly to Israel to offer support. "Thank you for coming. I could not imagine flying to a war zone, unless it was home. You remind me this is home for you too."

He sent me off with a jar of Israeli honey, inscribed *"Al Kol Eileh"*—the title of a song about the bitter and the sweet, so I would remember both from this trip.

After flying back to New York, I recounted my whole experience in my Sabbath sermon. The Torah portion for that Friday, entitled *Chayei Sarah*, literally means "the life of Sarah" but ironically begins not with her life but with her death and ends with the death of her husband, Abraham. A portion nominally about "life" is bookended with reminders of mortality. The heart of the portion, however, tells how Abraham and Sarah's son, Isaac, amid his grief and mourning, marries a woman discovered at a *be'er*, a "well," and settles at *Be'er L'Chai Roi*, literally "The Well of the Vision of Life."

After October 7, it was impossible for me to read *Chayei Sarah* and not think of the families I had met just days before who had settled near the Gaza border in the similarly named Kibbutz Be'eri, whose wells filled with blood on that horrible day.

My trip, which began with the families from Be'eri, ended with a hostage family from Jerusalem. Jack and Noam had two family members murdered on October 7 and three more held in captivity, including two teenagers. As I sat in their kitchen, their eight-year-old daughter bounced around with her friend on the living room couch, oblivious to the pain of our conversation. "That is our daughter, Be'eri," they introduced me. I raised my eyebrows. "Wow, that must be a complicated name to carry now." Noam smiled ruefully, explaining that she could not be more proud of her child's name and its new resonance. She told me that in the few weeks since October 7, five babies born in Israel had been given the name Be'eri. I thought to myself: Is there anything that captures the spiritual defiance of Israelis more than this? That they would give newborns, in the days after October 7, the name of a place that suffered unfathomable loss, and thereby reclaim the life-giving meaning of Be'eri, "my wellspring," which has sustained our people since ancient days? This is what it means for Jews to choose life. Not when it's easy but when it feels impossible.

For the rest of that year, every sermon I gave was related to Israel in some way. I spoke about everything from a daring hostage rescue to the glaring lack of women decision makers in this time of war. But in reality, I avoided the hardest subjects, the thorniest moral questions, because I was struggling for answers that did not come.

I was up at night with discomfort about the unfathomable cost of this war, grieving for so many innocents in Gaza, for young Israeli soldiers the age of my children and older reserve duty officers leaving families maybe forever. I wrestled with the military ethics of proportionate response and the agonizing calculation of how to value a life on one side versus the other. I was suspicious of those who spoke with such certainty defending Israel's use of MK-84 bombs, as well as those who confidently demanded a ceasefire, when it seemed impossible to know which would end the true threat of a terrorist group bent on wiping out the Jewish people. I was tormented by the faces of hostages who were sexually assaulted, tortured, sitting in airless tunnels without food, water, or light, wondering what price we would pay to bring them home. And the price if we did not.

The conflict reduced all nuance to rubble, and the lack of listening or compassion made me despair. A rabbi trains to have a non-anxious presence, to keep an appropriate distance from our own emotional response, but my own fear and disquiet, my anger and betrayal over the war and facile critiques of it, would sometimes short-circuit my own thinking and equanimity. I became the destination for many of my congregants' own pain and grappling. Rabbis often become a substitute, not only for moral authority or a loving parent but even for God. Congregants turned to me believing I could make it better. Expecting me to have answers.

"I don't have God's power to see. Or to know," I confessed in a quieter moment with a wise congregant who is himself also a rabbi. (Rabbis also need a rabbi.) "Of course you don't," he responded. "But what do you think God would want us to *do*?"

No one had asked me this before.

But with the bald question before me, I knew the answer: *God wants us to work toward a path to peace.*

Peace. A word that I had scarcely uttered in the last year. As if even the dream of it was unwise, unschooled, naive. But I knew that this is when faith steps in. Not a blind faith, but trusting in an outcome for which there is no other alternative, taking even the smallest steps to bring it about and not losing hope that it is still within reach.

Dimah
TEARS

Why do we cry?

It's not something we have to be taught. A newborn comes into the world wailing. There is something evolutionary and primal in us that understands tears as a way of communicating and bonding. While some animals can tear up from an irritant in the eye, human beings are the only species that sheds tears from emotion.

To cry is literally to be human.

Even our biblical ancestors wept, and no one more than Joseph, who has eight full episodes in tears. It's notable that Joseph doesn't cry early in his life when he's thrown into a pit by his jealous brothers or fished out of the hole and sold into slavery, or even when he is imprisoned on false charges of adultery.

Joseph cries when he sees his brothers after a long absence. And when he sees his beloved youngest brother, Benjamin, for the first time. When he asks his brothers "Is our father still alive?," Joseph weeps so loudly that his sobs could be heard in Pharaoh's house. Only then does he reveal, "I am Joseph."

His tears open the floodgates of his heart, allowing him to make peace with his brothers.

In the months after October 7, weeping became routine. I cried over lost lives, children held captive, young soldiers risking their lives to defend their country.

The Hebrew word for tears is *dimah*. It shares similar letters as the word *dam*, "blood," but includes the additional letter *ayin*, which is also the word for "eye." Our tears held the blood of our family that day.

The brutality of October 7 and the subsequent grief felt so enormous, the response from the rest of the world so callous and hypocritical, that initially, I struggled to find the emotional space or tears for the other side. It almost felt too threatening, a betrayal.

I received a needed spiritual rebuke from Rachel Goldberg-Polin, the mother of Hersh, an American Israeli whom Hamas murdered in cold blood after holding him in captivity for 328 days—just as Israeli soldiers seemed to be closing in on his location. In all of her speeches to Jewish groups, rallies, and meetings, she focused not on indignation or revenge but on morality and empathy. She chose words that insisted on the common love of every parent for their children. Early in the Israel–Hamas war, Goldberg-Polin addressed the United Nations and pleaded for its intervention. She began by reading her own poem.

> There is a lullaby that says your mother will
> cry a thousand tears

before you grow to be a man.
I have cried a million tears in the last sixty-
    seven days.
We all have.
And I know that way over there
there's another woman
who looks just like me,
because we are all so very similar,
and she has also been crying.
All those tears, a sea of tears,
    they all taste the same.

When Rachel, with a son in captivity, could remind us that her tears and those of a Gazan mother have the same salt, she embodied Joseph's teaching that our common weeping opens the heart for peace with our brothers and sisters.

Rachel's well of compassion gave permission for my own tears. I wept when I learned that Palestinian parents in Gaza have been writing the names of their children on their arms and legs so that they can be identified under the wreckage. Or seeing rows of small bodies lined on the ground in white shrouds. Or the image of a mother with a child in her hands sitting amid the rubble that was once her home. To cry for the other is to feel shared humanity. And to preserve our own as well. This is not a political or military strategy. It is a spiritual one, for our souls, so we might imagine a different day.

I thought of the power of weeping with the words of Psalm 126:

"Those who go out weeping, carrying seeds to sow,

will come back in joy, carrying sheaves with them."

The psalm instructs us to go out weeping, even to the most desolate places—perhaps the fields of the Nova music festival, the emptied orchards of Kibbutz Be'eri, or the rubble of Gaza City—and to carry seeds in an audacious act of hope. Our tears of empathy and compassion water those tiny seeds so that someday we might reap a different harvest.

Rachel finished her poem with the prophetic invitation to plant that hope in the ground and to soak them with our tears.

> Can we take them,
> gather them up,
> remove the salt,
> and pour them over our desert of despair
> and plant one tiny seed.
> A seed wrapped in fear,
> trauma, pain,
> war, and hope
> and see what grows?
> Could it be
> that this woman
> so very like me
> that she and I could be sitting together in
>   fifty years,
> laughing without teeth
> because we have drunk so much sweet tea
>   together

and now we are so very old
and our faces are creased
like worn-out brown paper bags.
And our sons
have their own grandchildren
and our sons have long lives,
one of them without an arm,
but who needs two arms anyway?
Is it all a dream?
A fantasy? A prophecy?
One tiny seed.

CHAPTER 30

Seoul National University

I joined two more missions to Israel in the year following October 7. Even though Israel was still at war, I felt strangely saner there, more able to exhale than while I was at home. It hurt my heart to walk through the streets of New York every day and see the torn hostage posters, ripped down by angry protesters unwilling to see them as victims. It was depleting to be asked over and over to defend the Israeli military response during a terrible war Israel neither started nor wanted. I felt gut-punched with every blacklist and boycott of "Zionists" by authors, students, doctors, or artists, which felt like a pretext for discrimination against Jews.

I grew up in the "golden age" of being Jewish in America and was never one to have the proverbial (or literal) "packed suitcase," a practice born of Jewish trauma in which we prepare for the inevitable expulsion of Jews from every host country throughout our history. America has been exceptional, and I still believe it is. But I thought of my husband's wholly assimilated German great-grandparents who felt they were German first, Jewish second, who had PhDs, sterling silver cutlery, and a Steinway grand piano, and I wondered at what point they packed their bags. They were among the fortunate to leave with their belongings before the Nazis destroyed everything. I surprised myself this year when I asked Jacob to look into German citizenship for himself and the kids. *A plan C, should things go horribly awry.* He looked at me like I had lost my mind. But in Israel, no one thought this was an alarmist idea.

Perhaps what worried me most for the Jewish future and American liberalism was what was happening on college campuses. I heard from so many of my Central students firsthand who recounted stories of intolerance, intimidation, and ideological litmus tests, with their peers and professors demonstrating a singular focus on Israel unlike any other conflict in memory. Protest can be an important tool for edification and attention, but when students refuse to engage in *any* conversation with a "Zionist" or to even allow them entry to parts of campus, universities have failed in their educational mission.

Sadly, students learn some of this illiberal behavior from professors and administrators who years ago started the practice of boycotting Israeli scholars and scientists. Following Hamas's 2023 attack, as Israel fought to return their hostages in an impossible war, more universities around the world shut their doors to Israeli academics, rescinding teaching invitations without warning.

But one notable exception of bridge-building improbably came from my birthplace. Seoul National University, SNU, Korea's oldest and most prestigious public university, planned to open the first Israel Education Research Center in November 2023. This was unquestionably a milestone. Since 1962, when South Korea became the first Asian country to open diplomatic relations with Israel, there had still not been a single Korean university that offered the academic studies of Hebrew, Jewish history, or Israeli culture. Establishing this new Israel center at Korea's flagship public university was overdue and not without controversy, especially in this fraught time. Not only was the opening postponed to June rather than the month following the October massacre, it was relocated off campus due to fear of a disruptive demonstration.

When the Israeli ambassador to Korea wrote to tell me of the creation of the new center and that SNU was inviting me to offer the keynote address at the inauguration, I couldn't believe it. Despite the headwinds of antisemitism, the university was undeterred in its vision. *Not everyone was closing the door on us.* It seemed impossible that my far-flung worlds were coming together for just this moment.

I flew to Seoul in the summer of 2024 for my first trip to Korea in my role as a rabbi. For most of my life, I had compartmentalized my Korean and Jewish identities, and depending on the context, one would crowd out the other. But here I was, returning to Korea *because* I was a rabbi. I came representing the wider Jewish community, but also as a *hangguk saram,* a Korean native.

The marriage of my two primary spiritual homelands of Korea and Israel had always seemed a little mismatched, like my tall American Jewish father and my tiny Korean Buddhist mother. But as I prepared for my keynote, I appreciated anew certain core similarities, much like the ones that had brought my parents together.

I had not focused before on the fact that Koreans and Jews, both from ancient cultures, established modern states within two months of each other in 1948: Israel in May and Korea in August. Both countries had to fight for their independence soon after their founding and have continued to face hostile neighbors on their borders, requiring national mandatory military service and a state of heightened awareness to threat. Both Israel and Korea have almost no natural resources to draw upon, so they have had to invest heavily in their people—their greatest resource—and have among the highest percentage of advanced degrees in the world. This helped explain my parents' obsessive focus on education. In addition, Israel and Korea are neck and neck for the most spending on research and development as a percentage of GDP. These factors make it less surprising that these two relatively new countries punch way above their weight economically and have become global IT capitals. On a spiritual level, both nations survived twentieth-century attempts to erase them—Koreans under Japanese occupation and Jews under Nazi reign. Grit and resilience undergird both peoples.

I stood on a dais of the large hotel conference room, filled with SNU faculty and leaders, the Israeli ambassador, members of the Israeli expat community, a dozen other ambassadors from other countries, Korean Christian leaders who helped fund the center, members of the press, and my Korean cousins and family who had made the trip. My talk was entitled "From the Chosun Dynasty to the Chosen People: The Meeting of Two Worlds." I shared my dream that these two extraordinarily enduring cultures, which historically had almost no interaction nor knowledge of the other, could finally see how deep some of their common values ran and how much each could learn from the other.

I talked about the blessing of belonging to both, as well as the gift of knowing the heart of the stranger in each, for it gave me the ability to observe both heritages three-dimensionally, as both an insider and outsider. Having the foil of the other allowed me to appreciate their differences. Korea has the most polite and hierarchical society I have known; just from the language, full of honorifics, you immediately know where you stand in the social order. Israelis are, well, *the opposite*. If you didn't know better, you might think the chutzpah was rudeness, but I have always experienced it as refreshing bluntness, informality. Koreans have a strong paradigm of gaining wisdom through silence, like a solitary monk on a mountain, while Jews traditionally discern truth in noisy study pairs called *hevruta*. While Korean culture values deference, Israeli culture values debate. These were some cultural norms I saw play out across my own family and in ways extended out to each culture and country.

And yet my mother was hardly deferential, and my father valued harmony more than argument. I learned that we are not only the products of our genetic makeup or cultural norms. We choose the pieces we want to keep. The irony is that the more we are rooted in the richness of our cultural legacies, the more confidence we have to journey far afield. This is the invitation my parents and my ancestors embodied for me as boundary crossers.

For so many decades, I'd assumed that my Korean identity was one I could never escape, since it was on my face and in my blood, while the Jewish identity was always discretionary. I not only could "pass" as not Jewish but was constantly challenged to prove that I was. But I now realize that while both my inheritances make a claim on me, it is always a choice to belong, to decide to do your part in continuing the epic story of those who came before you. I hoped, as I stood at that podium, I would look back and see this opportunity as one small way I contributed to my peoples' stories.

I closed my remarks by singing a mash-up of *"Yerushalayim Shel Zahav"*—"Jerusalem of Gold"—an unofficial anthem of Israel, and "Arirang," a beloved Korean folk song with rich history. As I sang in Hebrew, I looked over at the Israeli ambassador and saw his recognition and delight. When I sang "Arirang" the crowd rose to its feet singing with me, and I felt the emotional weight. Traceable back at least six hundred years, "Arirang" is sung by both North and South Koreans, a reminder of a shared history and culture that no border can erase. When

Japan occupied my Korean ancestors and forbade the singing of patriotic Korean songs, "Arirang" became the unofficial song of resistance.

Two songs of resilience against all probability, each an anthem of a buffeted people, ringing out into the hall—and just maybe into a gentler new day.

Am Segula
CHOSENNESS

There may be no more uncomfortable concept for the modern Jew than being a "Chosen People"—the biblical idea that Jews have a unique relationship with God. In an age of increasing multiculturalism, diversity, and inter-marriage, it can feel unnecessarily exclusive and uncom-fortably arrogant.

Unless we ask the question: Chosen . . . *for what*?

Jews were chosen not to *be* better but to *make things better*. In Judaism, we do that by upholding the obligations and teachings of Torah, learning our own particular Jewish language, customs, and rituals, by activating our ethics in everyday interactions—in our families, in business, in the public square. But in a world that increasingly celebrates the global and universal, embracing our particular traditions—

which often look so alien to others—can sometimes feel too narrow. Too provincial. Too tribal.

But tribalism is not all bad. Human beings need tribes: schools, congregations, sports teams, and sororities. They give us roots and community. They help us find our own unique place and purpose. Jews, like all people, need our tribe so we can know our story. So we understand who *we* are and what we were charged to do.

In Exodus, the first time that God calls Israel an *Am segula*, a treasured or "Chosen" people, it is phrased condition-ally: "*If* you obey me faithfully and keep my covenant, *then* you will be chosen among the nations" (Exodus 19:5). Di-vine Chosenness was not inevitably conferred; we have to *choose* to be Chosen.

Jews have no monopoly on righteousness or salvation. We are taught that *all* people are created in the image of God, each of us entitled to a place in the World to Come as long as we live a moral life. In the story of Noah—which pre-dates the existence of a Jewish people—a set of *Noahide* laws establishes moral codes and ethics that apply to *all* people.

Chosenness is not about being chosen *above others*.

Jews have been chosen to BE the other.

What do I mean by that—chosen to *be the other*? With apol-ogies to Rabbi Hillel, if I had to sum up the *entirety* of our Jewish teaching while standing on one foot, I would say,

You were a stranger, therefore care for the stranger. All the rest is commentary. Go and learn it.

Our Jewish master narrative is that we were strangers in Egypt, captive and then freed. Not only do we retell this story every year at our Passover Seders, among the most beloved of Jewish rituals, but we invoke it in our daily liturgy, our Friday-night blessings, and in countless laws in the Torah.

On Yom Kippur, the holiest day of the year, when our entire community is gathered, we read these words: "The strangers who live with you shall be to you like citizens, and you shall love them as yourself, for you were strangers in the land of Egypt."

But it's not just that we were strangers in Egypt. We Jews were strangers at the birth of Judaism. The first Hebrews, Abraham and Sarah, were commanded by God, *"Lech L'cha."* "Go forth from your land, from your birthplace, to a place *you do not know.*" God did not permit Abraham and Sarah to begin Judaism within the comfort of their hometown. They had to become immigrants. They had to be the Other in order to create a religion of the Other.

Moses, born of Hebrews, grew up as a stranger in the Egyptian Pharaoh's palace, and in his proclamation of being the "other," he names one of his sons Gershom (*Ger sham*), which means "a stranger there." And Ruth is the exemplary outsider, a Moabite turned most famous convert, who goes on to become the grandmother of the great King David and a mother in the line of the Messiah.

The Jew as outsider has persisted throughout the ages. We have made our way as strangers everywhere from Babylon to Brooklyn and survived the Crusades, the pogroms, and the concentration camps. Exile and endurance are the backdrop of everything we've become.

While today Jews miraculously have a homeland in Israel and generally feel secure here in America, we are commanded never to forget what it feels like to be *unwelcome*. We are mandated to recall being a stranger not just as ancient history but *as personal memory* in every generation—to taste the tears and eat the bread of affliction ourselves, to ingest the experience of being the stranger in our very bodies.

Knowing the heart of the stranger and the force of that Jewish memory is an ever-present caution against any feeling of superiority, bigotry, or indifference. As Jews, we know what it is to feel vulnerable and powerless. God chose the Jewish people to be archetypal strangers. *Why?*

So that we would never forget that the person behind the barbed wire, barricade, or checkpoint, that family forced to hide or run, or even the enemy on the other side of a conflict, are all within our circle of empathy. We are mandated by our tradition to remember, protect, and, yes, *love* the stranger, because that's who we are.

This is what we were Chosen for.

CHAPTER 31

Homecoming

My mother, my daughter, and I posed before the imposing, thirty-foot golden statue of fifteenth-century King Sejong on the main boulevard in Seoul. We looked like tourists, but we weren't there to sightsee. This was a pilgrimage for my mother's eightieth birthday, to her homeland, to our roots.

We asked a passerby to take a picture of us. He couldn't have known that this tiny Korean woman, with her biracial daughter and tall American granddaughter, were among King Sejong's eighteenth-, nineteenth-, and twentieth-generation great-granddaughters. My daughter's open face barely hints at the royal Korean ancestry she carries, but Rose has as much Sejong in her as any of the king's twentieth-generation great-grandchildren.

It was a typical, punishingly hot August day in Korea, and we sought shade by the side of the statue, where a summer camp of three-year-olds in matching yellow tank tops also took refuge and delight in the water fountains squirting from holes in the ground.

My mother, still carrying her silver handbag, jumped right in with the group of children. She wet her hands, water spraying up her skirt as she squealed her familiar laugh. We had come back to Korea to see where my mother grew up, and I marveled at the ways that she never will.

After exploring my birthplace of Seoul for a few days, we traveled to Taegu, Korea's fourth-largest city and the one nearest my mom's hometown, where her remaining family still lived. Restaurant Emo greeted us with tight hugs, glancing once-overs, and pronouncements over our looks: "*Aigo!* You're too skinny!" she told my mother. "Rose, *eepudah!* So beautiful." She had prepared a table full of my mother's favorites: dried fish jerky, seaweed salad, and Korean potatoes dug from the garden the day before. She peeled a peach for me, and I tasted childhood.

Restaurant Emo has two large refrigerators stuffed to overflowing in her small one-person apartment. Their innards uncannily resemble my mother's two refrigerators a world away: gallon jars filled with several types of kimchi; pots of doenjang and gochuchang; shelves stacked high with mismatched Tupperware containing pickled vegetables, leftover rice, and tiny crunchy anchovies; bottles and pitchers filled with home-brews of fermented sweet rice drink, boricha, and soy milk; and every kind of fruit and vegetable piled in colorful towers.

My mother's family lived through the Korean War and years of great scarcity, so a bulging fridge—or two—is comfort. Abundance. Blessing.

My emo only had air-conditioning in her bedroom, which she gave over to "the Americans," who couldn't bear the thought of sleeping in the stifling heat. Mom and her older sister put down a Korean mat for a bed on the floor of the living room, except they barely slept. They talked all night long like two little girls giggling at a slumber party. At one point I wandered out of the cool bedroom to say good night, and they were lying there with Korean face masks plastered on their cheeks and foreheads, laughing so hard tears spouted from the eye holes. I hoped that someday my sister and I would keep ourselves young this way.

The central event of our journey was a three-day retreat at the Donghwasa Temple to study meditation with a Korean Buddhist master, a friend of my mother's. We drove an hour north of Taegu, uphill, as virtually every Buddhist temple in Korea is set in the mountains.

Donghwasa Temple was established in 493 CE, though most of its many meditation spaces and gathering halls—still standing—date back to the early eighteenth century. My mother explained that this was the largest, oldest temple near Taegu, that her parents prayed here, and that this was where she had studied for six months at age twenty to prepare for the exam that qualified her for college.

This temple was also the site of frequent family outings when I lived in Korea as a child—not for prayer but mostly to hike the hillside, play in the nearby streams, and picnic under the trees. In fact, Donghwasa was the very first excursion my father took with my mom more than fifty years ago, when he left the US army base and came to visit her family in Taegu.

On this, my first return to the temple since age four, I arrived with generations of women in my family: my mother, her sister, the widow of my mother's youngest brother, and my daughter. Five women who don't appear, on looks alone, to be family, all sleeping together on the floor of one room in the temple guesthouse. Upon entering the temple, we were given uniforms—baggy purple pants tapered at the ankles and a green linen vest—so decidedly unfashionable that they required our first Buddhist practice: humility.

We gathered with twenty-five other guests in the main meditation hall, a long, wide space, centered around an altar featuring a large Buddha and many bowls for incense. The room was completely empty of furniture save the piles of seat cushions lining the wall. I took two cushions, knowing that we were about to begin hours of meditation. The teacher held a *jukbi*, a flat wooden stick with slats, which he would slap against his palm to draw us to attention or thwack against someone's back if they fell asleep. He lectured entirely in Korean, which my mother quickly translated for Rose and me as he went along—a few sentences for every paragraph. I knew much was getting lost in translation.

But the main question he kept asking was in simple enough Korean that I understood: *"Ee mok go?" "What is this?"*

He followed each student's answers with yet another question. As vexing as this methodology was, it also forced us deeper. I often hear a similar impatience from people exploring Judaism: "But can't you just tell me *what Jews believe*?" Both traditions operate under a similar principle: Faith does not come from getting all the answers, but from grappling with the questions.

The teacher instructed us that it was only in feeling frustrated and hitting a wall that we would be able to make discoveries. Then we would know that the true Buddha is not a statue that sits before us but rather an inner wakefulness, curiosity, and equanimity—that lives inside us.

My daughter had started meditating regularly earlier that summer and I had been practicing for more than a decade, but neither of us was prepared for hours of sitting without speaking, no break at all. I learned years ago not to expect any major epiphany during a single sitting. Instead, I had come to understand that meditation is a practice whose rewards come mostly *after* the silence: in renewed patience with others; in quieting the comparing mind; in greater clarity about what matters and what doesn't. Nevertheless, I still hoped that twenty-plus solid hours of meditation would produce *some* revelation in the moment. I tried to focus on anything besides my cramped legs and discouragement. My daughter, having absorbed some of the teacher's wisdom, whispered to me that this frustration probably meant I was doing something right.

After our first day, I overheard my emo bragging about me in an animated conversation with the teacher: "My niece, she is the first Korean rabbi! She lives in America and met the president!"

The teacher approached and asked if I would be willing to explain Judaism to the participants, all of whom had never met a Jew. So on the second night, I stood before the group, and in English, with my mother translating, explained that Abraham, the first Hebrew, lived at a time when people worshiped multiple gods. He questioned this practice from an early age and a midrash explains how he came to understand that there was not a separate god for the sun, moon, or stars but one God over all of Creation. One God meant that we were all connected to that single source. This became the foundation of our monotheistic religion.

I said that Abraham obeyed God's call to leave behind the familiar and to journey to "a place he did not know." He left his birthplace and found himself a stranger in a strange land, where he raised a family. Abraham opened his home to those even less at home than he was, to strangers wandering without a place to rest or eat, and in this act of instantaneous welcome, he began to feel a sense of belonging. It didn't happen immediately, but Abraham eventually understood that he had to leave home in order to find it.

I was recounting to this gathering of Koreans the story of Abraham, the first Jew. But I could see in my mother's wet eyes that she knew I was also telling her story. And her mother's. And mine.

The final morning, we woke before dawn and climbed up to the main ceremonial temple, atop the highest hill on the temple complex. We sat in darkness in a row of chairs lining the southern terrace wall and watched in silence as the sun colored the sky and then rose, in slow motion, over the lush forest below. Above the tree canopy were layers of mountains that each grew progressively lighter as they faded into mist. Here I was, at my mother's childhood 1,500-year-old Buddhist temple, meditating over the same mountains as the generations who came before me.

Ee mok go? What is this?

This is a mountain. This is a temple.

I am sitting here, but I am also part of this temple. This mountain. Part of this eternity.

I'm a stranger. But I'm also home.

After a good hour of silence, our teacher asked if I would sing a prayer. My first impulse—maybe surprisingly—was "Somewhere Over the Rainbow." It's a song that I love and often sing. I knew this standard would be familiar to a crowd of mixed-aged Koreans, and while it's not a Jewish prayer, it feels sacred to me. *Tablet Magazine* once hailed this classic, written by two Tin Pan Alley Jewish songwriters, as capturing the two-thousand-year-old longing of a wandering people—after all, "there's no place like home." They named it the number one Jewish song of all time: "The most beautiful exilic prayer ever set to music."

Singing this now universally beloved song of longing back in my birthplace, I realized that my own dream of finding a "homeland" had required that I leave this one. That America was the only place I could have fulfilled the promise of my particular divine blessing, as an immigrant Korean and as a Jewish woman with the heart of a stranger who dreamed of being a rabbi.

I stood up outside this pagoda-shaped sanctuary, and my voice carried over the trees. The retreat group sat with their eyes closed, meditating to my reframed "prayer." When I finished, my emo had tears running down her face. She turned to my mother and said, "I feel our parents here with us. And they understand now why you had to leave."

⁓

There was one final stop we had to make on this Korean pilgrimage: to HyunPoong, my mother's village, to pay homage to my grandparents. The winding road up the mountainside to our ancestral burial plot narrows to one lane before it goes to dirt. HyunPoong, my mother's tiny hometown, has modernized beyond recognition, but as we climbed upward, we traveled back in time: no buildings, no electric wires, no people. My cousin abruptly stopped the car as the unpaved road became unnavigable. We could only walk from this point. We took coolers of food and drink and a picnic blanket from the trunk and began the trek through the trees and tall grasses.

When we arrived at their plot, which I had last visited a decade before, I could barely recognize the two large mounds that marked my grandparents' burial place beneath all the overgrowth. It is customary for families to return to their ancestral hometowns during the fall

Chuseok holiday—a harvest festival known as Korean Thanksgiving—to visit the graves of their deceased relatives and bring a feast to "share" with the dead as they pay respects. All the shrubbery gets trimmed back for Chuseok, but our summertime offseason visit offered a glimpse of nature unbound.

My eldest uncle purchased this hillside when my grandfather died in 1953; my mother was eleven, and her youngest brother only a few months old. My halmuni had an infant and six other children to raise on her own and got them all to adulthood before she died of a stroke and joined her husband. "We picked a peaceful place for them overlooking the lake," I remember my mother telling me the last time we were here. "And we planted this circle of trees around them so that we would have shade when we came to visit." Seventy years later, the trees had grown so tall around the site that we could no longer see down to the lake.

I spotted two new neighboring graves, those of my mother's oldest and youngest brothers, who had died since our last trip to Korea. This was the first time my mother could say her goodbyes to them—Yi JaeYung, born 1934, and Yi InYung, born 1953. These two headstones marked the bookends of my halmuni's nineteen years of childbearing, during which she gave birth to nine babies, seven of whom lived past the age of five. Today her descendants number sixty-seven and counting.

We laid out the blanket and piled red bean rice cakes, pyramids of fruit, pajun pancakes, and almond cookies onto my grandparents' shared headstone so that they could enjoy the treats with us. My mother sprinkled halmuni's favorite pumpkin rice drink onto her grave. Emo bowed low three times, clasped her hands in prayer, and began talking to her deceased mother. I could barely understand what she was saying between the language and the tears, but I could make out names: those of her two children and her grandchildren; her son Uki, who was killed in an armed robbery more than twenty years ago; her dead husband. She filled her mother in on the news of the day. Asked for a blessing.

Because my mother is younger, she went second. She bowed and could not get out any words without heaving tears. She had promised her mother she would not leave Korea. And she didn't—until her mother died. But now she had returned. I listened to my mother speak to her mother in English, a language Halmuni could not understand. But I knew that as much as she was pouring her heart out to her mother, she was also sharing it with me and Rose. She spoke to her past to speak to her future.

Ancestor worship is foreign to Judaism, and though we have rituals for honoring the dead, we don't usually spend time "feeding" or addressing them publicly. But I stepped forward and spoke to my grandmother.

"*Halmuni, I last saw you when I was four years old, before we left this land. We moved to America and practiced religion as a Jewish family, but we never stopped being Korean. You were always with me. I became the first Korean American rabbi, and I hope that makes you proud. I have returned here with my daughter to pay our respects and to link our story to yours.*"

And then, because this is the way Jews honor our dead, Rose and I stood and recited the Kaddish memorial prayer in unison: a Jewish prayer, written in Aramaic, for our Korean ancestor, offered by her American family.

I know somehow she heard us.

Pardes
ORCHARD

In November 2018, my sister and I—together with our husbands and all five of our children—returned to Tacoma, Washington, to celebrate my parents' fiftieth wedding anniversary. We didn't take for granted that my parents had made it to fifty years of marriage intact, considering my father's health challenges, not to mention how they occasionally battled. There were times I thought they might have been better off apart, their many small grievances building up over years of bridging fundamental differences. But here they were, at the fifty-year mark, their marriage still chugging along, now mellowed into a kind of sweet symbiosis. They seemed as content as I'd ever seen them.

I know much of what kept them together was their joint investment in the project of their lives: our family. They never made either my sister or me feel guilty for moving away, Gina to pursue musical opportunities in LA, and me to New York, the Jewish hub of America. But all of us lost something in the physical distance between us. We spoke on the phone, but it was rare for our original foursome to gather in Tacoma with our families. So it was all the more meaningful to return for this golden anniversary over Thanksgiving weekend.

On Saturday night, after we'd recovered from all the turkey and stuffing, Gina and I brought together more than fifty people from the Korean and Jewish sides of our family at a restaurant in downtown Tacoma. Relatives came from as near as Seattle and as far away as Korea. My mom and her three sisters, looking like a set of round-faced, small-but-spunky quadruplets, held court at the center table. They fell into Korean chatter, as they always do when reunited. It would be one of the last evenings all four would be together before the death of my eldest aunt, Hawaii Emo.

At the party, the Yis and the Warnicks greeted each other with polite smiles before retreating to different sides of the room. Even as my parents had, for all these years, straddled their two worlds, and even as Gina and I moved easily between them, our extended families didn't really know each other and struggled to overcome the language and cultural differences. My sister and I—along with several cousins—toasted our parents, the grandchildren sang a joyful parody set to Billy Joel's "The Longest Time," and we shared a video montage of Mom and Dad through the years. My parents held hands through the entire program, tears filling their eyes as they basked in images of all they had built together.

The following day, my parents announced a surprise for us: the family orchard. Their unassuming home, overlooking the Puget Sound, sits high atop a steep ravine that had been overgrown with wild blackberry bushes, weeds, and "volunteer" trees—unwanted tree sprouts. They hired a professional weed whacker to clear out the growth and level a large flat surface. Over many months, my mother and father carried eighty bags of new topsoil down to their lower plateau and planted eighteen trees—eighteen being the numerical value of the two Hebrew letters that spell *Chai*, which means "life." My mother was excited that she'd found an Asian nursery nearby where she could purchase the rare persimmon and Korean pear trees that can thrive in the Pacific Northwest.

On this crisp November morning, all of Sulja and Fred's descendants climbed down the steep stairs alongside the house, as my parents proudly unveiled this new family orchard. We tried to hide our bemused disappointment; it looked to us like a smattering of four-foot sticks poking up from the ground.

"I know it's not much yet," my mother said, reading our faces, "but before I die, we will harvest bushels of fruit from these trees."

"This is a Red Delicious," she added, pointing to the nondescript stick in front of her, "the most famous apple of Washington state. And this is a fuyū persimmon tree, my favorite fruit as a child. And these are male and female kiwi trees; they won't grow fruit without each other." My mother cataloged every sapling and shared her vision of what they would become.

"Now I want each of you to pick one tree, it will be your tree and we will mark it. And every day, Dad and I will come down here and water and take care of each one of you. And when we miss you, we will talk to your tree."

My sister and the grandchildren each picked a sprig, while Jacob and I chose the mated kiwi. Each of us painted a wooden sign and attached it to our seedling with hopes of bounty to come.

The Hebrew word for "orchard" is *pardes*. It shares the same root as the word "paradise," recalling the original orchard—the Garden of Eden—a place that is interchangeable with "heaven" in Judaism.

The rabbis also used the word *pardes* to signify an important rabbinic mindset: the belief that a single text can have multiple levels of meaning, from the literal to the mystical. They read *pardes* as a four-letter acronym, PRDS, denoting four approaches to reading Jewish texts.

> *Pshat*: the simple, plain meaning of the text
> *Remez*: the allegorical significance of the
>   words
> *Drash*: the comparative or sermonic
>   interpretations
> *Sod*: the secret, mystical meaning

But this methodology is not just for holy texts. We can mine the same layers in the stories of our own lives.

As I walked through my parents' family orchard, I saw the *pshat*, the simple reading, right in front of me: the garden's eighteen trees, *Chai*, were good fortune, literally life—a source of nourishment, beauty, and fruit.

But the *remez*, the symbolism of the *pardes*, meant more: the trees connected my mother to her homeland, my father to his birthplace. Tending the garden gave my parents a way to nurture their family members who lived far away.

On the *drash* level, the family orchard proclaimed my parents' philosophy for a good life: clear ground for new roots; learn to transplant in distant soil; value honest, sturdy labor; and plant for generations to come.

But what was the *sod*, the secret meaning of the *pardes*?

My parents taught me that our task in life is to seed our own garden, to fill it with relationships, adventures, gambles, and wonder. They showed me how to make purposeful choices in what to cultivate: the mentors I needed, an inner compass. And what to weed out: the voices to ignore or prove wrong. They grounded me with the stories, rituals, and wisdom of all my ancestors—not just one side of the family. Their goal was not to root me in place, but to give me the sturdiness and security to stretch toward the light wherever it led me.

I spent many years of my young life apologizing for my mixed ancestry in communities that preferred monocultures. But I learned to embrace my outsiderness, no matter the discomfort or hurt, because it shaped my spiritual yearning, empathy, and grit. Every ecosystem ultimately thrives on diversity—and when I was among "mixed multitudes," I most easily could define what made me particular and distinct.

But the real secret of the *pardes* is revealed in the mythical Garden of Eden itself. Whether this story is part of your sacred canon or not, for a moment consider the message: Every person—regardless of religion or ethnicity—was descended from the same clay, animated by the same first breaths. In the end, we will return to the same shared soil—dust to dust. Adam and Eve, the ancestors of humanity, were exiled from Eden as the price for eating from the Tree of Knowledge; all of us were required to leave our first home in order to gain insight, independence, and responsibility. We had to leave God's orchard in order to grow our own. All of us have to make the journey, carrying the heart of the stranger from the safe to the uncertain. The wisdom we learn from our exile is the power that will help us finally find home.

Several years after that anniversary trip to Tacoma, I received a small box in the mail.

First harvest! read the note from my mother. *Enjoy some of Rose's persimmons, Eli's pears, and Gabriel's apples.*

More than fifty years after my parents first joined forces to build a proverbial garden—their family—once again their sweat, patience, and faith had borne fruit. I opened the box and tasted a bite of Paradise.

ACKNOWLEDGMENTS

Heart of a Stranger would not exist without Abigail Pogrebin, my book doula, master editor, and lifelong *hevruta*. She devoted countless hours and brought her wealth of writing experience to helping me clear each hurdle it took to complete this book—scrutinizing every last word, multiple times. Abby's honest and fierce friendship have made this book, and my life, immeasurably better.

I am so grateful to Brettne Bloom, my savvy and soulful book agent, for her patience and generosity at every step. I can't imagine a better champion. (And I would never have found Brettne if not for Dani Shapiro's perfect *shidduch*—thank you.)

Deepest appreciation for Pamela Dorman, one of the greatest editors in the business, for her belief in this book and wise guidance, and for her and Marie Michels's meticulous editing. The entire team at Pamela Dorman Books has shepherded this project with expertise and care: Brian Tart, Andrea Schulz, Kate Stark, Mary Stone, Alicia Cooper, Jason Ramirez, Rebecca

Marsh, Carolyn Coleburn, and Yuleza Negron. And I'm grateful for their partnership with my publicist Marion Brown, who helped bring this book to a wider audience.

Every draft was bettered by many friends who graciously gave feedback: Ariela Dubler, Jeremy Fielding, Mari Hinojosa, Julie Dobrow, Amy Zimmerman, Jenny Lyss, Jayne Riew, Rebecca Angelo, and crack editor Robin Pogrebin—and friends who shared their wisdom about the publishing process: David Leonhardt, Jodi Kantor, Ron Leiber, and Dan Senor.

I am indebted to Edgar Bronfman z"l* and the Bronfman Youth Fellowship in Israel for changing the course of my life at age sixteen, and to Les and Abigail Wexner and the Wexner Graduate Fellowship for greatly enabling and enriching my rabbinic and cantorial education. These Jewish philanthropists made investments in me and so many other young Jewish leaders, and I hope they see this book as one small return.

My path to the rabbinate felt shaky at times, but I was guided by important mentors and teachers along the way, who gently encouraged and inspired me: Rabbis Richard Rosenthal z"l, Michael Paley, Rick Jacobs, Peter Rubinstein, David Ellenson z"l, Aaron Panken z"l, Elka Abrahamson, and Lawrence Hoffman; Cantor Benjie Ellen Schiller; Shifra Bronznick; and Debbie Friedman z"l.

I am grateful for the remarkable colleagues in my Hartman Rabbinic cohort whose wisdom, humor, and support got me

---

* z"l—zichrono/a livracha—"may his/her memory be a blessing," indicating that they are no longer alive.

through the four years of writing, not to mention a pandemic; to my beloved B'not Zelophechad sisterhood, Rabbis Tamar Elad Applebaum, Sharon Brous, Sharon Cohen Anisfeld, and Delphine Horvilleur, who braid the world with their powerful Torah; to my dear friends Rabbis Elliot Cosgrove and Chaim Steinmetz, who make up my East Side trifecta; my HUC classmates and fellow alumni; and all of the colleagues and congregants at Westchester Reform Temple who gave me my first Jewish home as a young rabbi/cantor.

Never in my wildest rabbi dreams could I have imagined serving as the senior rabbi of Central Synagogue in New York City. I have learned so much about faith, courage, and belonging from this extraordinary community, and I am grateful every day for the privilege of being Central's rabbi. I could not possibly name everyone at Central who contributed to my journey or this book in some way, but I must thank Jeffrey and Nancy Goldstein for providing a retreat for me at the beginning and end of the writing; the incomparably gifted Annie Leibovitz, whose photography graces the covers of this book; and Dr. Shonni Silverberg and Jon May, presidents of the board during this project, representing the support I have felt from all the dedicated presidents and lay leaders at Central.

Marcia Caban, Central's executive director, exemplifies that one need not be a rabbi to have a calling at a synagogue. I am grateful she has been my trusted partner in building this vibrant community alongside her team of dedicated staff, security officers, and maintenance professionals. And I am so privileged to serve with the most talented, compassionate, and devoted clergy team: Rabbis Mo Salth, Ari Lorge, Rebecca Rosenthal, Lisa Rubin, Sarah Berman, Hilly Haber, Andrew Kaplan Mandel, and Sivan Rotholz; Cantors Daniel Mutlu and Jenna Pearsall; and Dr. Shira Epstein. Thank you all—as well as my former colleagues—for making this work together so inspiring and joyful. And I could not run my life at work without Chelsea Bassman's skilled command, or at home without Natalia Cansicio's steadfast stewardship. Together, they keep everything afloat.

I feel lucky to have a circle of close friends, many of whom met me and Jacob when we were kids and who know me first as just Angela, not as Rabbi. I thank this extended family by choice—you know who you are—for bringing so much depth, laughter, and richness to my life.

To Carol and David, Sara, Andrew, and Paul—I've said before that *you* could write the book on how to be the perfect in-laws. Thank you for always treating me like your daughter and sister.

To Mom and Dad, I hope this book honors what you taught me about life and embracing the heart of a stranger. I am beyond grateful for your unconditional love and the freedom you gave me to fly, even though it took me far away. Gina, thank you for being at the center of all my sweetest and craziest childhood memories—you own a corner of my soul. I recognize that sharing my story meant sharing our family's as well, and I am grateful to the three of you for your blessing in this, as with all things.

Gabriel, Eli, and Rose—you make my heart burst. You've been the greatest teachers and miracles of my life. There is no name I treasure more than *Mom*, and watching you grow into the people you are has been my greatest joy and blessing in this world.

Finally, to Jacob—I would not be the mother, rabbi, friend, or person that I am without your profound love, unwavering belief in me, and full-throated support of everything I have dreamed of doing. This book was no exception; as always, our countless conversations and your rigorous editing helped me understand what I wanted to say. All that, and you keep me laughing every day. Thank you, Jacob, for giving my heart its home.